Suspect Community

Suspect Community

People's Experience of the
Prevention of Terrorism Acts
in Britain

Paddy Hillyard

Pluto  **Press**
LONDON • BOULDER, COLORADO
in association with liberty

First published 1993 by Pluto Press
345 Archway Road, London N6 5AA
and 22883 Quicksilver Drive, Sterling, VA 20166-2012, USA

www.plutobooks.com

British Library Cataloguing in Publication Data
A catalogue record for this book is available from the British
Library

Library of Congress Cataloging in Publication Data
Applied for

ISBN 978-0-7453-0727-5 (hardback)
ISBN 978-0-7453-0726-8 (paperback)

Printed and bound by CPI Group (UK) Ltd, Croydon, CR0 4YY

To Fintan and Maeve
who have taught me so much about justice

Contents

About Liberty and Northern Ireland   xi
Preface   xiii

1: The Study in Context
    Introduction   1
    Background and History   2
    Suspect Legislation   4
    Official Reviews   8
    The Origins and Aims of the Project   9
    The Structure of the Book   12

2: Policing Ports and Airports: Examination
and Detention Powers
    Introduction   13
    National Ports Scheme   14
    National Joint Unit   16
    Unfettered Discretion to Examine   18
    Examination Rules   19
    Power to Detain Pending Conclusion of the Examination 22
    Power to Question   23
    Powers to Demand to See All Relevant Material   24
    Search Powers including Strip Searches   24
    Power to Retain Personal Documents   25
    The Duty to Comply   25
    Detention Power   26
    The Number of People Examined   27
    The Number of People Detained   30
    Conclusions   32

3: Examinations and Detentions at Ports
and Airports: People's Experiences
    Introduction   34
    Profile of the Cases   35
    The Examination Process   37

A 50 Minute Examination at an Airport 39
Other People's Experiences of Being Stopped 43
Women and Children and the Examination Process 49
Examination Conditions 51
Examination Questions 52
Examining Personal Documents 54
Seeking Redress 58
Examining Suspicion 59
Impact of Examinations 64
Conclusions 65

4: Arrest, Search and Detention Powers
Introduction 68
Arrest Powers 68
Search Powers 72
Detention Rules 73
Detention Rights 77
Detention Conditions 78
Interrogations 79
Fingerprinting, Intimate and Strip Searches 80
Length of Detention 81
Summary of the Differences between a PTA and
    a PACE Detention 83
Equal Before the Law 85
The Use of Arrest Powers 86
The Use of Extended Powers of Detention 88
Outcome of Detentions 90
Conclusions 93

5: Arrest and Detention under the PTA:
Two Case Studies
Introduction 95
Case 1: Sally's Experience 96
Case 2: Teresa's Experience 111

6: Arrests: People's Experiences
Introduction 121
Profile of the Cases 121
Arrests at Home 123
Arrests on the Streets 127
Arrests at Other Places 131

The Impact on Third Parties 132
Search of Premises 135
Material Removed 138
The Journey to the Police Station 139
Notification of Arrest 140
Media Coverage of PTA Arrests 140
Conclusions 147

7: In Custody: People's Experiences
Introduction 149
Initiation into Custody 150
Detention Conditions 160
Detention Regimes 169
Conclusions 181

8: Interrogation: Gathering Information
Introduction 183
The Context 184
Frequency and Length of Interrogations 187
Interrogation Techniques 188
Anti-Irish Racism 191
Types of Questions 193
Recruiting Informers 195
Conclusions 196

9: Exclusion: The Law
Introduction 198
The Power to Exclude 198
Making the Decision 202
The Submission to the Secretary of State 203
Failure to Comply 206
The Lifespan of an Exclusion Order 206
The Use of Exclusion Orders in Britain 207
Notification of Rights and Power of Removal 207
Representation 209
Reconsidering the Decision 212
The Review Process 212
Conclusions 214

10: Internal Exile: People's Experiences
Introduction 217

Notification of Exclusion   217
Explanation and Knowledge of Rights   219
Making Representations before Removal   220
The Journey   224
Representations after Removal   227
Conclusions   236

11: The Impact of the Acts
Introduction   238
Physical and Mental Health   238
Family and Social Life   242
Employment   245
Freedom of Movement   247
Financial Consequences   249
Confidence in the Law   250
Politics   252
Conclusions   255

12: An Assessment
Introduction   256
The Construction of a Suspect Community   257
Dual System of Criminal Justice   261
The Terror of Prevention   262
Normalisation of Emergency Legislation   263
Violation of Civil Liberties and Human Rights   264
Terrorism and Democracy   265
Conclusion   273

Appendix I: Research Methodology Used in this Study   274
Appendix II: Exclusion Order Notice under the Prevention of
   Terrorism (Temporary Provisions) Act 1989   276
Notes and References   278
Bibliography   291
Index   295

About Liberty and Northern Ireland

Formed in 1934 as the National Council for Civil Liberties, Liberty is an independent, non-party political campaigning organisation which works to defend and extend our civil liberties. As a voluntary sector membership organisation, Liberty depends for its survival upon members fees, grant aid and publication sales income, and donations.

Liberty believes in a society built on the democratic participation of all its members and based upon the principles of justice, openness, the right to dissent and respect for diversity. Accordingly, we aim to secure the equal rights and liberties of everyone - individuals and groups - (insofar as they do not infringe the rights and liberties of others), and oppose any abuse or excessive use of power by the state against its people. We also recognise that the erosion of civil liberties often begins with attacks on the rights of those who are marginalised within society: such attacks undermine the rights of us all.

Since its beginnings Liberty has been concerned about the situation in Northern Ireland. Our first major inquiry in 1935 called for the repeal of the Special Powers Acts. Since then we have consistently opposed emergency measures which, whilst failing to defeat terrorism, have effectively institutionalised the suspension of fundamental civil and political rights. Far from suppressing violence, these powers – directed predominantly at the Catholic community in Northern Ireland but with a devastating impact on the civil liberties of everyone - have arguably helped perpetuate the conditions in which terrorism flourishes

Recent years have also witnessed the abolition of the right to silence in Northern Ireland, the ban on broadcasting the words of members of Sinn Fein and other political parties, the renewal of all the most oppressive features of the Northern Ireland (Emergency Provisions) Act and calls for the reintroduction of internment. Meanwhile, allegations of ill-treatment at police stations, the denial of access to lawyers by suspects in terrorist cases and threats against defence solicitors continue.

1991 saw the condemnation of the government's record in Northern Ireland by several international human rights agencies, including Amnesty International, Helsinki Watch and the UN Committee Against Torture. Taking this international human rights perspective on Northern

Ireland further, Liberty – together with other organisations working in the field – organised an ambitious three-day Human Rights Assembly to measure the government's alleged breaches of human rights against the standards set by various international agreements to which the UK is a signatory.

Liberty has also been concerned about the erosion of civil liberties in Britain arising directly from the conflict in Northern Ireland. We were one of the few organisations to oppose the PTA's introduction in 1974 and its subsequent renewal in 1976, 1984 and 1989. Over the years we have advised hundreds of people who have been stopped, questioned, arrested and detained under the PTA. We campaigned against its extension to terrorism not related to Northern Ireland – which meant it was no longer 'temporary' and linked to the current 'emergency' but here to stay – and have actively challenged abuses under the PTA of civil liberties enshrined in the European Convention on Human Rights. Indeed, any success in limiting the Act's draconian provisions has come about as a result of decisions from the European Commission and Court of Human Rights. Even this avenue has now been blocked, at least temporarily, because the government, deciding that it no longer needs to obey the rulings of the Court, has derogated from the Convention under Article 15. At the time of writing Liberty is actively challenging this decision, as well as pursuing ground-breaking cases such as our representation of two women who are suing the police for assault and false imprisonment under the PTA.

We have collaborated closely with the author on this book. As well as providing a comprehensive picture of the extraordinary powers available under the PTA, it describes in detail how a whole community has been targeted and criminalised. This process – consistently sanctioned by official reviews of the legislation's operation – stands as an indictment of the state of human rights in this country. We hope that this book will contribute to the campaign for change and look forward to the time when Irish people are free of harassment and the PTA is no more.

If you believe that civil liberties are important and worth fighting for, join us now. You can take an active role in our campaigns or simply ask to be kept informed of civil liberty developments. Either way, your support is vital to our survival and the continuation of our work. For a free information pack, contact Liberty, 21 Tabard Street, London SE1 4LA (tel: 071 403 3888).

Preface

One day when this book was nearly completed I was joined at lunch by a sociologist, who has an interest in policing. We discussed a number of issues concerning the criminal justice process in Britain and eventually the discussion came around to the Prevention of Terrorism Act (PTA). I argued that most detentions under the PTA were significantly more traumatic than most of those under the ordinary criminal law and I proceeded to describe a PTA detention. After I finished he remarked that he did not think from my description that there was a difference and implied that he did not see either form of detention as particularly stressful or traumatic. The comment reflected an inability to empathise with the experience of someone in police custody.

It also reflected a reluctance to move beyond an analysis of criminal justice as a system of rules and procedures to one which places the individual at the centre of the process. He is, however, not alone in this. Over the last 20 years the British criminal justice system has been the subject of an unprecedented amount of research, yet very little of it has been focused on the 'consumers' – those arrested, detained and charged. While many of the studies have obtained information from suspects about a specific aspect of the system, for example, access to a solicitor, the interest is not on the person, but on the extent to which the law may or may not be working. It has been principally legal and not sociological research, and has been directed at analysing the system rather than understanding the experiences of those drawn into it.

The focus of this book is on individuals and their experiences of being examined, arrested or detained under the PTA in Great Britain. The study does not consider the experiences of those arrested or detained under the PTA in Northern Ireland. Although the complexities of the law are spelled out to provide the context, the overall objective is to let those affected describe how they perceived the operation of the law and its procedures. It is principally a study from below and not from above and is part of the sociological tradition of the 1960s when there was a widespread interest in the powerless rather than the powerful.

While some people who were interviewed or made a statement did not seem to be unduly perturbed by their experience under the PTA, many had a harrowing tale to tell. In a few cases people openly wept as they told their story. For some it was the first occasion they had re-lived the trauma of their incarceration. Most were able to recall every important detail of a detention which in some cases had occurred eight years previously. For many, clearly, the experience will never be forgotten and it will affect them for the rest of their lives.

I have tried as far as possible to let people tell their own story in their own words. Very little editing has been done to those parts of the interviews which have been used. Some changes were made to keep the statements anonymous. Although most people said that they did not object to being named in the study, some did wish to remain anonymous, and, in the interests of consistency it was decided to make all quotes anonymous, except in a few cases where the individuals concerned already had a high public profile.

There are many people to thank. To begin with, I would like to thank all those who gave interviews and completed statements. Without their time and effort the study would have been impossible. I would also like to thank the many individuals connected with the numerous Irish and other organisations in London and elsewhere who encouraged people, whom they knew, to come forward and make a statement. I would also like to thank the many solicitors and other lawyers who have helped in various ways.

All research projects rely on the help and support of many people and it is always invidious to select anyone for special thanks, particularly when a project continues over a number years, as this one did. But the greatest debt is to Lia Dover, who got the project off the ground, and to Sara Huey and Fran Russell, who did much of the detective work in tracking people down, obtaining statements and helping prepare a research report on earlier cases, which was submitted to the London Boroughs Grants Committee in 1989. Sara Huey wrote up the material on exclusion for the research report and I have incorporated a large part of it with amendments and new material. Fran Russell prepared a number of drafts on the interview and legal material and has been a constant source of support throughout. Many others provided valuable research help at various times: Jacqui Beavington, Judith Carlson, Sister Sarah Clarke, Mary Connolly, Jo Delahunty, Father Faul, Marcelle Fletcher, Brenda Henson, Brenda McCarthy, Mary McKeone, Father Murray, Wendy Pearlman, Gareth Peirce, Claire Reilly, Sue Rolfe, Father Paddy Smith and Libby Volke; my thanks to them all.

The project would not have happened if it had not been for the skill and patience of Sarah Spencer, the then General Secretary of Liberty, and would not have seen the light of day without her support and that of Andrew Puddephatt, the current General Secretary.

The Greater London Council funded the initial project and further money was provided by the London Boroughs Grant Scheme. A small grant was provided by the University of Bristol's research committee to survey more recent cases and analyse the data. A number of people – Michael Ellman, Conor Foley, Malcolm Hurwitt, Mike Tomlinson, Fran Russell, Joe Sim, John Wadham and Jane Winter – read the manuscript, providing valuable comments. Renée Harris was a very efficient and long-suffering copy-editor. I am very grateful to them all.

Finally, the most important debt of all is to Margaret Ward, who provided considerable research expertise and advice and remained patient and supportive as other demands delayed the completion of the book.

Paddy Hillyard
Department of Social Policy and Social Planning
University of Bristol
May 1992

1 The Study in Context

Introduction

In 1986 a couple were asleep in bed when they were awoken at 5 o'clock in the morning by a terrible banging downstairs. The next moment they were surrounded by armed, uniformed and plainclothes police, who had used a sledgehammer to knock down the front door. They were told to get up and get dressed. The man was subsequently arrested, taken to Paddington Green police station, held for five days, questioned extensively and then released without any action being taken against him. His experience was not exceptional. He is one of 7,052 people who have been arrested or detained in Britain in relation to Northern Ireland affairs between 29 November 1974 and 31 December 1991 under successive Prevention of Terrorism (Temporary Provisions) Acts (PTA) and then released after periods of detention in police custody ranging from a number of hours to up to seven days.

The first Prevention of Terrorism (Temporary Provisions) Act was introduced in 1974 following the bombings in the Birmingham pubs in November 1974. At the time there was widespread public outrage at the carnage and demands for greater police action against the IRA. Irish people were attacked at work and some were driven from their homes. The police acted quickly and within a few hours of the bombings had arrested five people as they were boarding the boat at Heysham and another person in Birmingham. They were all subsequently convicted. The government, for its part, finalised the Prevention of Terrorism (Temporary Provisions) Bill, which had already been prepared, and placed it before Parliament within a week of the bombings. Although the police at the time were opposed to special legislation for dealing with political violence, it went through Parliament without a division and the Prevention of Terrorism (Temporary Provisions) Act 1974 (hereafter the 'PTA 74') was on the statute book within 24 hours.

Although there have now been three major reviews and a number of yearly assessments of the legislation, not one of these has ever conducted any systematic research into any aspect of the Acts.[1] Similarly the Home Office, which carries out a considerable volume of in-house and supervised research, has never supported any project on the PTA.[2] There is, therefore, no *systematic* evidence on how the Acts operate nor, more importantly, what people experience from the moment of their arrest or detention, through a period of custody to their eventual release.

This book provides the first independent research into people's actual experience of the operation of the Acts and the first systematic analysis of the impact of the legislation in Britain. People's experiences of the operation of the Acts in Northern Ireland are not examined except in relation to the review procedure of those excluded from Britain to Northern Ireland. It is based on written statements, mostly transcribed from taped interviews, of 115 people who have been examined, detained or arrested in England, Wales and Scotland under the Acts between 1978 and 1991. These experiences have been supplemented, where appropriate and with due care, by unverified newspaper and other reports.

Background and History

The PTA 74 was based on two different sources which, in one way or the other, had been introduced to deal with Irish political violence. It drew upon a number of key elements in the Northern Ireland (Emergency Provisions) Act 1973, particularly the powers of arrest, detention and proscription and the Prevention of Violence (Temporary Provisions) Act 1939, which had been introduced to deal with a previous IRA campaign.

It is, however, part of a much longer line of exceptional measures directed against Irish people. Between 1800 and 1921 there were no fewer than 105 separate Coercion Acts initiated in Ireland.[3] Between 1921 and 1973 when the Northern Ireland (Temporary Provisions) Act was introduced, there were always some form of special powers operating in Northern Ireland.[4] In Britain, the use of terror by the Fenians (1865–7) led to the suspension of *habeas corpus*. Another wave of bombings led in 1884 to the creation of a separate anti-terrorist unit, the Special Irish Branch, later to become today's Special Branch.[5] These campaigns led to much anti-Catholic feeling and attacks on the Irish in Britain became commonplace. By far the worst attacks occurred in Stockport in 1852 when one person was killed and 100 injured. There were other attacks on Irish people in London, Liverpool and Yorkshire, culminating in the anti-Catholic Murphy riots of 1867–71.[6]

Migration of labour was a crucial element in the development of perceptions and reactions to the Irish.[7] As a direct consequence of the economic and social relations between Ireland and England, large proportions of Irish people had no option but to leave and seek work elsewhere. There have been two main waves of migration to Britain: the first in the early to mid part of the nineteenth century and the second from the late 1920s to the present day. The first was heavily influenced by the potato famine in 1846 and 1847 and had a big impact on the towns where Irish people settled. For example, by 1861 one quarter of Liverpool's population was Irish-born. By the turn of the century there were over 630,000 Irish-born living in Britain.[8]

By this time the notion of the Irish as an inferior race was firmly established in English popular consciousness and within the state. It was underpinned by pseudo-scientific theories of race. Not only were Irish people conceived of as a race with distinct physical differences and only slightly higher than black people in the evolutionary scale, they were also attributed with a number of negative social and cultural characteristics. They were seen as violent, drunken and dishonest or, as Disraeli put it in 1836, 'This wild, reckless, indolent, uncertain and superstitious race has no sympathy with the English character.'[9] In short, they were seen as a problem population, a dangerous class which needed regulation, discipline and control.[10]

In the second wave the proportion of Irish-born increased from half a million to over one million in 1981. The increase has been fairly consistent over the whole period except in the early 1970s when emigration from Ireland slowed down and Irish people living in Britain were either attracted home because of the improved economy in Ireland or pushed out as a result of the recession in Britain. In the 1980s the emigration from Ireland increased again and it has been estimated that over 500,000 people left Ireland over the last decade. This would suggest that there must now be around 1.3 million Irish-born people living in Britain. While some seldom return to Ireland, most have never lost their roots and make frequent visits back to Ireland. There is, therefore, a constant flow of Irish people back and forth between the two islands. Although the precise numbers involved has never been estimated, it must come to millions of return journeys every year.

It is against this background of a large settled population which makes frequent visits back to Ireland, as well as a large migrant population seeking work and Irish students studying in Britain, that the PTA must be placed.

The Irish now constitute the largest single ethnic minority group in Britain. There is, however, very little recognition of this at the official level: as yet Irish people are not considered to be a separate ethnic group. Similarly, in the numerous studies into the criminal justice system, there is seldom any separate discussion of the Irish although their experiences of policing in Britain are likely to be very different from other groups.[11] The Home Office now collects information on the number of black and Asian people in prison, but no statistics are produced for the number of Irish. The Irish, although they form a sizeable minority, remain invisible in the social administration of the state and academic discourses in crime and criminology.

Suspect Legislation

The PTA 74 provided the police with extended powers of arrest and detention and gave them new powers to control the movement of persons entering and leaving Great Britain and Northern Ireland. It also gave the Secretary of State the power to issue an exclusion order banning a person from living in any part of the United Kingdom. In addition, it proscribed the IRA and made the display of support for it illegal. Mr Jenkins, the then Home Secretary, described the powers as 'draconian' and went on to argue that: 'In combination, they are unprecedented in peacetime.' He then added: 'I believe they are fully justified to meet the present danger.'[12]

This unprecedented and draconian legislation has now been on the statute book for 18 years. It has been amended and extended on three occasions – in 1976, 1984 and 1989 – and although it must still be renewed annually there is no longer any expiry date. It has thus gained a permanency on the statute book which belies its title.

The introduction of the legislation created a dual system of criminal justice in Britain. The existing powers and procedures for dealing with the most horrific offences (465 homicides, 429 attempted murders, 58,000 woundings of one sort and another and 1,000 rapes were notified to the police in England and Wales in 1973[13] – the year prior to the introduction of the PTA) were considered to be insufficient to deal with those people suspected of being involved in political violence connected with Northern Ireland affairs. As a result, radical new powers and procedures were introduced for dealing with 'terrorism'. In the meantime, the violent robber, rapist and other ordinary decent criminals – ODC as they are now called[14] – continued to be arrested and tried under the ordinary criminal procedures. Although there have been important changes over the years, the dual system still operates today.

The PTA, however, not only created a different system for dealing with those against whom there was some independent evidence suggesting that they were involved in or had committed offences relating to terrorism, it also created a system with the potential to bring into custody and interrogate *anyone,* irrespective of whether or not there was any evidence against them, because the principal arrest required no reasonable suspicion of an offence.

Inevitably, a very different culture and atmosphere quickly developed around PTA arrests. Security in police stations became much more intense, there was heightened tension and the dissemination of information to the media was more carefully handled. One of the aims of the study is to explore these differences not only in the law but also in the way in which PTA detainees are perceived and treated by the police.

Until 1984 the PTA was solely directed towards dealing with political violence arising from Northern Ireland affairs. In 1984 it was extended to cover international terrorism, that is, political violence arising in any part of the world. This, however, did not radically alter the use of the Act. As can be seen from Figure 1.1, the legislation was, and still is, primarily used in relation to Northern Ireland affairs. While there has been a significant reduction in the number of people detained each year under the PTA, whether at ports and airports or elsewhere, on average 96 per cent of all those detained each year since 1984 relate to people picked up in connection with Northern Ireland affairs. Although the official statistics provide no information on the nationality or other characteristics of those detained, all the available evidence from this study and elsewhere suggests that most of those examined, arrested and detained under the PTA in Britain have been Irish or have had strong Irish connections. Irish people living here and/or moving between Britain and Ireland have, therefore, become a suspect community. In subsequent chapters we will show how this suspect community has been constructed.

There is another key feature of the PTA. Of the 7,052 people who have been detained in connection with Northern Ireland affairs under the PTA, over 6,097, or 86 per cent, have been released without any action being taken against them.[15] In terms of the figures for Britain, it means that one person has been detained and then released for at least every day the legislation has been in force. If it is assumed that people are detained for two days on average, this group has in total spent 33 years in custody – an abuse of power which must be considered

6

Figure 1.1 Number of Persons Detained under the PTA in Connection with Northern Ireland Affairs and International Terrorism, 1974-1991.

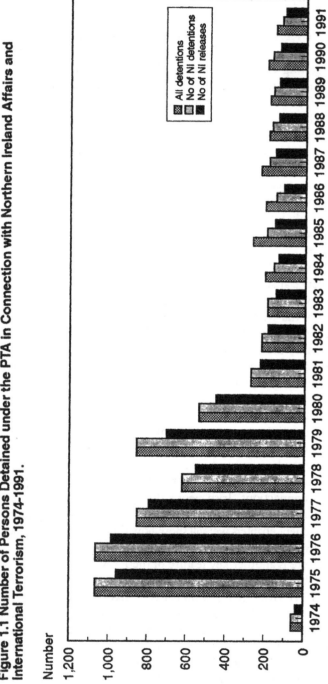

Source: Home Office Statistics

alongside the combined total of 200 or more years of wrongful imprisonment of the Birmingham 6, the Guildford 4 and the Maguire 7.

What is abundantly clear is that a person who is drawn into the criminal justice system under the PTA is not a suspect in the normal sense of the word. In other words, they are not believed to be involved in or guilty of some illegal act. As we will show in subsequent chapters, people are suspects primarily because they are *Irish* and once they are in the police station they are often labelled an Irish suspect, presumably as part of some classification system. In practice, they are being held because they belong to a suspect community. The distinction between the two different categories was succinctly put by one person in the study when he asked rhetorically: Irish *suspect*? or *Irish* suspect?

Eighteen years after the introduction of the PTA, the dangers of hasty and precipitous reaction to political violence is only too apparent. The Birmingham 6, as the world now knows, were innocent of the bombings but were beaten up by the police, made false confessions under duress, and were convicted and sentenced to 21 life sentences in a top security trial in Lancashire castle. It then took the criminal justice system 16 years to admit its error and release the six from jail.[16]

Other injustices were to follow, and the PTA played a significant part in these cases. The first person arrested under the PTA was Paul Hill. Along with Gerry Conlon, Patrick Armstrong and Carole Richardson he was subsequently charged with bombing public houses in Guildford and Woolwich. They had all been arrested along with tens of other Irish people and subjected to various degrees of violence. The four were subsequently convicted on the basis of confessions which were beaten out of them. They spent a total of over 60 years behind bars before being released.[17]

Another group arrested at the same time as the Guildford 4 under the PTA were six members of the Maguire family and a neighbour (the Maguire 7). They were all subsequently convicted of possessing explosives solely on the basis of forensic tests. Guiseppe Conlon, Gerry Conlon's father, died in prison and the rest served their sentences. Their convictions too have now been quashed.[18]

Judith Ward was also arrested under the PTA in 1974. She was subsequently convicted – on the basis of contradictory statements and similar forensic tests as the Birmingham 6 and carried out by the same forensic scientist – of killing 12 people with a bomb in an army coach on the M62. She spent 18 years in prison before being released from her life sentence by the Court of Appeal in May 1992.

Official Reviews

There have now been three major reviews of the legislation by Lord
Shackleton, Lord Jellicoe and Lord Colville and a number of yearly assessments of the operation of the PTA. They have all, however, suffered
from a number of fundamental weaknesses. To begin with, the terms
of reference for the three major reviews were very restrictive and
began with the phrase, 'Accepting the continuing need for legislation
against terrorism ...' All the reviewers accepted this condition either
implicitly or explicitly in conducting their reviews. The Shackleton
Report made no comment on it. The Jellicoe Report was satisfied that:
'from preliminary enquiries and from a close perusal of the parliamentary debates ... that some form of special legislation was indeed required
to deal with the continuing threat posed by terrorism throughout the
United Kingdom'.[19] The evidence obtained from these preliminary
enquiries and the parliamentary debates is not, however, presented
nor an argument developed for public scrutiny. The Colville Report
was unhesitating in its belief, following a review of the Act in 1986, that
there was a need for continuing legislation.[20] Again, no further details
were given and no argument developed.

Second, they have focused almost exclusively on obtaining information
from only one group – those responsible for implementing and operating
the legislation. They relied principally upon official files and statistics,
visits to observe at ports, airports and police stations, and discussions with
those responsible for implementing the legislation and those using the
powers. While some attempt was made to seek the views of people other
than those, in the words of the Jellicoe Report, in 'the Establish-
ment'[21] – through press advertisements and letters of invitation – these
techniques initiated a response mainly from academics, politicians,
political parties and organisations concerned with civil liberties. They
did not produce a significant response from the many thousands of people
who have been examined, arrested or detained under the Acts.

No attempt was made to conduct any systematic research in Great
Britain to assess rigorously the impact of the Acts upon individuals, their
families or upon the Irish community in general. This, however, did
not prevent the inclusion of the claim, in the latest Colville Report, that
the committee had 'built up a detailed picture of the legislation as it is
actually experienced by ... *those whom it affects...*' (emphasis added).[22]

The third weakness of the reviews is that although they have been
described as independent, and successive governments have emphasised
this point, this is misleading. The men who carried out the three major

reviews of legislation have all been closely associated with government over many years. For example, Lord Jellicoe is a former SAS officer and ex-head of the secret National Security Commission. It would, therefore, be surprising if their politics and past experiences did not incline some of those appointed towards supporting special powers[23] irrespective of any restrictive terms of reference.

The Origins and Aims of the Project

Since the introduction of the PTA, the National Council for Civil Liberties (since 1989 known as Liberty[24]) has been concerned about the implications of the Acts for civil liberties. In various publications it has drawn attention to the many infringements of civil liberties and has campaigned against the legislation on the grounds that the ordinary criminal law has provided sufficient powers to deal with political violence.[25] No systematic research had, however, been carried out into the operation of the Act.

In 1983 the Troops Out movement applied for funds from the Greater London Council to monitor the legislation and conduct research into its impact on the Irish community in London. There was uproar when news of the application was made public. Nearly every newspaper carried the story and it was an item on the BBC TV news at 9 o'clock. The committee meeting to consider the application was postponed and the application was subsequently rejected.

Later in the year, Liberty submitted a grant application to examine the impact of the legislation on Londoners and to provide advice to those affected by the legislation. Funds were granted. Further support for the project was provided by the London Boroughs Grants Committee. By the end of 1988, 81 statements had been obtained from people examined, detained, arrested or excluded under the PTA. A research report based on these 81 cases was then submitted to the London Boroughs Grants Committee in February 1989. At this point, although there was no further money to continue with the project within Liberty, I offered to continue to collect cases and publish a book on the findings. A further 34 statements were obtained by the end of December 1991. The book is therefore based on some 115 statements as well as newspaper reports and many letters received over the years by Liberty from people who have been detained under the PTA.

When the grant to Liberty was announced a number of papers carried the story. The *Daily Telegraph*, for example, carried the headline

'GLC to pay for inquiry into Terror Act effect on Irish'.[26] Some reports either explicitly or implicitly suggested that the research would assist terrorism. The climate of opinion is now very different. After the release of the Birmingham 6, the Guildford 4, the Maguire 7 and Judith Ward, there is now widespread recognition that much is radically wrong with the British criminal justice system. Lord Denning expressed it more strongly at the time of the release of the Guildford 4 when he described the system as 'being in ruins'. The Government's response, after the release of the Guildford 4, was to set up a Royal Commission on Criminal Justice.

Initially there were two major aims to the project. The first aim was to examine people's experiences of being detained or arrested under the PTA and to explore the wider impact of the legislation on the Irish community in London. A second aim was to study the operation of the legal powers and ascertain whether or not people's very limited rights under the PTA were being upheld. In other words, the focus here was on the legal powers and rules and not specifically on people's experiences. As the study progressed, the first aim became the central focus. This was in part due to the nature of the interview material. In many cases people did not know their precise legal status at any point in time. For example, many did not know whether they were being examined, detained or arrested. Moreover, they were often confused about when the authorities did specific things. Hence it was impossible to make any precise assessment of the operation of the rule of law.

Another factor, however, was also important in influencing this shift in focus. As the study progressed the results of other work on the operation of the criminal justice system were being published. Almost without exception, these focused on the operation of the legal rules and the extent to which rights introduced under the Police and Criminal Evidence Act (PACE) in 1984 were being applied. In general the narrow legal approach tends to ignore what people experience and what they consider to be important in the criminal justice process. All too often people are treated at best as objects and at worst as statistics. Seldom is there any attempt to ask people what they felt. As the descriptions of people's experiences in this study were so vivid and detailed, it was considered important to focus on these aspects rather than on the application of the legal rules and infringement of civil rights.

This study, therefore, adopts a very different approach from many of the recent studies of the criminal justice system and also from that adopted in the official reviews of the PTA. It examines the operation of the PTA from below rather than from above by focusing upon the experiences of those directly affected by the legislation. Such a focus, it must be emphasised, involves a moral and political act of commitment to understanding the world from the perspective of those who are powerless.

It was impossible, for obvious reasons, to obtain a random sample of all those detained. Instead the study adopted a networking approach. This is described in more detail in Appendix I. Essentially this involved building up a sample through making contacts within the Irish community and elsewhere. This produced a sample of some 115 people. Eighty were men and 35 were women. Fifty-eight were Catholics from Northern Ireland and 20 were of Irish Catholic backgrounds living in Britain. There were nine people from the Republic living in England and a similar number of English people in the sample. In terms of outcome, 66 per cent were released without any action being taken against them compared with the 86 per cent of all detentions under Acts between 1974 and the end of 1991. Some 26 per cent were excluded, 8 per cent were charged with offences compared with 5 per cent and 10 per cent respectively of the 7,052 people detained overall. The gender breakdown and the outcome of the cases in this study are therefore somewhat atypical of the general pattern. But there is no evidence to suggest that their range of experiences was different from those of the other 6,097 people who were examined, detained or arrested under the PTA in Britain.

Some people may challenge the truth of the accounts. It can be argued that as so many people in the Irish community are opposed to the Act, they therefore have a vested interest in exaggerating their experiences as a means of helping to bring about change. Clearly this is always a possibility. However, there was little to suggest that the contents of the statements had been distorted for political purposes. What emerged was a uniformity of experience which would have been hard to achieve if people had not been prepared to describe their experiences in a frank and truthful manner. In any event, many of the experiences were painful and do not put the informant in an heroic light and people are most unlikely to lie in such circumstances.

The principal problem with the interview material was not the accuracy of the accounts but how to select material from the often extensive descriptions of experiences, in some cases covering 20 pages of transcript. The overall aim was to capture what happened to people at particular stages throughout the criminal justice process. Typically this type of research involves making selections from all the statements to describe a particular stage or process, for example, the initial stop, the examination or an interrogation. A large element of judgement is required in making the selections. Moreover, this approach, focusing on a particular stage or process, does not capture a person's complete experience or their overall feelings. The reader is presented only with a snapshot at one point in time and the cumulative impact is lost. To overcome this problem three case studies are presented in full – one of an examination lasting 50 minutes is presented in Chapter 3 and two detentions – one four-day and one one-day detention – are described in Chapter 5.

The Structure of the Book

People's experiences of the PTA are described in Chapters 3, 5, 6, 7, 8, 10 and 11. Apart from Chapter 5, each chapter describes a number of people's experiences of some particular aspect of the PTA. For example, Chapter 3 explores what happened to people who were stopped and examined at ports and airports. Their experiences are broken down into the initial stop, the examination conditions, the type of questions asked, the personal documents which were examined and the overall impact of the detention. The other chapters follow the same pattern with a description of a number of people's experiences of different processes. Chapter 5 is different. It provides case studies of women who were arrested at home and detained in Paddington Green and a local police station.

Although the main purpose of the book is to describe people's experiences, another aim is to provide detailed information on the powers and procedures under the PTA. The different aspects of the law are described in Chapters 2, 4 and 9, and are interspersed with the chapters dealing with people's experiences. It must be emphasised that these have been written from a civil libertarian perspective and aim to inform the public of what their very limited rights are under the PTA. The aim is therefore to provide people with a succinct summary of the law so that they can either assess their own experiences against this information or be better informed of the law if they are arrested or detained in the future.

Finally, Chapter 12 offers an assessment of the PTA. It confirms the findings of other work carried out by Liberty: that the Acts have severely undermined the principles of natural justice and that the provisions violate international standards on human rights. At the same time, they have had a profound impact on the Irish community in general and on a large number of individuals who have been either arrested or detained under the legislation.

2   Policing Ports and Airports: Examination and Detention Powers

Introduction

The introduction of the PTA in 1974 gave the Secretary of State considerable new powers to control the movement of people between Ireland and Great Britain. It provided extensive powers to establish a comprehensive system of port controls and a process of internal exile which gives the Secretary of State the power to remove people who are already living in Great Britain to either Northern Ireland or the Republic of Ireland. Although the legislation was extended in 1984 to cover international terrorism the port powers were devised, and have been principally applied, to control Irish people travelling between Britain and Ireland. In both substance and practice, therefore, the PTA is a discriminatory piece of law in that it is directed primarily at one section of the travelling public. In effect it means that Irish people in general have a more restrictive set of rights than other travellers. In this sense, the Irish community as a whole is a 'suspect community'.

Establishing a comprehensive system of port controls involved a number of factors. The police were given extensive new powers and the powers of immigration officers under the Immigration Act 1971 were greatly expanded. The National Ports Scheme, set up in 1968, was expanded to deal with the new work introduced by the PTA. To coordinate the overall policing of ports and airports a special unit, about which very little is known, was established at New Scotland Yard in the mid–1970s under the title of the National Joint Unit (NJU in official parlance).

The system of internal exile is based on the power of the Secretary of State to issue an exclusion order to a person prohibiting their presence in one part of the United Kingdom and forcing them to live either in Northern Ireland or the Republic of Ireland. Under this system the person has no right to see the evidence against them and no right to go before a court: the decision is purely an executive one.

These two systems of control have a significance which go beyond the immediate requirement of policing the movement of people between Britain and Ireland. They are likely to form the blueprint for policing the movement of people in Europe with the advent of 1992. Although the official aim is to create an 'area without internal frontiers', the reality is likely to be very different. As Michael Spencer has pointed out, the concept of a ring fence surrounding what has been dubbed 'Fortress Europe' has rapidly come to dominate the planning of EC governments. Plans are now being made not only to intensify checks at external borders, but also to introduce random internal checks. 'For some people', as Michael Spencer remarks, 'all this begins to look like less, rather than more freedom.'[1]

Much has already been agreed. Under the Schengen Agreement to which France, Germany, Belgium, Luxembourg and the Netherlands are already signatories, there will be far greater cooperation between the police, coupled with a harmonisation of immigration and other policies. More specifically, there will be increased policing of external borders and many internal checks. For example, anyone who stays in a hotel or lodging house, and even on a hired boat or at a camping site, must fill in a form and show proof of identity. And most important of all, a computerised Schengen Information System is to be established. This will store a wide range of information including details on wanted or missing persons and vehicles and details of non-EC nationals who have been refused admission, as well as persons who have been extradited or expelled. In addition, it will store information on people or vehicles who are under surveillance. This information will be available to a range of agencies responsible for policing within as well as outside the community.[2]

Many of the features of the PTA policing system can be readily identified within the Schengen proposals, and there can be little doubt that far from seeing an increase in the freedom of movement within the new Europe, certain sections of the population – immigrant workers and gypsies, for example – will be subject to greater surveillance and control. The way in which the policing of ports and airports operates under the PTA at the moment therefore sheds important light on how so-called 'suspect' populations are likely to be treated in the new Europe.

The aim of this chapter is to consider various aspects of the policing of ports and airports under the PTA. It begins with a brief description of the National Ports Scheme and then looks at the various powers available to examine and detain people entering or leaving Britain.

National Ports Scheme

The National Port Scheme was inaugurated in 1968. Its principal aim was to coordinate the policing of ports and airports. Initially, it was

15

Figure 2.1 Location of Designated Ports and Airports in the United Kingdom.

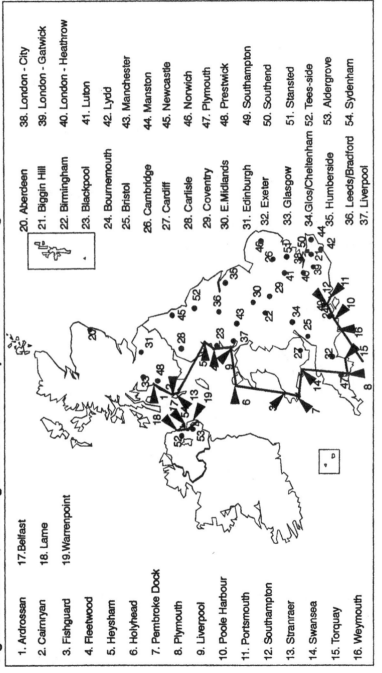

1. Ardrossan	17. Belfast	20. Aberdeen
2. Cairnryan	18. Larne	21. Biggin Hill
3. Fishguard	19. Warrenpoint	22. Birmingham
4. Fleetwood		23. Blackpool
5. Heysham		24. Bournemouth
6. Holyhead		25. Bristol
7. Pembroke Dock		26. Cambridge
8. Plymouth		27. Cardiff
9. Liverpool		28. Carlisle
10. Poole Harbour		29. Coventry
11. Portsmouth		30. E.Midlands
12. Southampton		31. Edinburgh
13. Stranraer		32. Exeter
14. Swansea		33. Glasgow
15. Torquay		34. Glos/Cheltenham
16. Weymouth		35. Humberside
		36. Leeds/Bradford
		37. Liverpool

38. London - City	
39. London - Gatwick	
40. London - Heathrow	
41. Luton	
42. Lydd	
43. Manchester	
44. Manston	
45. Newcastle	
46. Norwich	
47. Plymouth	
48. Prestwick	
49. Southampton	
50. Southend	
51. Stansted	
52. Tees-side	
53. Aldergrove	
54. Sydenham	

located at New Scotland Yard but it was moved to London Heathrow Airport in 1983. It is staffed by Special Branch officers and provides 24 hour coverage.[3] Under the PTA the number of points of entry between Britain and Ireland is restricted to certain 'designated ports'.[4] These are shown on Figure 2.1. As can be seen, all major western seaports and a number of southern seaports are designated and together they form a barrier running from the Isle of Arran to the Isle of Wight.

Very little information about the working of the scheme, however, is publicly available. The annual reports of Her Majesty's Chief Inspector of Constabulary, however, do provide some details of the impact of the PTA on the scheme.[5] By the end of 1974 the total number of ports or groups of ports covered by the scheme in the United Kingdom was 66, to which 37 police forces contributed 559 officers. This included 160 extra officers to assist in fulfilling the requirements of the PTA.[6] By 1989, some 780 police officers were deployed permanently and another 110 were deployed on an occasional basis. It is reported that 'much of this manpower was responsible' for monitoring the PTA.[7] In short, there appears to have been at least a sixfold increase in the manpower deployed at ports and airports to fulfil the requirements of the PTA. This increase, however, needs to be set against the huge increase in the volume of passenger traffic. For all ports and airports, it totalled 134.4 million passengers in 1989 – a 10 per cent increase over the previous year alone.[8]

In 1985 a former Inspector of Constabulary was asked to carry out a study of port facilities.[9] This report was never made public but the overall purpose of the various recommendations was to achieve a more standard form of port policing and to improve the overall efficiency and effectiveness of police operations. In September 1987 a national coordinator of ports' policing was appointed to provide advice and assistance to chief officers and to promote coordination of the work of port units.[10]

The National Joint Unit

The most important organisation in the policing structure of ports and airports is the National Joint Unit which is based in Scotland Yard. There is also very little public information available on its organisation and functions. In 1991 the Home Secretary was asked to describe its role. He said:

The role of the National Joint Unit at New Scotland Yard is to prepare, on behalf of all police forces in Great Britain, applications to the Secretary of State for extensions of detention and exclusion orders under the Prevention of Terrorism (Temporary Provisions) Act 1989, and to provide advice to police forces on the operation of the Act. The unit is staffed by 17 police officers, most of whom are seconded to it for short periods from provincial forces.[11]

This is an incomplete answer. The NJU clearly has other functions. First, to work together with other sections of the police and security forces to collate all the data on wanted and suspected terrorists. Second, to circulate this information to the ports and airports on a regular basis. Third, to answer all enquiries from ports and airports about specific passengers.

It is not known whether the unit has its own computer or whether it makes use of other computers run by the police or security services. As will be seen from the number of queries made by ports and airports every year, the NJU would require fast access to a database. What probably happens is that the NJU updates on a daily basis a list of wanted and suspect persons from various sources. This information is then probably stored on the Police National Computer. This database will then be checked if a query is received from a port or airport. If a person's name appears on the database, then they are likely to be stopped and examined if they are due to pass through the port or, if already detained, to be held for further examination. In the meantime further information may be obtained from a variety of other sources, possibly from the Special Branch or the army or RUC in Northern Ireland.

For security reasons, there is no way of knowing the number of people who are defined as suspects or the type of information which is stored on them. Nor is the Home Secretary prepared to make public the total number of records on the database currently in use. He reported that it is not available in the form requested.[12] The Data Protection Act 1984 provides people with the right to see certain computerised records but does not apply to databases which are designed for the purposes of law enforcement. There is therefore no way in which a person can check the accuracy of the information held on them. Yet the information may lead to long periods of detention at a port or airport and considerable inconvenience, such as missed flights and extra costs. In addition, there is no way of knowing whether the list of suspects systematically discriminates against any particular section of the community, such as all people living in Nationalist areas in Northern Ireland.

The work of the National Port Scheme and the NJU is made easier by a number of important requirements under the PTA. Captains of ships and aircraft, if required by an examining officer, must provide on arrival at all designated ports a manifest of all passengers and crew.[13] It is not known what proportion of ships and aircraft are required to provide a passenger manifest. Captains must also ensure that passengers embark and disembark in accordance with the arrangements approved by the examining officers.[14] In addition, examining officers have the power to insist that all passengers complete a landing or embarkation card.[15]

Unfettered Discretion to Examine

The powers to stop anyone entering or leaving Great Britain are very wide. The legislation provides an examining officer (typically Special Branch Officers but also immigration and HM Customs and Excise officers), with the power to stop and then examine anyone who has arrived in or is seeking to leave Great Britain by ship or aircraft.[16] The stated purpose of the examination is to determine whether the person is or has been concerned in the commission, preparation or instigation of acts of terrorism, is subject to an exclusion order or whether there are grounds for suspecting that the person has committed an offence under the Act.[17]

Unlike the inland arrest power under the PTA,[18] there is no requirement when a person is stopped that the examining officer must have reasonable suspicion that the person is involved in terrorism. This position has been confirmed by Lord Donaldson. He argued that:

> ... an officer has to satisfy himself of the only matter upon which he must be satisfied, namely, that the person whom he seeks to examine is in the category of person where he can say to himself *bona fide* 'I wish to find out whether this person has, for example, information which he or she should have disclosed under section 11'. He does not have to have any grounds for thinking that they have the information, but merely that the person concerned shall be in a category or there should be special circumstances which in his view make it reasonable that he should find out and that he should ask questions.[19]

This power provides the examining officers with almost unfettered discretion in the sense that they may stop anyone and subject them to examination and the courts have virtually no power to intervene except to enquire whether the examining officer 'is acting *bona fide*' and 'whether ... his conduct is *prima facie* such as no reasonable person could have taken'.[20]

Random investigations, as Walker has pointed out,[21] are therefore lawful under the PTA. But more importantly, the law appears to allow examining officers to go much further than carrying out random investigations, permitting them to stop particular categories of people. As Lord Donaldson put it: 'He does not have to have any grounds for thinking that they have the information, but merely *that the person concerned shall be in a category* ...'[22] (emphasis added).

In other words, it is lawful for examining officers to stop and examine someone simply because they are Irish. This is a much more insidious power than one which permits only random investigations. Under a system of random investigation, in theory at least, everyone has an equal chance of being stopped. This, after all, is the meaning of random. The examination powers, as interpreted by the Court of Appeal, permit categories of people to be picked out. They are therefore discriminatory.

At this point it is helpful to note that there is a difference between an examination, detention and arrest. As we will discuss in more detail later in the chapter, a person can be examined without being detained; they can be detained for the purposes of the examination; and they can be arrested. There must be reasonable suspicion for an arrest to take place, but it is not required for an examination or for a detention for the purposes of an examination.

Examination Rules

In the early years of the PTA's operation an examination could continue for up to seven days. In 1984, certain time limits were placed on the examination process. One hour after the beginning of the examination the examining officer is now required to hand the person being examined a notice of their rights. The notice is in a standard form and is reproduced in Table 2.1.

It has been argued that the notice 'ensures that persons are cognisant of their rights and emphasises that an examination is in process even if an individual has not been detained'.[23] The reality is very different. To begin with, the Notice of Examination is factually wrong. It refers to 'under that Order'. There is no such Order under the 1989 legislation. The Colville Report recommended that instead of being contained in Statutory Instruments, i.e. Orders, all port powers should be enacted in primary legislation.[24] In other words, all powers should be noted in the main Act itself. This recommendation was accepted and therefore the notice should read 'under this Act' rather than 'under this Order'.

Table 2.1 Notice of Examination Recommended in Home Office Circular, No. 27/1989.

PREVENTION OF TERRORISM (TEMPORARY PROVISIONS) ACT 1989

Notice of Examination

You are being [examined] [detained for examination] under the Prevention of Terrorism (Temporary Provisions) Act 1989. Under the Act you have a duty to give the examining officer all such information in your possession as he may require for the purpose of his function under that Order.

[The examining officer has authority under the Order to detain you if necessary pending the conclusion of his examination.]

Do you want someone informed?

If you wish, you may at public expense have one person known to you, or who is likely to take an interest in your welfare, informed that you are being [examined] [detained] and where you are.

Do you want to contact a solicitor?

You may consult and communicate either in person, in writing or on the telephone with a solicitor.

Delay

If a delay in meeting your request is considered necessary, you will be so informed.

If you do not want to make any request now, you may make it later.

This failure to update the Notice of Examination not only reflects the apparent lack of concern within the Executive concerning civil liberties but it must also cause considerable confusion to switch from talking about an Act to a non-existent Order.

Secondly, the notice does little to clarify a person's legal status at this point in time. It is headed Notice of Examination but, as shown below, a person may by then have been detained. In other words, the examination stage will have come to a halt and the detention stage begun, but there is nothing on the form to explain this important distinction; it has to be inferred from the deletion of the word 'examined' in two places on the form. The person being detained experiences no change whatsoever in their state of confinement as they pass from a process of examination to one of detention.

Thirdly, the form's content is confusing. It asks if people want someone to be informed that they are being examined/detained, or if they want to contact a solicitor. But then it immediately states that 'if a delay in meeting your request is considered necessary, you will be so informed'. No information is provided as to which grounds may make such a delay necessary. Nor is there any requirement for the examining officer to state a reason. In effect people being examined have no rights. They are dependent upon concessions which may or may not be granted by the very same authority which is carrying out the examination.

Power to Detain Pending the Conclusion of the Examination

The detention powers under the PTA have also given rise to considerable confusion. An examining officer may detain a person being examined at any time during the examination. It is often assumed that the examining officer may detain someone only when they have formed a reasonable suspicion that they have been concerned in the commission, preparation or instigation of acts of terrorism. But no such suspicion is required to detain a person pending the conclusion of an examination. The PTA thus provides examining officers with the unfettered power to detain and question anyone.

There are certain time limits on the examination process which are shown in Figure 2.2. If the examining officer does not have reasonable grounds at the end of a 12-hour period for suspecting that the person has been concerned in the commission, preparation or instigation of acts of terrorism, the person must be released. But if there is reasonable suspicion, it is solely at the discretion of the examining officer whether or not a person is formally detained at the end of the 12-hour period.[25] Whether or not the person is to be examined further or detained, they must be issued with a notice stating that one or other stage is to continue.

While it is likely that most people will have been formally detained by the end of the 12-hour period, there is no requirement that they should be. Indeed, the Home Office circular on the law goes as far as to point out that: 'In a very few cases, however, the person may be willing to cooperate and it may not prove necessary to detain him or

22

Figure 2.2 The Examination Process at Ports and Airports.

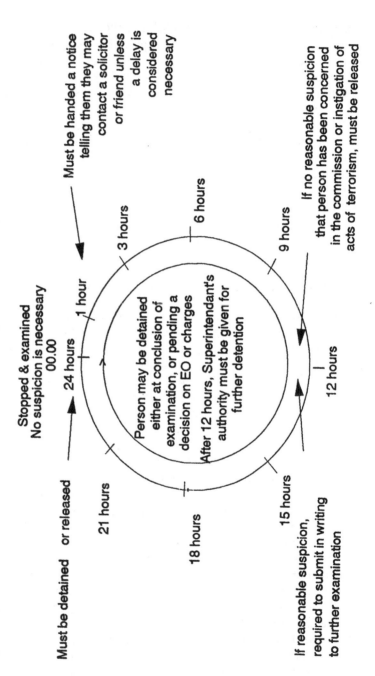

her.'[26] The law however does not permit any further examination after 24 hours. At this point the person must be detained, if the examination is to continue, or be released.[27]

Power to Question

One of the most contentious aspects of the PTA has been the power of examining officers to ask whatever questions they wish and no attempt has ever been made to restrict the type of questions that can be asked. The Colville Report noted:

> There are some critics who say that people are detained and then questioned about a whole expanse of their political affiliations, their activities and their friends; associates and family members also receive attention.

It concluded that:

> It would doubtless be accepted that the police should not use their authority to bring in at random Irish or other passengers and then subject them to a general inquisition on their life-style, leisure activities and other personal details.[28]

The Report then went on to argue, however, that it could see no way of banning what it called 'fishing expeditions'. It gave two grounds. First, as terrorists are trained in anti-interrogation techniques – they stay silent for long periods – the police therefore need to roam over a variety of subjects in the hope that clues will emerge. This is a *non sequitur*. If terrorists are trained, they are likely to remain silent, particularly for any examination period of up to 12 hours, and there is no reason to assume that any clue is likely to emerge by asking a wide range of questions which are not being responded to in any event. The second reason given is even more spurious. It is argued that 'if people are innocent and unconnected with terrorism they will not know that there are methods employed by terrorists to waste time and generally sap the progress of an inquiry.'[29] In short, a person's innocence and lack of knowledge is used as a justification to subject them to the traumatic experience of being interrogated about their politics and lifestyle.

Powers to Demand to See all Relevant Material

There are a number of further powers relating to the examination. A person who is undergoing an examination must produce a valid passport or some other document which will satisfactorily establish their identity and nationality or citizenship.[30] Moreover, they must say whether they are carrying or conveying documents of any 'relevant description' specified by the examining officer and they must produce the material if asked to do so.[31] The phrase 'relevant description' is defined in a very loose and open-ended way and simply covers anything which appears to the examining officer to be relevant for the purposes of the examination.[32] The legislation therefore makes no attempt to specify the types of documents which may be examined and leaves this entirely up to the discretion of the examining officers.

These powers constitute a significant invasion of a person's privacy. They give the police the unfettered discretion to ask for any material, however personal, including address books, diaries and cheque books. It is significant that none of the reviews considered the privacy implications of these powers. All focused on the problems facing those carrying out the examinations. The Shackleton Report said nothing about the powers other than that the police were under no illusions about the potential for forging documents.[33] The Jellicoe Report was principally concerned about the satisfaction and morale of those conducting the examinations.[34] The Colville Report, however, did note that there had been complaints that documents are removed and held for a period, but then argued that 'these powers are part of the price to be paid for keeping terrorism at bay'.[35]

Search Powers including Strip Searches

The legislation also provides extensive search powers and these are often used to obtain documents to examine. As with so many of the PTA powers, the discretion allowed is extremely wide and permits an examining officer to search anyone who has been stopped and also any baggage which they may be carrying.[36] The only restriction is that the search of a person may only be carried out by someone of the same sex.[37] If the authorities wish to carry out a strip search it is recommended, but it is not obligatory, for the person to be formally detained and taken to a police station to be searched. Since 1989 the PACE Codes of Practice have applied to these searches.[38] In addition to these powers of search, the examining officers may search any ship or aircraft.[39]

Power to Retain Personal Documents

The authorities are under no obligation to return immediately any material which is demanded during an examination or found during a search, even if the owner is examined for only a matter of minutes and released. They are allowed to keep letters, diaries, cheque books and other personal documents for up to seven days.[40]

The legislation makes no reference to material which is photocopied by an examining officer. It is unclear whether photocopied material is covered by the seven day retention rule and must therefore be returned. The law as it stands states only that 'anything produced' or 'found under examination' should be returned after seven days. But there is considerable ambiguity over the word 'produced'. If it means only that which is given up or handed over by the person examined, then photocopied material would not be covered. If 'produced', however, is defined more widely to mean any material which is either handed over or *generated* in the examination such as a photocopy, then photocopies of material would have to be returned as well.

Even if the law does mean that photocopies of documents should be returned at the end of seven days, there is no guarantee that this will occur. There is no independent scrutiny of the examining officers' files. There is also nothing to stop examining officers from taking extra photocopies during the seven days of which the person would not be aware.

The Duty to Comply

These draconian examination and search powers apply to everyone who is stopped. No one can object to a specific power; everyone has a duty to obey. All the separate powers are ultimately underpinned by a single coercive sanction:

> A person who knowingly contravenes any prohibition or fails to comply with any duty or requirement imposed by or under this Schedule is guilty of an offence and liable on summary conviction to imprisonment for a term not exceeding three months or a fine not exceeding level 4 on the standard scale [£1,000] or both.[41]

This sanction, coupled with the requirement that a person must produce 'all such information' which the examining officer requires 'for the purposes of his functions', effectively abolishes the traditional right of a person to remain silent. In the Committee Stage of the PTA Bill in 1989, Peter Archer distinguished between three very different meanings of this ancient right to silence and what its curtailment actually means. First, it can mean that if a suspect is interrogated and fails to answer questions or make a statement, the court can draw an adverse inference. Second, it can mean that if the suspect does not answer questions or provide a statement then they have committed an offence, separate from the original one of which they are suspected. Third, it can mean that someone who is not a suspect, but has simply been stopped and examined, and who fails to answer questions or provide an identity, is then guilty of an offence. It is not necessary for there to be a shred of evidence against them, but they will be asked to provide evidence against themselves. As Peter Archer argued, each meaning is more sinister than the next as far as the erosion of civil liberties is concerned. 'We have gone from the top of the bank to the bottom and have cleared all three stages in one.'[42]

The abolition of the right of silence at a point where people have been detained not on the basis of suspicion or even reasonable suspicion but simply at the whim of the examining officer, has fundamental importance if they are subsequently detained on reasonable suspicion. At the heart of the adversarial system of British law is the privilege against self-incrimination. This means that a person has the right to remain silent in order not to incriminate themselves. As the PTA removes the right to remain silent, it contradicts one of the traditional principles of English law and the examination process effectively deprives the defendant of a fair trial. Examinations may, therefore, radically increase the chance of miscarriages of justice.

The PTA, in making it an offence not to provide information or to answer questions, further indicates that those drawn into the criminal justice process at ports and airports under the PTA experience more coercive powers regarding the provision of information than those drawn into the process inland under the PTA or under the ordinary criminal justice system.

Detention Power

It has already been pointed out that there is no clear rule concerning when an examination must come to an end and a detention begin. Under the PTA an examining officer may authorise the detention of the person who is being examined either at the conclusion of the examination, or pending decisions of the Secretary of State, the Director of Public Prosecutions or the Attorney General.[43]

Once detained, a person can be held for a period not exceeding 48 hours from the time when they were first stopped and examined.[44] The Secretary of State must then approve a further period or periods not exceeding five days.[45] These procedures are similiar to extensions to detentions following an arrest and will be dealt with in more detail in Chapter 4. It should be noted that it is recommended in the Home Office circular that 'formal detention should be treated as beginning as soon as it becomes necessary to prevent the person from leaving the examination area rather than when a person is removed to a place of detention – usually a police station'.[46]

While it is possible for the person to be detained for the seven days at the place where they are examined, it is normal practice to take them to a suitable police station unless the port or airport has proper detention facilities.

The Number of People Examined

There has been considerable confusion over the years about the extent to which the examination powers have been used. This stems principally from the failure of the authorities to provide detailed and comprehensive information. The main confusion has arisen over the number of annual inquiries made to the National Joint Unit, which were recorded for a number of years in Her Majesty's Chief Inspector of Constabulary reports for England and Wales. It was assumed that each enquiry meant that a person was physically stopped and examined.[47] This is not necessarily the case.

What typically happens is this. The manifests of passengers and vehicles made available to the authorities under the PTA will be looked at and a number of checks will be made to the NJU. Similarly, landing cards which have been handed in on the outward leg will also be checked. If a person or vehicle is recorded for some reason on the Police National Computer (PNC), then they will be stopped by examining officers as they pass through the port or airport. Thus, only a proportion of those checked will be examined. At the same time, people who are stopped by the examining officers on the basis of some stereotype, may also be checked against the PNC.

The published figures on the number of enquiries made to the NJU therefore provide no information on the total number of people stopped and examined. However, they do provide some indication of the hidden or secret examination process in which thousands of people, without their knowledge, are having their name and other particulars checked against the records stored on a police computer of whose existence they are probably totally unaware. The computer may contain a record on them, but they have no right to know this and no right to see the contents. The Colville Report[48] questioned the value of these statistics published by Her Majesty's Inspector of Constabulary, but they are of some value in showing the workings of what is best described as the secret state.

Figure 2.3 shows the number of annual enquiries to the NJU for the period from 1978–90. The most noticeable feature is the steady increase in the number of enquiries over the period. In 1975, the first full year of the PTA, there were around 30,000 enquiries. In 1989, this figure stood at 101,000 – more than a threefold increase in the period. Put another way, some 250 enquiries are made every day of the year or about 10 every hour. Only in the early 1980s was there any downturn in the level of activity.

Figure 2.3 Number of Inquiries Made to the National Joint Unit at Scotland Yard, 1978-1990.

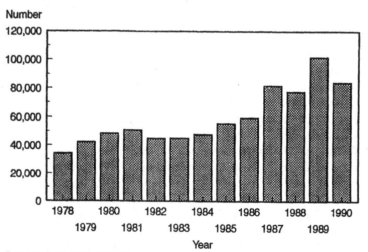

Source: Home Office Statistics

The use of examination powers are often compared with the huge volume of passenger traffic and they are then shown to affect a minuscule proportion of the total number of passengers. But this is an inappropriate comparison when one considers that the use of the powers is widely believed to be targeted at a particular section of the population: principally young men living in Ireland and Irish people living in Britain. It is impossible to tell what proportion this group makes up of the total travelling public. But even if it is assumed that the suspect travelling population was as large as four million people, it would still mean that one in every 50 are subject to a search by the NJU. This provides some picture of the extent of the secret surveillance which is now being carried out.

Since 1984, examining officers have been required to record the number of people who are stopped and examined for more than one hour. Nearly 1,000 people have now been examined but not detained for more than one hour in the period 1984–91. Figure 2.4 shows the number of people examined for longer than one hour. As with the enquiries of the NJU, there has been a steady increase. In 1984 only 31 were recorded as being examined for more than one hour. By 1991 this figure had increased to 247 – an eightfold increase. In 1991 one third were examined for between one and two hours, 56 per cent for between two and four hours and 11 per cent between four and 24 hours.

Figure 2.4 Persons Examined for More Than One Hour Under the PTA in Connection with Northern Ireland Affairs but not Detained, 1984-1991.

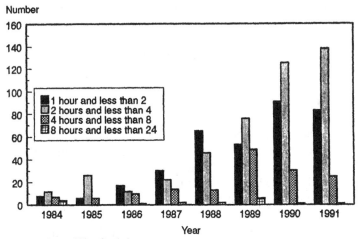

Source: Home Office Statistics

These statistics on examinations reflect only the tip of the iceberg. Some idea of the use of the powers is provided in the Colville Report.

Lord Colville observed the arrival of one ferry, which carried about 600 passengers, of whom 200 were drivers or passengers in cars, or lorry drivers. The police apparently spoke briefly to all of these people, and to nearly two-thirds of the foot-passengers. He noted that a few cards were completed and two telephone checks were made. He argued that as this was not untypical, there must be *'millions'* of examinations every year (emphasis added).[49]

As examining officers are only required to record the numbers actually detained there is a dearth of information on the amount of time the 'millions' are held. Some may be held for only a few minutes but many may be held for just under an hour. The crucial question is, how many? Even if the examining officers used their powers to question one per cent of all people for 59 minutes, it would mean that 10,000 were being detained. It would be surprising if examining officers did not use the licence given to them and use the full 59 minutes to conduct their examination.

The Colville Report, however, concluded that there do not 'seem to be any useful statistics for events which affect a passenger for less than one hour'.[50] This view seems to imply that an examination of less than one hour is of no great significance: it is just like any other inconvenience that travellers endure on entering or leaving a country. This is clearly unreasonable. As this study will show, an examination under the PTA is a very different experience from having one's baggage checked or being asked whether you have anything to declare. Many people find it a very traumatic event, particularly when the examination takes longer than a few minutes. Moreover, a delay of even half an hour may mean a missed connection and considerable extra expense.

The Number of People Detained

Figure 2.5 shows the number of people detained at ports and airports in connection with Northern Irish affairs since the introduction of the PTA in 1974. In the early years of the legislation, hundreds of people were detained each year. The highest number of detentions occurred in 1976 when 812 people were held. The figure remained high until the start of the 1980s. Since then the number has declined, reaching the lowest number in 1991 when 49 people were detained. Information on the number of women is not presented in the official statistics. However, a Parliamentary Question in 1991 produced data on the number of women held under the PTA. It recorded that between 1985 and 1991 520 people were detained, of whom 33 – or 6 per cent – were women.[51]

Figure 2.5 Persons Detained at Ports and Airports in Connection with Northern Ireland Affairs, 1974-1991 (showing gender for 1985-1991).

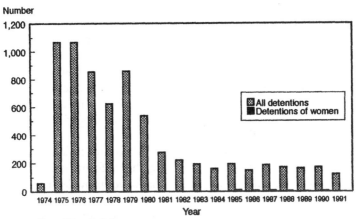

Source: Home Office Statistics

The official statistics record an aggregate figure only for the outcome of detentions; they are not broken down showing the outcome of detentions at ports and airports and those inland. But if it is assumed that there is no significant difference in the outcome of those who enter the system by way of detentions at ports and airports or arrests inland, the figures suggest that of the 4,744 people detained at ports and airports up to the end of 1991, over 4,000 were neither charged with an offence nor excluded. If each person was held on average for two days, this group as a whole spent a total of 22 years in custody.

As the content of the interviews described elsewhere shows, the principal objective of the use of the examination power is to gather intelligence, and huge trawling operations have been mounted – particularly in the early years of the legislation – to achieve this aim.

Fewer people are now being held and consequently it has been suggested that the use of the powers is much more targeted. But there is little evidence to support this. Although the proportion not charged or excluded has dropped from an average of 82 per cent during the first five years of the Act to 79 per cent during the last five years, the use of the powers can hardly be said to be targeted when nearly nine out of every ten people detained are being released without any action being taken against them.

Conclusions

This chapter has described various aspects of policing ports and airports under the PTA. It has shown the enormous powers vested in the examining officers. Their use is extensive: there are probably millions of examinations every year. In 1991 nearly 250 people were examined for more than one hour and only eight were subsequently charged with any offence. In the early years of the legislation, massive trawling operations were mounted and people pulled in for questioning. The failure of the law to restrict the type of questions that could be put to members of the travelling public no doubt encouraged the police to gather low-level intelligence.

It is, of course, very difficult for the authorities to admit that the primary purpose of questioning is to gather information. To begin with English law, unlike Scottish law, has never provided the authorities with a power to hold someone simply for questioning. Secondly, it would be seen as discriminatory because the main target is Irish people. Thirdly, such a power would involve an extensive infringement of civil liberties. It is far easier to attempt to justify an unrestricted power to question in terms of a spurious argument of unmasking terrorists travelling between Ireland and Britain.

Since 1974 there has been significant growth in what has been described as the 'secret state'. There has been a considerable expansion in the number of people who are considered suspect and an exponential increase in the amount of information which is collected and stored. Every hour of every day 10 people are having their details checked out on the police computer for PTA purposes. Moreover, the system of control is constantly expanding. There has been a threefold increase in the extent of surveillance – the checks to the NJU – and there has been a sixfold increase in the number of people stopped and examined for more than one hour. Whether the PTA is considered to be temporarily permanent or permanently temporary, in practice it has gained a permanency which is constantly drawing into its net of suspicion an increasing number of the suspect population.

Many of the policies associated with the development of a comprehensive system of policing at ports and airports have not originated in, let alone been comprehensively discussed, by Parliament. Apart from the specific powers to stop, examine, detain and search introduced under the PTA itself, the system of policing has been developed within the Home Office and higher echelons of the police. The public and, indeed, Parliament, has been presented with only a minimum of information. A similar, undemocratic form of policy making is also taking place in relation to the development of port and airport controls in Europe. The Schengen Agreement has been agreed between a small group of top civil servants and other state officials without reference to the European Parliament.

In attempting to prevent the spread of political violence to Britain, anyone living in Ireland as well as anyone with an Irish background living in England can be seen as falling within a category of people who may legitimately be stopped. The Irish community as a whole can therefore be legally viewed as a suspect community. Insofar as the port powers give examining officers unfettered discretion to stop and examine anyone who falls within a 'category of person' from whom further information is sought, the PTA is an example of institutionalised racism.

The development of the system of control at ports and airports has led to a substantial diminution of the civil rights of one section of the population – mainly those people travelling between Britain and Ireland. Their rights of citizenship have been undermined. They are now subject to extensive secret surveillance and when they are stopped and examined their right to silence has been abolished.

This erosion of civil liberties will only intensify as the system of port and airport control is further consolidated around Fortress Europe after 1992. The official policy is to eliminate all internal borders but the United Kingdom is likely to maintain the current controls at ports and airports under the PTA. If it is forced to abandon these controls, as is likely, it will then introduce a comprehensive system of random internal controls based presumably on some form of identity card. At the heart of the whole policing operation will be the computerised Schengen Information System which will differ little from the computerised system operated by the NJU at Scotland Yard.

3 Examinations and Detentions at Ports and Airports: People's Experiences

Introduction

The aim of this chapter is to analyse people's experiences at ports and airports. It describes the examination process and then presents a case study of one examination lasting 50 minutes, before describing a number of people's experiences of being stopped. The chapter also describes the conditions under which people are held, the type of questions they are asked and the information they are requested to provide. It is concerned predominantly with the initial stages of examination and detention, before people are taken to a police station. What happens to them at the police station and to all those arrested inland is dealt with in Chapter 7.

In the last chapter it was pointed out that the law makes a formal distinction between three powers available at ports and airports: a very general power of examination 'for the purposes of determining' who the person is, a more specific power of detention based on 'reasonable suspicion', and a power of arrest. Since 1984 the examining officer must give detainees a form telling them whether they are being examined or detained and they have always been required to inform a person that they are being arrested. Yet most of those stopped had little idea of their precise legal status at any particular point in time. It is therefore impossible to differentiate accurately between those who had been examined without being detained, those who were detained and those who were arrested.

It was very difficult locating people who had been stopped and examined at ports and subsequently released. Although thousands of people every year are likely to have been stopped for more than a few minutes and examined for up to an hour, most people, for very obvious reasons, do not want to draw attention to the fact and shun any publicity. They are only too aware of the possible adverse consequences of being held under the PTA. A large section of the public still believe that 'there is no smoke without fire' and that anyone who is stopped is therefore not totally innocent. In short, they are stigmatised. In a climate of sensational and biased reporting of terrorist incidents, this could hardly be otherwise. It is, therefore, eminently sensible to remain silent about the experience in case one loses friends or even one's job.

This point is clearly illustrated by one case in which a couple and their two children were stopped at Holyhead at 1 o'clock in the morning at the start of a family holiday in England. It was a freezing cold night, there were no facilities and they were held at the dockside until 7 o'clock in the morning. Their two children were forced to sleep in their vehicle and when they arrived at their guest house they were able to get only an hour's rest before having to vacate their room. They did not report their experience to the press nor did they make a formal complaint to the police. Their case came to light only by accident when one of the researchers was on holiday in the West of Ireland and was introduced to the family (580F/79, 6 hours, released).[1]

Of the 115 cases in this study, some 69 people were stopped at ports and airports. After careful consideration of the evidence, it appears that 15 people were examined, 51 were detained and three arrested.

Profile of the Cases

No systematic attempt was made to collect comprehensive personal details on those stopped at ports and airports in case this inhibited people from talking about their experiences. Some information, however, did emerge during the interviews and this is presented in Table 3.1.

Of those examined, eight were men and seven were women. Half were Catholics living in Northern Ireland, one was from the Republic and four were living in England. One third of them were attending either conferences or meetings in Britain or Northern Ireland and another third were looking for work. The others were on holiday or attending football matches.

Table 3.2 presents similar information for those who were detained or arrested. Of the 54 people, 41 were men and 13 were women. Forty four were from Northern Ireland, of whom 41 were Catholic and three were Protestant. Of those whose purpose of visit was known, 30 per cent were attending conferences, a quarter were attending football matches and 30 per cent were looking for work.

Table 3.1 Sex, Origin, Purpose of Visit, Outcome and Average Detention of Those Examined and Not Detained at Ports and Airports

	Examined only
Sex	
Male	8
Female	7
Origin	
Catholic living in Northern Ireland	7
Catholic living in the Republic	1
Irish, living in England	2
English, living in England	2
Other	3
Purpose of visit	
Attending conference/meeting	5
Looking for work in Britain	5
On holiday	3
Attending football match	2
Outcome	
Released	15
Average length of detention:	2 hours, 20 minutes
Total number of people examined only	15

As can be seen, all those who were examined and not detained were subsequently released without any action being taken against them. Their average period of detention was 2 hours and 20 minutes. Of the 54 who were detained, 30 were released after being in custody for a total of 34 days between them or 28 hours each on average. The other 23 were excluded, 22 from Britain to Northern Ireland and one from Northern Ireland to Scotland. The majority spent seven days in custody before being deported. The overall average length of detention was 81 hours.

Table 3.2 Sex, Origin, Purpose of Visit, Outcome, Average Detention of Those Detained at Ports and Airports

	Detained/Arrested
Sex	
Male	41
Female	13
Origin	
Catholic, living in Northern Ireland	41
Protestant, living in Northern Ireland	3
Living in the Republic	2
Irish, living in England	5
English, living in England	2
English, living in Ireland	1
Purpose of visit	
Attending conference/meeting	9
Looking for work in Britain	5
On business	2
Visiting family	1
On holiday	3
Attending football match	8
Other	2
Don't know	24
Outcome	
Released	30
Excluded	23
Charged	1
Average length of detention:	81 hours
Total number of people detained	54

The Examination Process

It is possible to build up a fairly clear picture of the examination process from official reports, people's experiences and by a little guesswork. Much of the key activity goes on behind the scenes and the travelling public are unaware that a series of checks is being carried out. Two sets of information are vital to the whole process: the passenger manifests of ships and aircraft and the embarkation and landing cards which passengers may be required to complete. Some of the smaller airports require these to be completed as a matter of course; others, such as Gatwick and Heathrow, ask a selected group of passengers to complete the cards. Landing cards are coloured pink and embarkation cards are green.

Prior to any ship or aircraft leaving or arriving at a designated port, the police probably carry out an inquiry or check of the passenger manifests against the NJU records. These form part of the 100,000 inquiries made every year of the NJU records.[2] If a person is on the database or is noted as being a relative or friend of someone who is under suspicion, these people will be 'flagged' to be stopped as they pass through the security check. How the examining officers pick out those they want to examine has to be guessed. But in some cases they will probably have a photograph of the person. Alternatively, they will rely on either picking up the person when they present an embarkation or landing card, or when they are requested to show some form of identity.

Other people are likely to be stopped and examined because of some official policy to stop everyone who falls into a pre-defined category, for example, all people living in republican areas of Northern Ireland or those who are unemployed. Landing cards play a crucial role in this process. As they are handed in, the examining officer can quickly check whether the person lives in a particular area or fits any of the other pre-defined categories. If they do they can be stopped and examined.

After a boat or flight has arrived or left, it is probable that a random selection of the cards will be checked against the NJU records. If the check is positive in some way, then the person will be 'flagged' to be stopped and presumably this information will be circulated to all other ports and airports.

The remainder of those examined are either simply stopped at random or because they fit some stereotype held by the examining officers of what a 'terrorist suspect' looks like.

Once a person has been stopped at a security desk, they will typically be asked to produce some form of identification. This will be followed by a few further questions about the purpose of their visit, the nature of their employment and where they were going to stay. If the person is stopped going through customs, the initial set of questions will be accompanied by a search of their luggage. In either event, if the examination, for whatever reasons, is to proceed beyond these initial questions, the person will typically be removed to some room away from the main check points or baggage search areas. If a more extensive examination is considered necessary, the person will normally be detained, if this has not already occurred, and taken to the nearest police station.

As was noted in the Introduction, space does not permit us to present every person's experience in full; it is therefore necessary to make selections from the statements to describe people's experiences of different aspects of the examination process. But in order for the reader to obtain an overall understanding of a full examination, we begin with a description of one person's particular experience.

A 50 Minute Examination at an Airport

In 1987 a woman who was seven months pregnant was travelling from England, where she was living, to Dublin to carry out some research for a biography she had been commissioned to write. She was stopped on the way out and asked a few questions. On the way back she was again stopped and examined. The examination lasted about 50 minutes and therefore forms no part of any official statistics: only examinations lasting over an hour are recorded.

> On my way back on Friday, I handed in my pink card and everyone queued. I was about the last person to go through customs because I had stopped to go to the toilet and was called over by a woman customs officer who asked me if I knew my quota. I said, 'Yes, I've just got this one bottle of alcohol.' She asked me for my passport and I replied that I'd only come from Dublin, why do I need a passport? She said: 'Of course you need a passport.' I said, 'You don't need a passport for England' and finally a customs man behind her said, 'It's all right, she doesn't need a passport for Ireland.' These were simply delaying tactics because by this stage the woman had taken over my bag and was going very carefully through everything, and as she did this the Special Branch man who had taken my pink card had come in and he was going through my big yellow bag, which contained all my files of work. He was reading them while she was going through my bag of possessions, looking through everything very carefully. I had the *Linen Hall Review* magazine which she was reading and at the same time this guy was going through magazine cuttings that I had. He then started to read my notes. He asked me questions on the notes, he said, 'What's that word?' I said 'It's Treaty.' He said, 'What Treaty does that refer to?' and I was getting

cross – by this stage everybody else had gone and there was just him and me and the woman customs officer – and I said, 'Do you want a lecture on Irish history because its quite a long process, but basically the Treaty between Britain and Ireland in 1921' and he said, 'Oh, and what government was in power then?' I said, 'Where?' and he said, 'In Britain' and I said, 'I haven't a clue' and he said, 'Liberal' and I said, 'Yes of course it was and Lloyd George was Prime Minister', thinking if I show that I don't know anything about history he would get suspicious. Then he went through all the photos in the journal, saying, 'Oh, I've never seen a picture of Michael Collins before' and such-like, saying that he was very interested in Irish history and that he had studied it.

I thought maybe he's just peculiar like that, he's being deliberately annoying and he has a little bit of knowledge and he wanted to show it off. I showed my impatience. I kept looking at my watch and sighing; at this stage I was sitting on the long bench, my big bag was repacked and he continued to read everything else that I had. I think then he went through my diary as well. I was making remarks like 'Wouldn't it be much handier if you had a photocopier here, you wouldn't have to sit and read it all now, you could just take it home and read it'. And he looked at the things as he was packing everything up and then he said: 'Well right, I now have to inform you that I have to detain you for questioning under section 4 of the Prevention of Terrorism Act.' Something about 'grounds for suspicion about,' or 'sympathising with terrorism' something like that, I can't remember the formula now. I said, 'You must be joking.' I just couldn't believe it was true. And he said, 'Come this way with me please'.

He called for a woman to come as well, and brought me down back to where we came, into this little room. The door was closed and he went off, leaving just this woman there with me and she said she had only been there for three days and she had no idea what it was all about. And I said, 'Well, I just think it's crazy.' She was sort of lying against the door as if I was about to break it down. Then he came back with another Special Branch man, and this Special Branch man started going through my bag of clothes. I said, 'All of that's been gone through very thoroughly' and he said, 'Yes, but not by me.'

So everything got taken out again, and the original man then started going through my handbag in great detail. He took out my diary, asked me if I belonged to *Spare Rib*. I said no, it was just a diary you could buy anywhere in any shop. I had been given photos by my cousin – family photos – and he started asking me about them. And then there was a letter from my father that had just arrived the morning I was getting the plane and he opened that. I said, 'That's just a letter from my father', he said, 'Oh, right' but he kept on reading it. The first paragraph congratulated me on getting a contract for the book, so it was quite obvious that I was telling the truth about the whole thing. The other thing was that I had lots of National Library reference material that would have indicated the fact that I had been working in the library. But he just kept on reading the letter.

At this stage I was getting really anxious about the fact that my partner and my two year old son would be waiting for me. I had said at the beginning that I was being met, so they said that they would tell the people meeting me, 'inform them of the situation', or something like that, and I heard a PA going out for anyone meeting me to contact the desk, and then they said that they had been told, but they didn't tell me what they had been told.

As it turned out, my partner at that stage wasn't in the terminal building because we had arranged that he would just hover in the car outside. So he missed the PA and they didn't repeat it, so he wasn't told anything.

I felt fairly confident that it was all just a terrible mistake, that they could see I was completely innocent, I had absolutely nothing in my possession that could be in any way incriminating, and then the next letter he drew out was an old letter I had from friend, written in 1984, which I had kept and taken to Dublin because the address was in Irish and I wasn't sure what it was and it had the telephone number on it and I wanted to bring that because I wanted to go and see her. It had mentioned in the letter that she had tried to visit prisoners in Long Kesh, and then I felt really anxious, I felt that maybe they would use that to show that I was in sympathy with republicanism or had close connections with republicans. I explained it was a letter from a very old lady, they could see it wasn't recent, and they could see that she referred to my book at the very beginning. And I said that I talked about her in my book and I went to pay a courtesy call on her.

The first thing they had asked me when I went into that little room was: 'Are you a member of any republican organisation, are you a republican?' I said no, I wasn't, I was a researching writer and I would regard myself as a feminist. About that time the first Special Branch guy went off with my notepad and my diary, he had also gone through my cheque book and its transactions and wanted to know why I still had my account in Belfast. I explained it was for convenience. They went through all my ID cards and there was an old swimming card from Belfast that I still had and it had my old address in Belfast; they asked me who lived there, so that was put down to check.

They wanted to know who I lived with – they had also seen the photos of my partner and our son because they were in my diary – and wanted to know his date of birth and where he was born and what he did. So I think that was all the information they were able to get from my personal possessions. With all of that to check out, the first fellow left, leaving me in the room with the Special Branch guy.

After a while I pretended to go to sleep and just sort of sat in this really warm little room. He told me I could stretch my legs if I wanted to, I said, 'When you're as pregnant as I am, you want to rest them, not stretch them'. He said, 'Oh, I wouldn't know anything about that, never having been pregnant'. And I expressed again my anxiety about my son and his disappointment about not seeing me and the fact that they were waiting. I got no response from this. We just sat there.

I closed my eyes for about 15 minutes or so, and then the Special Branch guy came back, with all my stuff, and he said that he was satisfied that I was what I said I was, which was a *bona fide* researcher and writer, and I said, 'That means I can go?' and he said, 'It does'. And I said, 'Great, it was pretty obvious all along that I was what I said I was' but he said something like 'If you weren't what you said you were you would now be going to a prison cell'. And I said, 'Well, I'm a completely innocent person, I can't see why I should be grateful for that'.

I got my stuff together. I must say they weren't particularly gallant, nobody pushed my trolley or anything like that.

There were two other things to say about the experience. One was the complete disregard for the feelings of anyone who is seven months pregnant, obviously very tired, quite obviously doing nothing but going about her own business. Through a complete quirk, (because I wouldn't normally carry family photos like that, I certainly wouldn't carry them if I didn't want them to know all about me) by the end of it they knew an awful lot about me. The other thing was that all I had, as I said, was the article about Sean MacBride, and my library notes, and nothing was incriminating about that, but they made me feel it was incriminating.

The last point to make is the terrifying implications of the PTA in terms of its power to exclude a person from Britain. After a while, all I could think was that they might exclude me, put me on the next plane back to Ireland, and I wouldn't be able to live with my partner and our son in England. Our family would be broken up and there would be nothing we could do about it. I felt very vulnerable on that score, because I knew that it has happened to people in the past. And that was why I was talking to the Branch men, desperately trying to convince them of my 'respectability'. (500F/87, 50 minutes, released)

This brief examination of only 50 minutes illustrates how an event considered to be insignificant by the authorities for recording purposes can have a very different meaning for the person examined. It is not only a very frightening and stressful ordeal but it also affects other members of the family who are expecting to be able to meet their friends and relatives. This case also shows how the various powers in the PTA combine together. First, the respondent was stopped under the examination powers, then held under the detention powers, and over-riding the whole experience was the knowledge that she could be excluded without ever having to go before a court of law. Finally, it is difficult to understand how such an examination can be of any use whatsoever to the prevention of terrorism. The person's identity could obviously be checked in a matter of minutes. The rest of the examination seemed to be nothing less than harassment of someone going about their lawful business between Britain and Ireland.

Other People's Experiences of Being Stopped

It is clear from the study that landing cards play a crucial role in the policing of ports and airports. We begin our analysis of other people's experiences by considering those stops which occurred immediately after a landing card had been handed in.

In 1985 a full-time official of the Social Democratic and Labour Party – the party which represents the majority of Catholic opinion in Northern Ireland – was stopped while entering Scotland to address a meeting on the political situation in Northern Ireland.

Everyone on the plane had to fill in a landing card and stand in a queue to hand them in at one of the three booths. The middle one was free and I was sent to it. I handed in my PTA card and was asked to produce further identification. I produced my driving licence. The woman then queried the fact that I had stated that I worked for John Hume and if this meant John Hume the politician. I said yes, that the

card said John Hume MP. I was then asked if I had any further identification – I did not. I was then asked for proof that I worked for
John Hume and I produced my pass for Westminster. After looking
at this the woman made a phone call and asked me to sit on one of
the seats at the side. I was taken to a locker room. (230M/85, 1¼ hours,
released)

In the summer of 1985 a woman was travelling over to London with
two others to visit a friend who had been detained under the PTA in
Scotland.

While the plane was taxi-ing in everyone was asked to fill in a
landing card. These were collected at the bottom of the ramp by two
policemen and two policewomen in plain clothes. From where we
were at the back it seemed that all the women coming off the flight
were being asked questions as they handed in their cards. Five
women were detained off our flight; including the three of us.
(248F/85, 1½ hours, released)

In other cases, people who are not listed to be stopped and examined
are detained after the landing card details are checked. For example, an
NUS official from Northern Ireland was returning with a colleague from
a conference in England.

We were waiting to board the flight when we were approached by
two plain clothes officers, these were the same officers who had
accepted our destination cards as we passed through the checkpoint.
They said, 'We are holding you both under the Prevention of
Terrorism Act' and to come with us. (233F/85, 2 hours, released)

In another case the person was sitting on the plane, having gone
through the check out and filled in the embarkation card.

Before the take off a plain clothes officer got on the plane and he
walked up into the pilot's cabin and spoke to the pilot. I was sitting
near a door where two uniformed police were standing whilst their
chief was sitting outside. The plain clothes detective came walking
down the aisle and asking for me by name. I stepped up and said,
'What's the problem?' and he said, 'No problem, I just want to
search your luggage'. I was taken off the plane, by which time an
officer had already thrown my baggage onto the tarmac. When I got

outside the plane I was surrounded by police and airport officials. I was put into a Landrover and driven to the airport police station. (421M/87, 3 days, excluded)

Anyone who refuses to fill in a landing card or fills in only part of it immediately gives rise to suspicion.

The first time I was stopped I was flying from the States to enter England, and the form that they give you says occupation. I didn't want to fill that out because I just resent the notion of categorising people by their occupation. I didn't put anything down. And I wasn't thinking customs, police, customs, the State, I just wasn't thinking like that. And then the other thing was that I gave my permanent address with my sister who lives in Belfast. The first man I spoke to didn't like the fact that I hadn't put down occupation, and then he asked me about the address. (393F/85, 3 hours, released)

In 1984 two Irish Members of the European Parliament in transit between Dublin and Brussels refused to complete landing cards in London on the grounds that they were Europeans and Irish and that the requirement is contrary to the Treaty of Rome which guarantees freedom of movement between EEC member states to all European citizens. They were detained for 15 minutes while an immigration official satisfied himself that they were MEPs and waived the landing card requirement.

Another person who objected to completing all the details on the grounds that it infringed their civil liberties was not so fortunate. The officer requested him to give the missing details which the passenger continued to refuse to do. When asked for further identification, he refused to give this, even though he was able to do so. He was then detained and subsequently charged under the PTA with failing to provide the necessary information. His response:

It is terrible when one cannot move from one part of the apparently un-United Kingdom without being detained by the police and then summoned to appear before a court several hundred miles away for refusing to complete a card. How long will it be before one has to carry an identity card to cross from Devon to Cornwall? (501M/83, 1½ hours, charged)

People who object either through their manner or directly to questions put to them are likely to be examined at greater length then and there or on the return leg. This occurred in the case study, presented at the beginning of the chapter. This is not untypical. An American visiting Ireland was waiting to board the ferry to Dublin when he was approached by a police officer.

> On hearing my American accent, he asked for my US passport, then proceeded to ask questions which I took to be none of his business. I did not attempt to conceal my annoyance at being asked where I was going, the purpose of my trip, who I was going to see, and whether I had any relatives in Ireland. I also observed him taking photographs of me sitting in the car, as I watched him in the rear-view window.

On his return a week later the American was again approached by the same officer.

> Upon my recognizing him and mentioning that fact, all my personal belongings were taken out of the car and examined. The curious rummaging through my effects wherein likely objects for examination like the heavy black box in which my typewriter was housed were in fact ignored; he preferred to read copies of my personal correspondence from a letter to American Express to one to Barclay's Bank to a journal and personal notes. (504M/85, 1 hour, released)

In some cases no landing cards are completed but people are picked out and examined. At first sight it appears that they are being stopped at random, but often the stop is far from random and has been ordered by the NJU. Their name and presumably photograph have been circulated to all ports.

In 1988 the parents of a young boy who had been shot dead by a plastic bullet fired by the army, travelled over to England. Since the death of their son they had joined a campaign whose aim was to stop the use of plastic bullets. The purpose of their visit was to join a protest group outside the factory which made the lethal weapons.

> Just as we were coming through the terminal with all the rest of the passengers there was a person standing behind this desk – actually, the wife was already past him and I was near enough past him too – and he started shouting, 'You, you, you' and ran after us and called me

back again. And I says, 'What do you want?' and he says, 'Your name' and I says my name and he says, 'Have you any identification?' Well, I showed him identification. He says to me, 'Have you any other identification?' so I showed him more identification. He says, 'No, we want something with a photograph on it'. I says, 'Well, I haven't got it'. So the next thing the wife came up and he turned round and says to her, 'Are you travelling with this man?' She says, 'Yes'. He handed us two wee pink cards and he says to me, 'You wouldn't mind filling them in. It's only for security reasons'. So we looked over them and filled them in and I says, 'Well, what was the reason why we were getting stopped?' He says, 'It's just a routine spot check'. I says, 'Well out of the whole lot we were the only ones being spot checked and you ran out after us'. (600M/88, 50 minutes, released)

In 1986, one of the young workers who had picketed Dunne's store for over a year after refusing to handle South African goods, was invited to address an anti-apartheid meeting in Birmingham. He was stopped at the airport.

I was travelling over to address a meeting of the anti-apartheid movement, as well as Birmingham Trades Council. I had my passport as my ID. I was stopped and asked where was I staying? Who was meeting me? And why was I here? I was also asked about the Dunne's store strike. (576M/86, 50 minutes, released)

In these two cases it is apparent that the police already knew about their reasons for travelling to England. In other cases people are examined and subsequently detained after allegedly political material is found in their possession. In one case the occupants of a car were requested to fill in pink PTA forms. The driver was then asked to open the boot of the car and the police examined the contents.

After 30 minutes or so we were told that we were detained under the PTA. The police stated that this was due to documentation which was in the car which they said was of a republican nature. The documentation referred to was booklets which are sold openly in Dublin and probably Britain also. (508F/85, 28 hours, released)

One feature to emerge from the analysis is the high proportion of people who appear to be stopped and examined at greater length on the return leg of their journey. Half of those who were examined only and two-thirds of those who were subsequently detained and taken to a police station, were stopped on their return. In the majority of cases they had completed a landing card on the way out. It is clear that in a number of cases the examining officer had carried out a check at the National Joint Unit at Scotland Yard.

In one case a person who had served a prison sentence in Northern Ireland journeyed to Scotland for a football match. He was expecting to be stopped at the port.

When we arrived by bus at Cairnryan two police came on and handed out Boarding Passes which everyone filled in. They then let the bus go and I thought that was the end of the matter. When we came back after the match the police were waiting and asked everyone for ID. I showed my work pass and was immediately arrested and brought to a small waiting room by two policemen in civilian clothes. After an hour or so two special branch came and told me I was officially under arrest and was to be brought to Stranraer barracks. (196M/80, 7 days, excluded)

In another case a group of people who had been over to Ireland for the Easter Rising Commemorations caught the night ferry, arriving back in Liverpool at about 7.30 a.m.

Coming off the boat, my companion and I were stopped by the same man who had taken our names and addresses on the Saturday evening. He said that we had been 'checked up on' since Saturday and took us to a room where he told us we were being detained under the PTA. (165F/83, 31 hours, released)

Some people appear to be regularly stopped and harassed as a matter of course as they travel to and from Ireland. In one case a Catholic who lived in Scotland started travelling over to Northern Ireland to play in a flute band at St Patrick's Day parades, Ancient Order of Hibernians and other rallies. He also started a relationship with a Belfast woman who is now his wife.

From 1979 on, nearly every time I returned home to Scotland after visiting Belfast I was detained at Stranraer harbour, never arrested, but just held long enough – one hour or one and a half hours – so that I would miss my connecting train to Glasgow which was at 6.30 p.m. When I missed this train I had to make other arrangements to get home or sleep rough in Stranraer because the next train was not until 7 a.m. the next morning and Glasgow is about three and a half hours train journey from Stranraer.

After being detained a few times he wrote and visited his local MP complaining about this harassment. The MP was sympathetic and contacted the authorities at Stranraer but their excuse was that it was just routine questioning and they were sorry for any inconvenience to passengers. The harassment continued. In 1981 his fiancée and her sister arrived in Scotland so that they could be together for Valentine's day. When travelling back to Belfast they were arrested at Stranraer. His fiancée was detained for three days and then released without charge. Her sister was held for seven days and was given an exclusion order barring her from entering Great Britain.

In May 1981 he was detained again at Larne harbour for two hours. Then in June he was again detained at Larne while returning home after his girlfriend's twenty-first birthday. He was taken to Castlereagh, held for five days and served with an exclusion order preventing him entering Northern Ireland. (389M/81, 5 days, excluded)

Women and Children and the Examination Process

All the official reports make the assumption that the travelling public consists only of men and no reference is made to women or children. Without exception, all the reviews have been gender blind. Women and children, of course, do travel and form a sizeable proportion of the travelling public between Britain and Ireland. Women's circumstances, however, will differ substantially from those of men. Many will have a range of family responsibilities to which they are returning and any delay may cause considerable problems with a whole network of arrangements. Some may be pregnant. Others may be travelling with babies or young children. No special facilities, however, appear to have been provided and children travelling with parents who are stopped and examined may end up in the care of the local authority unless other arrangements can be made.

In this study, there were a number of cases when women were stopped while travelling with children. In one particularly horrific case the mother of two young children aged one and two was not allowed to change their nappies and then the two children were wrenched away from her at the airport, before she was taken to Paddington Green police station.

> I was just at customs – you know, as you come off the aeroplane and collect your luggage ... They had taken my cases away and the kids, they were one and two at the time and they were both in nappies, and they wouldn't let me get their nappies out of the cases. They had their nappies on from eight o' clock that morning till about eleven o' clock that night, the whole time, they wouldn't let me change their nappies. I asked for something to eat for the children at tea time, they were going mad, going crazy crying, and they brought in a plate of bread and jam. It was all confusion, it was terrible. They never explained why we'd been stopped.
>
> They took the children off me at the airport. The policewoman had to drag the youngest away from me – it was awful. They kept telling me they'd got in touch with my mother and father and they were coming to fetch the children, then from Saturday to Tuesday they kept telling me that they (the children) had been put into care. I found out after that they hadn't, my parents had collected them at the airport. I was under the impression the whole time I was held that they were in care. The children had been alright for a little while and then they were hungry and tired and their nappies needed changing, and then they were upset, especially when they took them away. Cathy, she's the youngest, she was only one, she clung onto me and they pulled her off me, she kept screaming and it was just terrible, they just pulled her off me and told me they were putting her into care. It was terrible, because they'd never been away, they were only babies and had never been away from the house, they'd never stayed with anyone. (318F/79, 3 days, released)

In another case, three women were taking 16 children to Glasgow on holiday and they were stopped and detained at Stranraer. The children were subsequently taken to Glasgow by the bus driver, who had travelled from Glasgow to meet the party. It was reported in the *Guardian* that he was told that if he didn't take the children they would need to be taken into care of the local authority.[3] Two of the women were held for 44 hours and one for 22 hours before being released. (512F/85, 44 hours, released)

It is not only women travelling with children who encounter problems. In one case a man who was travelling with his nine year son was detained.

I was detained under the Prevention of Terrorism Act at approximately 6 p.m. ... while passing through security at Stranraer. After completing a landing card I was told I was being detained under the PTA and taken with four others to Stranraer police station. We had been travelling with a coach load of other Celtic supporters to a match in Glasgow. I was very concerned about my nine year old son and wanted him to remain with me but I was told that he would be put into care if I did not allow him to be taken on to Glasgow by a friend who remained in the coach. (252M/83, 23 hours, released)

In all three cases, had the children not been cared for by relatives or friends at the port or airport, they might well have been taken into care.

Examination Conditions

After the initial set of questions, if an examination is to continue the person is normally taken to an examination room. The various reviews into the working of the PTA have all commented on the physical facilities at ports and airports. The Jellicoe Report noted that the accommodation at Irish ports 'at best tends to have a temporary and makeshift air, and at worst – at some of the sea ports – is quite simply unacceptable'. It recommended that HM Inspectors of Constabulary for England and Wales should examine the adequacy of accommodation for police anti-terrorist controls at ports and make recommendations about the minimum levels which should apply.[4] This has now been carried out, but the report was not published.

The Colville Report noted that accommodation arrangements were 'woefully inadequate' and recommended that the minimum needed was:

a separate room ... in which the person under examination may be placed, and if necessary interviewed. This room should be immediately and discreetly accessible from the arrival or departure channels, preferably round a corner so that the door is not seen by everyone else.

It made no comment about the conditions in the room except to say that a lavatory, cooking facilities and even a cell are optional extras.[5]

People's views of the examination facilities were mixed. In some places a locker room typically serves as an interview room. In 1985 a person was stopped at Glasgow airport:

I was taken to a locker room that had a small table with a chair on either side. It had staff notices and statutory employment notices on the wall, some of which had rather lewd graffiti. It surprised me whenever I was left on my own in what was obviously a locker room. (230M/85, 1¼ hours, released)

No improvements had been made to the facilities by 1989. The locker room was still in use.

They then marched me through the airport to pick up my bag and then brought me into a very small room, like a box room, it was actually being used as a store room by cleaners, because there was a mop and bucket. There were three chairs and a table by the wall. As well as a filing cabinet and the cleaning materials there was also a large plastic bag like a bin sack for embarkation cards which had been filled in by people previously. This was obviously how they stored them and they were in such a way in elastic bands in bundles of twenty. You could actually read the top one and as I was amusing myself reading some of these cards they came in and threw a jumper which looked to me like it was lost and found, which was also in the room, they threw that over the bag so that I couldn't read these government secrets. (555M/89, 1 hour, released)

The accommodation at Birmingham airport appeared to be reasonably satisfactory but there was an notice on the door which a detective admitted was offensive and explained that it was a joke.

So they took us into the room. It was just an ordinary square room, nothing in it, just a desk, like a visiting box in any jail, just a table with a couple of chairs, that's it. It said on the door, something about 'Aids' and he said, 'Ah, we're only joking about this' and they pulled the thing off it. He says, 'We're only slagging somebody' and they pulled it off and rolled it up and threw it away. He said, 'We're bringing you in here.' (600M/88, 50 minutes, released)

Examination Questions

In practice it is difficult to differentiate between the use of the power to question a person on any topic and the power to demand to see all relevant material. Typically, when a person is stopped and asked to produce some form of identity, this is followed by a number of questions. Initially, the questions cover the person's identity, place of residence and the purpose of their travel. If a person is to be examined further, then the range of questions is typically much broader and deals with their family and friends – where they live, how old they are, whether they are married and the number of children they have, including their dates of birth. A typical example of this form of questioning can be seen from a case in 1985.

> Then one of the two original police officers came and closely questioned me about my life, family and activities, for about another 30 minutes. It was then that it must have been realised that I had no connection with terrorism and I was returned to a room where my luggage was. I was asked to check and I signed that everything was in order. (233F/85, 2 hours, released)

Another person stopped at Heathrow was asked:

> How long was I staying; was I married; did I have children; did I work; and my husband's date of birth and whether he was working. (248F/85, 1½ hours, released)

It will be observed that the husband's date of birth was requested. In a large number of cases the date of birth of the husbands or partners, relatives and friends is sought by the examining officer. This information, together with a person's name, provides a unique method of identification for both manual and computerised records. As women, in contrast to men, tend to know the birthdays of other members of the family, they are often therefore of more use to the intelligence gathering process.

Once the personal information is collected the questioning typically moves on to politics, and people are asked about their political beliefs and those of their friends and relatives. For example,

> We were then separated and I was closely questioned on my family and friends, details of them and our political affiliations. I was questioned on my political beliefs and perceptions and the nature of my work. As far as I was concerned I was not questioned about anything of a terrorist nature apart from 'did I know anyone in the IRA'. (234M/85, 2 hours, released)

In other cases there was extensive questioning about politics. The SDLP official who was visiting Glasgow University Labour Club was asked:

- What was I going to Glasgow University for?
- Why was I going to the Glasgow University Labour Club?
- Who had invited me?
- Did I personally know the people who had called the meeting?
- What did I know about the GULC?
- Did I know the Sinn Fein speaker?
- What was I going to say in my speech?
- Why had I not a written speech?
- Why were some of the GULC booklets in my document wallet?
- What did the list of statistics in my document wallet mean?
- Did I think I would win the debate?
- How long had I worked for John Hume?
- Did I like John Hume?
- Would John Hume be closer to the SDLP or the Labour Party?
- Had I always supported the SDLP?
- Did I have any relations in Britain?
- Did I have any relations who had ever been to Britain? (I said I had a sister and a brother who had attended Keele University.)
- Were the members of my family involved in the SDLP? (Apart from such questions I was asked very little about my family.)
- What was my previous involvement in student politics?
- What had I been doing at the time of the H-Block protests etc? (230M/85, 1½ hours, released)

A councillor who was returning from a Labour Party delegation to Northern Ireland recorded the following observation.

The police seemed mostly interested in my participation in the Labour party delegation and asked whether we intended to invite speakers from the Republican movement to Britain. (507F/85, 2 hours, released)

She was also asked her views about internment and plastic bullets.

Examining Personal Documents

The power to demand to see relevant material was used extensively. Many of the questions were related to what was produced. Most of the people in the study were required to produce a range of documents, but examining officers were particularly interested in diaries, letters, address and cheque books.

For example, in one case:

A letter to my wife, which I had forgotten to post, was opened and read. My diary was also closely read. (506M/85, 2 hours, released)

The novelist Dervla Murphy has drawn attention to the privacy implications of these practices:

The young woman then spent twenty minutes scrutinising my baggage ... She did ... read a few of my personal letters and she carefully studied my bank statements ... As I lead a very humdrum life, both personally and financially, I have in fact no objection to the general public reading my letters and bank statements. But it did occur to me that there must be many other equally law-abiding citizens who would object, for valid reasons, to such an intrusion into their private lives. (Letter in the *Irish Times*, 5 May, 1983)

The practice of examining personal documents however, appears to go much further than an intrusion into people's private lives. Most people find it an extremely distressing and humiliating experience and there is considerable evidence to suggest that these feelings are not some indirect consequence of a necessary practice, but are part of a deliberate strategy, particularly as far as women are concerned. A disproportionate number of women reported that they felt humiliated and a pattern emerged suggesting that this was far from accidental. This is how one woman described her experience at Heathrow:

Then she (the examining officer) came back and asked me questions based on the papers. I had my address book, my personal diary, letters, and then I had a small collection of ordinary *Newsweek* and *New York Times* articles about Northern Ireland that my sister had asked me to bring over, they were very straight type articles. So then she asked me questions about that material and she had really read the stuff, she asked me what I was doing in Indiana. In my diary I had written down that I had been there and she said that she had been there or some personal thing to prove that she had read through that material very well and I'm sure made copies of things, and asked me questions about my religion. I actually almost started crying because they had read a personal letter sitting in front of me. It felt like rape, that's what it felt like. That was when she told me what legal rights I had and how they could ask me things. (393F/85, 3 hours, released)

The same person was stopped on another occasion when returning from France. Again, her personal documents were examined. By now her feelings had changed from distress to rage.

The worst thing was the first time when I knew this woman had been reading my personal diary, and the second time I was pretty angry because it seemed pretty clear that I was going to be let back into the country because there wasn't any reason for me not being allowed in. (393F/86, 3 hours, released)

In another case the police read aloud the contents of a woman's diary.

They also went through my diary from January to December, reading every single page of it out loud to each other. There was nothing really personal in it, just shopping lists and all sort of ridiculous things – mostly to do with work 'see so-and-so at 7.30' and things like 'period'; because of PMT I would mark that in my diary. I was not asked any questions about it, they just read the diary from beginning to end – which is a very humiliating thing. (240F/81, 2 days, released)

In these examples, as well as in the case study presented at the beginning of the chapter, male officers were involved in reading the personal documents belonging to women. In any other setting this type of behaviour – where men use their position of authority to intimidate and humiliate women – would constitute sexual harassment. But because it takes place within a police setting this overt form of sexism goes uncensored.

The sexism of examining officers was reflected in another case. A man was stopped and the officers went through his personal effects and papers in his brief case.

The dark haired officer in particular examined contents of personal letters, one of which contained a photograph of a girl. This was a photograph of a personal friend who was properly dressed. Their remarks included such expressions as 'Look at the size of the boobs on her', 'She would keep you warm in bed at night'. He further remarked, 'I see you like blondes' then, 'Did Sheelagh screw' or words to that effect. I found these remarks extremely distasteful. (234M/85, 2 hours, released)

Apart from personal documents, examining officers were also interested in anything that might seem to be political material. In one case, having inspected personal documents, the examining officers went through a person's conference papers.

They came and went through all our personal documents, diaries, you know. I had a diary with lots of phone numbers and things in and we objected to this sort of thing – they were doing it anyway, so short of physically getting up and trying to stop them, there was nothing we could do about it, no matter how much you protested about it. So they went through all our conference documents and any other documents we had, through all our luggage and personal effects and then began to question us about our political involvements – asked us were we members of a political party in Northern Ireland. (271M/81, 5 hours, released)

The SDLP official experienced a similar examination at Glasgow airport.

The police read the papers in my document wallet. The woman police officer took my diary out of the room for about four or five minutes returning it with the comment that I did not keep it very well. I told her that this was just as well. It had names and addresses in the back; friends and associates, media contacts, names and phone numbers for different pressure groups and organisations, numbers and extensions for people in different government departments North and South. (230M/85, 1½ hours, released)

The parents of the boy killed by a plastic bullet were interrogated about the material they were carrying.

I had booklets and he took them out and said, 'What are you doing with these?' and the wife turned round and said, 'My son was shot by a plastic bullet'. He said, 'Well, what are you doing with these?' and we said, 'We were coming over here'. He also took out the statement we had to read out at Astra, who make the plastic bullets, and he turned round and said he was going to have to put these through the computer. So he went out and left us by ourselves for about 10-15 minutes and came back in again and turned round and says, 'It won't be too long, we're waiting for it to come back through the computer'. (600M/88, 50 minutes, released)

The trade unionist, who was stopped in 1986, had a similar experience. Police demanded to see the texts of the speeches he intended to make and also the notes of the speeches. His notes and also a book on the anti-apartheid movement were taken away and not returned to him.

A number of people in the study were concerned about what happened to the material which was taken away to be examined. Most suspected that it had been photocopied before it was returned. In one case the examining officer told the person that the document was being photocopied.

It is obvious from the nature of the questioning and the type of documents read that the principal aim of the examining officers is not to establish a person's identity nor to ascertain whether 'the person is or has been involved in the commission, preparation or instigation of acts of terrorism', but to gather intelligence. Although, as the Colville Report noted:

> ... it would doubtless be accepted that the police should not use their authority to bring in at random Irish passengers and then subject them to a general inquisition on their life-style, leisure activities and other personal details.[6]

This is exactly what they are doing.

Seeking Redress

The powers under the PTA either to demand to see any material which a person is carrying, or to ask any questions, are unchallengeable. People may, however, make a complaint to the Police Complaints Authority concerning the manner in which the examination was carried out. The American who was visiting Ireland made such a complaint and received the following reply concerning his complaints of incivility and oppressive conduct in respect of alleged photography and the reading of correspondence:

An investigation has been made and there is no evidence at all that any photograph was taken of you and the Detective Constable denies that he took any photograph. He also denies reading your correspondence although he acknowledged that when replacing some papers in a suitcase he could not avoid giving them a cursory glance. He has explained that it is his normal practice to say to people with whom he deals at Holyhead 'Have a nice day', which is a practice which he picked up from the many Americans passing through. He has asked me to say that he is sorry if you felt that it was meant other than sincerely. I appreciate that you will probably not find this very acceptable but as no independent evidence is available, as to what occurred, there is no other way in which the matter can be resolved. (504M/85, 3 hours, released)

The American did find the response unacceptable and argued that an independent investigating body would be more impartial and effective. From a broader perspective the case illustrates the impossibility of seeking redress through the Police Complaints Authority because in the majority of cases there will be no independent evidence.

In this case the explanation given for this examining officer's behaviour is very untypical. Normally, examining officers, as has been shown, read this type of material. A final observation is that the Police Complaints Authority does not appear to be particularly familiar with the PTA because there was no need to investigate whether or not personal documents had been read as the police officer was perfectly entitled, if he so wished, to read any material which the American was carrying.

Examining Suspicion

Since 1974 over 4,700 people have been stopped and detained at ports and airports. In addition an unknown number, totalling tens of thousands, have been examined for varying periods of time. The vast majority have been released without any action being taken against them. The key question is: who is likely to get stopped and examined or detained and why?

There have been numerous studies about the way the police exercise their discretion to enforce the law in relation to ordinary crime. But there have been no studies of the way examining officers at ports and airports use their discretion. Official reports, however, have been aware for some time of the problem of examining officers applying stereotypes. One of the major criticisms of the examination power has been that examining officers have a stereotype of what a 'terrorist' might look like. The Jellicoe Report noted that examining officers had said that 'with experience and practice they develop a "nose" for passengers with terrorist links'.[7] But the Report did not wish 'to make too much of this from the point of view of inconvenience to the travelling public' because so few people are formally detained, and those that are stopped are seldom held for more than one hour. The Colville Report also noted: 'There is no doubt that some officers are activated by a stereotype of the person who might be a terrorist.' It went on to say that 'an approach based on stereotypes is a mistake and an irritation'.[8]

This study suggests that these sorts of crude stereotypes certainly play a part in the policing of ports. The woman in the case study presented at the beginning of the chapter was stopped because of her anomalous position and 'stuck out like a sore thumb in the midst of the businessmen and the priest'. When the author asked an examining officer on one occasion what factors made him suspicious, the first factor he noted were tatty, dirty shoes. Even the casual observer at any port or airport cannot fail to notice that the most likely candidates for 'the passenger with terrorist links' appears to be young men in jeans and Dr Martens or trainers rather than older and more conventionally dressed people.

While stereotypes certainly play a part, the abuse of stereotypes by examining officers should not be over-emphasised. From all the evidence gathered from this study, it appears that the operation of the PTA is much more systematic and targeted than is generally assumed. Many people are stopped and examined because a search has been made of the NJU records. In other cases, the information on the landing card gives rise to suspicion. Here stereotypes may well play a part in constructing the suspicion; for example, if the occupation recorded is incongruent with the style of dress. But what gives rise to suspicion is much more likely to be a product of a set of policies determined by the higher echelons within the security services.

It appears that at least five factors played a key role in the social construction of suspicion of people stopped in this study. First, any sign or information which suggests that the person is politically active. Here even the most innocuous of political activities, such as wearing a badge publicly declaring one's position on some topic, may be sufficient to cause suspicion and for a person to be stopped and examined, as Dervla Murphy found to her cost.

I was stopped in the customs shed of Holyhead by a young woman in plain clothes who explained: 'This is a security check under the Prevention of Terrorism Act.' As proof of identification I produced my AIB banker's card, my RGS Fellow's card, my An Taisce member's card, and my HTD out-patient's card. Next I stated the purpose of my visit to the UK – to get my new book off to the printer – and listed the six English friends with whom I had stayed; all, as it happens, of mind-boggling respectability.

I was the only person to be checked that afternoon though hundreds of passengers, including scores of hairy young men, were boarding the Dun Laoghaire ferry – some of them looking much more like targets for PTA vigilantes than an elderly female, grey and lined and bowed beneath the weight of printed matter. Of course it is reassuring to know that such spot-checks are made and the young woman was polite and chatty and we ended up the best of friends.

When eventually I boarded the ferry – the gangplank had to be replaced to allow me on – I got into conversation with an elderly Englishwomen to whom I expressed my puzzlement at having been singled out for PTA attention. She said: 'You're wearing three anti-nuclear badges, I've learned to take mine off, just to save time, when passing these security checks.' Then I saw the joke. If one is opposed on ethical grounds to the nuclear deterrent – the ultimate form of terrorism – one may be suspected of subversion by those who operate the Prevention of Terrorism Act. Mankind is surely in a muddle like it never was before. (Letter in the *Irish Times*, 5 May, 1983)

At the other end of the political spectrum is anyone who is a member of Sinn Fein. Although this is a legal political party in Northern Ireland and draws support from around one-third of the nationalist community, its members are seen as potential terrorists because of its refusal to condemn the IRA. In between these two positions are a range of political activists which included, in this study, two local councillors, a trade union official, a couple protesting against the use of plastic bullets and a full-time official of another political party.

In a number of these cases, the person was stopped before handing in a boarding card. For example, the trade unionist who was visiting England to speak at an anti-apartheid meeting and the couple over to protest outside the factory making plastic bullets, were stopped immediately they were recognised, which suggests that their names and photographs had been previously circulated to the ports and that they were 'terrorist suspects' before landing. In the case of the couple protesting against the use of plastic bullets, a file had already been opened on them.

A second, related, factor, in the construction of suspicion, is whether or not the person is a student, or more importantly, active in student politics. In the late 1970s the NUS argued that students had been regularly subject to harassment and it published a list of students who had been examined under the PTA (reproduced in Table 3.3).

Table 3.3 Students examined, detained or arrested under the PTA as reported by NUS in the late 1970s.

In December 1977, delegates to the NUS Conference from colleges in Northern Ireland travelled by air from Belfast to Blackpool; seven of them were held for 30 minutes at the airport on the basis that they could not name the hotel in which they would be staying. One was held overnight on the grounds of alleged association with the Provisional IRA, which proved to be totally unfounded.

In February 1977, three students were detained at Leeds/Bradford Airport and later released without being charged or given an idea of the suspicions against them.

In June 1978, the Student Community Action worker from Nottingham University was taking a party of young people to Nottingham for a holiday away from Belfast. Two 16 year old Catholic boys were detained for three hours, searched, photographed, fingerprinted and repeatedly abused by police as 'dirty Irish scum'.

In November 1978, a group of students and trade unionists came over to Britain from Northern Ireland to tour student unions as a central feature of the NUS 'Peace, Jobs, Progress', campaign. Two of the students were detained at the airports in Belfast and Manchester and subjected to considerable abuse.

In February 1979, the then NUS Vice-President and NUS Treasurer was stopped by officers of the Special Branch at Belfast International Airport while on union business, and detained for three hours. She was held for two hours at Heathrow Airport on her return. During her detention she was searched, fingerprinted and had all the documents in her possession photocopied. All the officers taking part in the interrogation, including the search, were male. She was advised that the number of visits she was making to Northern Ireland was excessive and should be cut down.

In December 1979, two members of the Northern Ireland delegation to NUS conference were detained at Liverpool Airport under the PTA. One of the students, a woman, had to endure a full body search in front of six male police officers.

Unfortunately, the NUS does not appear to have maintained a register of students stopped since 1979. But from the evidence which is available, students travelling between Ireland and Great Britain are still subject to special attention. This study includes a student and two NUS officials who were stopped and examined.

All the evidence suggests that the PTA is used to deter perfectly legitimate political activity and people are viewed as suspicious simply because of their politics. As well as the inconvenience to those stopped and examined, the overall impact on political expression must, over time, be considerable.

The third factor which helps to construct suspicion is where people live. The official statistics recording the number of people examined and detained at ports and airports do not provide any social information such as age, gender or place of residence. The evidence from this study, however, suggests that the PTA examination and detention powers are heavily directed towards policing Catholics living in Northern Ireland, and in particular those living in nationalist areas. Half of all those examined and 85 per cent of those subsequently detained were Catholics living in Northern Ireland.

The fourth factor in the construction of suspicion is whether or not the person has had previous contact with the law. It is known that of those who were subsequently stopped, seven per cent had a previous conviction in Northern Ireland and one third were ex-internees. In another case, the person had a relative in prison. The computerisation of all criminal records as well as information on internment makes the routine examination of all these people relatively straightforward. It also means that it is very difficult for anyone in this category of suspect to begin a new life elsewhere.

Finally, people who challenge the authority of the examining officer often become a suspect. It is hard to comprehend why, logically, such action generally leads to more extensive examination. If the person was a genuine terrorist the last thing they would wish to do would be to draw attention to themselves by, for example, not fully completing a landing card or objecting to the type of questions asked. These are the actions of civil libertarians who feel indignant at the erosions of rights. Yet in a number of cases people were detained for a further period after challenging the authority of the examining officer.

Whether or not these factors are important in relation to all those who are stopped is impossible to say, because this study is not based on a representative sample of all people stopped at ports and airports. Nevertheless, there have been numerous allegations over the years that the PTA is being used to police those actively engaged in politics around the Northern Ireland question.

Impact of Examinations

Any examination which lasts more than a few minutes can at best be an unpleasant experience and at worst a terrifying ordeal. Here we consider only the impact on those who were examined and not those who were detained or arrested. As this latter group was on average detained for a much longer period of time, the impact on their lives is much greater and is considered in Chapter 11 alongside those who were arrested and detained inland.

Some of those examined considered the experience of little consequence. Others objected to having to answer questions about the purpose of their visit, where they were staying and the nature of their work. Most felt acute embarrassment when their personal letters, diaries and other documents were read by some stranger. Those who were familiar with the potential powers of the legislation – such as the powers of the Secretary of State to exclude people – or knew about the many injustices which Irish people have experienced in British courts, experienced a sense of fear of what might happen to them.

The impact of short examinations, however, is much more than psychological: they often caused considerable inconvenience to those examined. People were delayed in their travels. Others missed their connecting flights and had to pay for extra accommodation or travelling expenses.

> It was then discovered that there were no more flights from Manchester or Liverpool and we would have to fly from Manchester to London and get connecting flights from there. This cost us an additional £32 each and wasted 5½ hours journey time. I am not complaining about any particular police officer or official but I am complaining about the inconvenience that I was put to on that particular day and the additional expense incurred on me that day when I, as a private citizen, had no connection with terrorism. (233F/85, 2 hours, released)

Families too are affected even by short examination periods. A family meeting a person from a boat or a flight will not know what has happened to them when they do not emerge with all the other passengers. Their immediate assumption is that they have missed the flight or the crossing and may be put to extra expense trying to establish where they are. For up to one hour the authorities are under no obligation to inform relatives or friends waiting for a passenger who has been stopped. Even if the examination continues after one hour, the police have a qualified discretion to refuse notification. In these circumstances, for those waiting at the port or airport the person simply disappears.

The examination powers have curtailed people's right to take part in public affairs and do perfectly ordinary things such as carrying out research, attending meetings, going to conferences, and visiting friends and relatives.

Moreover, they have an impact on political activity. As we have seen, a number of people who were involved in politics were stopped and examined for a short period of time. These experiences must either strengthen the person's political resolve or it may curtail their commitment and therefore subsequently reduce the amount of political activity around certain issues. The extent to which students have been stopped and examined coupled with the surveillance to which they are subjected must have played an important part in reducing the amount of student politics around the Northern Ireland problem. Opposition to the presence of British troops in Northern Ireland or to special legislation such as the Northern Ireland (Emergency Provisions) Acts or the PTA is now far less common than in the early 1970s. People who do not concur with the bipartisan position of successive British governments are treated with suspicion and often seen as supporters of the IRA and terrorism.

The broader impact of even the short examination procedure is to force people to change their behaviour and restrict their freedom of movement and the type of material which they carry on them. Some people have admitted that they no longer travel through Britain if it can be avoided. Some avoid particular ports. Others have pointed out that they no longer carry personal documents on them in case they are stopped.

Conclusions

This chapter has focused on people's experiences of being stopped and examined under the PTA at ports and airports. It has shown how the very extensive powers of questioning and the requirement to produce any material which people have in their possession have been used not for the specific purposes laid down in the legislation but to gather a mass of intelligence information. As most of the information is collected from people who have no connection with terrorism, its value must be highly questionable. Notwithstanding the increasing sophistication of computer software, the sheer volume of information must make it extremely difficult to distinguish between valuable and worthless intelligence.

The role of the NJU is crucial. It is clear that certain types or categories of people are targeted, particularly those who are in some way involved in Irish politics and those who have previous convictions in Northern Ireland. This is not to deny that many innocent people are regularly stopped and examined because of some crude and inappropriate stereotype of 'the terrorist'. What emerges, however, is that the construction of suspicion is generally far from a random process. It reflects a structured set of policy objectives among the higher echelons of the police and security services.

The high proportion of those stopped and examined in our study who are involved in political affairs suggests that there is a deliberate policy to use the PTA to police Irish politics. In most cases the activists who were stopped did not appear to have been stopped at random but were already known to the authorities. The authorities may not like their politics, but all these people are involved in perfectly legitimate activities and in a democratic society should be able to travel freely without being subject to detailed interrogation.

The use of the port powers goes much further than 'a minor inconvenience',[9] as the Jellicoe Report expressed it. The collection of the information, as has been shown, involves considerable intrusion into people's privacy including, in some cases, sexual harassment by male officers who insist on reading women's diaries and other personal information in their presence. These experiences are often extremely embarrassing and stressful even when the examination lasts for less than an hour.

At a broader level, there is much evidence to support the allegation – often been made by members of the Irish community – that the powers are used simply to harass Irish people travelling to and from Ireland. To begin with, many of those examined are stopped and questioned only on the return leg of their journey. It is possible that new information comes to light between their outward and inward journeys which alters the examining officer's suspicion. But if new information emerges and the authorities are concerned with the prevention of terrorism, why wait until the return leg of the journey to detain people? It would be more sensible to arrest them immediately than let them go about their business and wait for them to return. In any event, after the examination most people are allowed to go on their way without action being taken against them. Secondly, as we have seen, the types of questions asked and the documents read appear to have little to do with either establishing the person's identity or ascertaining whether they are involved in 'the commission, preparation or instigation of acts of terrorism'.

There is a body of academic opinion which argues that some emergency powers are necessary to deal with political violence. Clive Walker, for example, argues that the port controls 'contribute significantly to the prevention and control of terrorism in Britain'.[10] He does not, however, produce any evidence to support this view but refers to sections of the Shackleton and Jellicoe Reports.[11] The Shackleton reference is not relevant to the point and the Jellicoe Report argues that the primary purpose of the controls is to deter those involved in terrorism from entering a particular territory and to demonstrate that they are likely to be caught. But no evidence is produced to support the deterrent argument. While the belief in the role of deterrence in the prevention of crime has been with us since the time of Jeremy Bentham and is currently enjoying a revival in criminological studies, not one of many studies has found sufficient evidence to support the view that specific legislation deters criminal behaviour.[12] In the case of those who are actively committed to a political cause, the deterrent effect is likely to be even less significant.

Even if it is assumed that the port controls prevent some terrorism, this must be weighed against the negative impact of the legislation. The evidence from this study as well as that presented to the various reviews suggests that the port powers have alienated sections of the Irish community and made them less willing to cooperate voluntarily with the authorities, thereby making it more difficult to prevent and control terrorism in Britain. At the same time, the use of the powers may have contributed towards a few people rejecting democratic politics and turning to violence as a direct result of their experiences.

But whatever the arguments about the effectiveness or otherwise of the port controls in preventing and controlling terrorism, a number of features are incontrovertible. The controls have led to a reduction in the travelling public's civil liberties, involving a considerable restriction on their freedom of movement and their right to participate in public affairs and, more specifically, creating a frontier between Northern Ireland and the rest of the United Kingdom. In addition, they involve an extensive invasion of people's privacy and cause considerable distress to a large number of people. Finally, using the powers to police politics rather than terrorism is undemocratic.

4 Arrest, Search and Detention Powers

Introduction

The introduction of the PTA in 1974, as we have noted in Chapter 1, created a dual system of criminal justice in Britain. 'Ordinary decent criminals' (ODCs) suspected of the most petty to the most horrific offences are dealt with under the ordinary criminal law. Yet those suspected of being involved in terrorism in connection with Northern Ireland are dealt with under the PTA. Although there have been a number of changes to both tracks – mainly extending police powers – the differences between the two systems remain.

The aim of this chapter is to describe the powers of arrest, search and detention which were introduced under the PTA, and where appropriate, to make comparisons with the ordinary criminal justice system. The law for both systems is now extremely complex, involving reference to the statute law, schedules to statutes, Home Office circulars and quasi-legal Codes of Practice. This complexity makes it difficult for anyone drawn into the system to know their rights. In addition, crucial aspects of the law are vague or contradictory. It is not possible to present a complete picture of the law in the space available here and the analysis which follows is therefore necessarily selective, focusing on those aspects of the law which provide a context for the experiences described later. The final section of the chapter provides a brief analysis of the charges brought against those arrested and detained under the PTA.

Arrest Powers

Under the PTA, police officers may arrest anyone without a warrant where they have reasonable grounds for suspecting that they are either subject to an exclusion order or guilty of some offence under the PTA, or are or have been concerned in the commission, preparation or instigation of acts of terrorism in connection with Northern Ireland affairs or, since 1984, with international terrorism.[1]

There is a further power of arrest permitting examining officers to arrest and detain anyone pending their examination or a decision by the Secretary of State whether or not to make an exclusion order against them.[2]

There are a number of points to be made about these powers. To begin with, it must be emphasised that the power to arrest any person who is suspected of 'being concerned in the commission, preparation or instigation of acts of terrorism' permits a police officer to arrest *where no actual offence has been committed,* where there is no suspicion that any offence has been committed, and *where the person is not suspected of committing any offence* [emphasis in original].[3] This arises because 'acts of terrorism' are not offences in the ordinary criminal law and no specific acts are defined under the PTA. Thus, in practice the legislation provides the police with the power to arrest people for questioning.

As Hall has pointed out, one of the difficulties with the arrest power is knowing what constitutes reasonable grounds in terms of justifying a suspicion.

> A suspicion is based on reasonable grounds though the grounds do not prove guilt, do not amount to a case to answer in a court of law, and may even be, at a trial, inadmissible in evidence against the person arrested. Grounds may be unreasonable where there is an 'excess [of] sentimentality, romanticism, bigotry, wild prejudice, caprice, fatuousness or excessive lack of common sense' but this is not an exhaustive list.[4]

The official reviews of the legislation have encouraged a broad interpretation of the law to allow people to be detained solely for questioning. The Shackleton Report argued:

> ... the police are bound to follow up any information or suspicion about involvement in terrorism ... The prevention of terrorism is not simply a question of arresting people who can promptly be charged with offences...[5]

The Jellicoe Report took a more restrictive interpretation and argued that a person could be arrested provided they themselves were suspected of terrorist involvement.[6] In other words, the power could not be used as a general method of intelligence gathering. The Colville Report did consider the issue of suspicion, but it made no comment on whether it could be used for intelligence gathering.

These conflicting interpretations of the extent of the arrest and detention powers are also reflected in the Home Office circular to Chief Officers. It begins by stating that

> The prime objective of the exceptional powers in section 14 is to enable sufficient usable and admissible evidence to be obtained as a result of the *additional investigations they make possible* so that proceedings can be instituted against persons involved in the kinds of terrorism covered by the section. [emphasis added][7]

A careful reading of these words suggests that the Home Office is advising Chief Officers that it is lawful to arrest anyone if it will enable usable evidence to be obtained for *other* investigations. There is no requirement that the evidence or the proceedings need to be connected with the person arrested. The police are being encouraged to arrest someone in order to investigate the behaviour of someone else altogether. In fact, of course, it is quite contrary to English and to international law to arrest someone in order to investigate the activities of a third party. Whether the wording is deliberate or ambiguous it is impossible to tell, but it clearly gives approval for the police to use the law of arrest for information gathering.

The circular proceeds, however, with a totally contradictory statement. It notes that

> Any arrest of a person under section 14 and subsequent detention must have as its purpose the bringing of charges or, when this is not possible, the consideration of an application for exclusion ...[8]

The circular is now saying that the power of arrest may not be used for intelligence gathering but solely to initiate some action against the suspect. The advice to Chief Officers is therefore contradictory and leaves the law open to interpretation. While the Home Office circular gave conflicting advice, the Home Secretary, Leon Brittan, was in no doubt about the extent of these powers. In 1985, on the RTE programme *This Week* he said in response to the interviewer's point that 87 per cent of detainees were released without charge:

> I think that is a very misleading figure because that suggests that the purpose of detention is simply to bring a charge. If that were so, there might almost be no need for the legislation. What the figures do not tell you is how much information was obtained, not only about the

people concerned but about others, and how many threats were averted as a result of obtaining information from those who were detained. *The object of the exercise is not just to secure convictions but to secure information.* [emphasis added][9]

The Circular points out that the power to arrest without warrant for up to seven days without specific charges being brought is 'clearly exceptional'. As a result it places special obligations on both the police and Secretary of State to ensure that 'all proprieties are observed'. These are to be observed in part in their own right, but also and more cynically:

to enable them (Chief Officers) to rebut allegations about the abuse of power, for example, that a person has been arrested for reasons connected with his [sic] political views or activities or simply to gather intelligence and not because he [sic] is reasonably suspected of being involved in terrorism.[10]

This suggests that the Home Office is more concerned with avoiding adverse criticism of the police than upholding the rule of law. It may be argued that this is an extreme interpretation of the statement. But further confirmation of the Executive's attitude to those detained can be obtained from an earlier circular. This carried the same advice but continued: 'This consideration will not be particularly important in cases involving the arrest of suspected international terrorists.'[11] In other words, there was no need for the police to cover their backs in the case of international terrorists presumably because they were less likely to be in a position to complain or, if they did complain, they would be in a weak position. Significantly, this sentence was dropped from the 1989 circular.

The law is also very vague on the amount of force which can be used in effecting an arrest. The Criminal Law Act 1977 says that the amount of force must be 'reasonable in the circumstances'.[12] But this is very unhelpful. What is reasonable in one circumstance may be totally unreasonable in another and in any event it can often only be determined retrospectively. For example, it may be reasonable to smash down someone's front door at 6 a.m. in the morning and for armed police to rush in and make arrests if an armed gang is in the house. But it is clearly unreasonable to use this amount of force when there is no armed gang and the arrests are solely for information gathering.

An arrest does not necessarily involve a single action, but is made up of a number of different elements. An arrest at a house, for example, will require the police to enter the building, search for the suspect and then make an arrest. Does the force have to be reasonable at each of these stages or overall? As Walker has pointed out, the law is also uninformative in regard to the most dramatic employment of force, namely the firing of lethal weapons.[13]

Apart from extending the arrest powers to cover international terrorism, there have been no significant changes to the arrest powers since their introduction in 1974. The Jellicoe Report recommended that the police throughout the United Kingdom should be reminded by the appropriate Secretary of State that the power of arrest under the PTA should be exercised only where there is no other power appropriate to the end sought.[14] This was accepted and the police notified. But the reminder carries no legal basis and can be ignored by the police if they so wish.

Search Powers

The search powers under PTA 89 have been substantially extended. In Chapter 2 we described the powers of search at ports and airports. Inland the powers are also considerable. To begin with, a justice of the peace may grant a search warrant authorising a constable to enter premises for the purposes of searching for and arresting anyone liable to arrest under the principal arrest powers.[15] Secondly, a police officer may search a person for the purpose of ascertaining whether they have in their possession any document or other article which may constitute evidence that he or she is a person liable to arrest.[16] After an arrest a person may be searched for the purpose of ascertaining whether they are in possession of any document or other article which may constitute evidence that they are the person liable to arrest.[17] The police also have the power to carry out intimate and strip searches when a person has been detained. These powers are dealt with below.

In addition, there is a power to search premises for ordinary material. If a terrorist investigation is in progress, an application may be made to a justice of the peace for a warrant if there are reasonable grounds for believing that there is material on the premises, provided that it is not subject to legal privilege, which is likely to be of substantial value to the investigation.[18] A warrant, however, can only be granted if (a) it is not practicable to communicate with any person to grant entry to the premises; (b) the entry would not be granted without a warrant, or (c) if a search might be frustrated or seriously prejudiced unless the police can secure immediate entry.[19] The warrant gives the police not only the power to search the premises but also anyone there, without the need to have any reasonable suspicion in relation to the person searched.[20]

A terrorist investigation is defined in very broad terms and includes any investigation relating to Northern Ireland or international acts of terrorism, any acts which are connected with specific offences under the Act, investigations into the resources of proscribed organisations and investigations designed to assess whether there are grounds to proscribe any such organisation.[21]

'Ordinary material' is defined in negative terms. It is everything which is not covered by two categories of material – excluded material and material handled by special procedures. Broadly speaking, excluded material covers personal records which are held in confidence, human tissue for medical diagnosis and some journalistic material.[22]

Detention Rules

Prior to 1986 the treatment of a suspect in custody was regulated principally by Police Force Standing Orders and what were known as the Judges' Rules. The former had no force in law and the latter, which were created in 1912 and revised in 1964, were quasi-legal. They were embodied in no Act of Parliament, yet a breach of the Rules could be punished in certain circumstances by the court refusing to accept evidence obtained in breach of them. From 1986, with the introduction of PACE and the Codes of Practice made under it, the treatment of *ordinary* suspects in police custody has been more closely regulated. The extent to which this tighter regulation has improved the position of the suspect is the subject of considerable debate, which is considered below.

It was widely assumed that as the Codes of Practice made numerous references to the treatment of PTA detainees in custody they automatically applied to them as well as 'ordinary decent criminals' (or ODCs). However, this does not appear to have been the case in *all* police force areas. In one case in 1987, a person who had been detained at Liverpool requested a copy of his custody record, via his solicitor. An Assistant Chief Constable replied that since he was not arrested or charged with any criminal offence, he was therefore unable to accede to the request. His solicitor then wrote again pointing out that the Codes of Practice allow a detained person or their legal representatives to apply for a copy of their custody record within twelve months and there is no stipulation that a person be either arrested or charged with an offence. A Deputy Chief Constable replied, standing by the original decision.[23]

The Liverpool police had read the legislation very carefully. Notwithstanding the numerous references in the Codes of Practice, PACE itself provides that a person is in detention only if they are arrested for a specific type of offence or for an arrestable offence.[24] Under the PTA, people are normally either not arrested for a specific offence but for terrorism, or they are simply detained. In the Liverpool case, the person had not been arrested but detained under the PTA. The PACE Codes of Practice therefore did not apply. Other police forces, particularly the Metropolitan Police, do not appear to have taken such a legalistic position and have applied the Codes of Practice to all detainees. The loophole in the law was partially closed in the PTA 1989 when it provided that the Codes applied to all people *arrested* under the PTA.[25] But they do not appear to apply to people *detained* at ports and airports. The Home Office, however, had this advice:

> Chief Officers will nevertheless wish to consider carefully whether procedures in such cases should be brought into line with those for section 14 arrests. The view may be taken ... that the spirit is more important than the letter, and that the safeguards contained in Code C should in principle apply to all persons detained in police custody under the 1989 Act.[26]

In the following sections we describe the position before and after PACE, but it should be borne in mind that as most of the people in this study were arrested or detained prior to 1989, they were not subject to the Codes of Practice which was amended in 1991, but to the Judges' Rules and Police Standing Force Orders.

The Review Procedures

Prior to the introduction of PACE, detention under the ordinary criminal law required that a person charged with an offence which was not serious had to be brought before a Magistrate's Court within 24 hours or be given police bail.[27] Since the introduction of PACE, a suspect under the ordinary criminal law can be held for up to 96 hours.[28]

Although this reduces the discrepancy in terms of the time a person can be held between the PTA and the ordinary law, the PTA procedures are very different.

Under PACE a suspect can initially be held for questioning for up to 24 hours from the time of arrest or arrival at the police station, whichever is earlier. At the end of 24 hours the person must be released or charged unless she or he is suspected of committing a 'serious arrestable offence'. If the individual is suspected of committing such an offence, then an officer of at least the rank of superintendent can authorise the extension of the detention for up to 36 hours, after which the suspect must be brought before a Magistrates' Court. The Court can then authorise detention for a further 36 hours, bringing the total detention period to 72 hours. If the police wish to detain the individual still further, they must bring their case before a Magistrates' Court again, which can authorise an additional detention of up to 24 hours, bringing the total possible detention to 96 hours.

Following the recommendations of the Colville Report, a review procedure for detention under the PTA was introduced in 1989.[29] There are, however, substantial differences between the two review processes. The most important difference is that there is no independent element in a review for a PTA detainee and the police are not required to bring the case before a Magistrate's Court after 36 hours.

The PTA review procedure requires that an initial review should be carried out as soon as practicable after the beginning of the detention and subsequent reviews should be carried out at 12 hour intervals.[30] The reviews, however, may be postponed if it is not practicable to carry them out because the person is being questioned or if no review officer is readily available.[31]

The detention may only be continued if it is necessary to obtain or preserve evidence specifically related to offences under the Act or in terms of the vague and nebulous concept of being involved in terrorism. In addition, continued detention may be authorised if the person is being checked out to see if they are subject to an exclusion order or if the Secretary State or the DPP are considering making an exclusion order or bringing charges.[32] These caveats are either so vague or so broad that it is hard to see how the review officer, who must be someone unconnected with the case, can reach a decision to release the person.

Apart from the different time periods for review and the numerous qualifications, the major contrast in law between the PTA review procedure and PACE is that no outside authority is involved in the former. Under PACE, a person must be brought before a Magistrates'

Court after 36 hours and if an extension is granted they must be brought back again within 24 hours. In other words, in the four days a body other than the police has the opportunity to hear the reasons for further detention and, more importantly, has an opportunity to consider the condition and state of health of the detainee. The effectiveness of the procedure is debatable; nevertheless, the point which is being highlighted is the difference in law. Under the PTA, however, a person can be held for up to seven days without any outside assessment. The detainee has only a right to make representations to the review officer.

The Colville Report did not discuss whether there should be any external scrutiny of detention. However, the Jellicoe Report did discuss this issue and rejected the proposal on the basis that the Magistrates' Court is not the forum for discussion of '*issues of extreme sensitivity*' (emphasis added); and because not very many extensions are applied for under the PTA, magistrates would not be able to develop the necessary expertise. He also rejected a proposal that applications be made to a High Court judge on the grounds that:

(a) he could not see any real advantage;
(b) unacceptable problems of security would arise;
(c) the criteria upon which a decision to extend a detention are not susceptible of judicial assessment;
(d) there would be problems of availability whereas Ministers are on call virtually 24 hours a day; and finally
(e) the Ministers are answerable to Parliament for their decisions and he believed this to be the best way of ensuring that the power is properly operated.[33]

The Jellicoe Report, however, does not explain why information pertaining to a suspected 'terrorist' is considered too sensitive while information, for example, relating to a suspected child molester or rapist can be brought before a magistrate. One possible explanation is that some magistrates are not to be trusted with handling the information. To acknowledge this point, however, would cast doubt on the integrity of the magistracy. In any event, the list of reasons why a magistrate should not be involved apply only to a very small minority of cases. Nearly nine out of every ten people detained under the PTA are released without any action being taken against them.

Whatever the details of the argument, making a distinction between what is or is not acceptable to bring before a Magistrates' Court, or indeed a High Court judge, yet again emphasises the very different treatment of those suspected of ordinary crime and political violence. In this respect, the law makes a clear distinction between the way ordinary crime and political crime is dealt with in the criminal justice system.

Detention Rights

Prior to 1989 there were no rules governing how long a PTA detainee could be held incommunicado, and thus unable to contact a friend or solicitor. It was possible to hold someone incommunicado for the whole seven days. Since 1986 a person arrested under PACE may request to have one person known to them informed as soon as practicable of their whereabouts.[34] In addition, they may at any time consult and communicate privately – whether in person, in writing, or on the telephone – with a solicitor.[35] Although the legislation refers to these provisions as rights, this is an incorrect use of the term: both provisions may be delayed for up to 36 hours at the discretion of the police. They are better described as concessions.

Since 1 March 1989, these concessions have been available to PTA detainees.[36] These too may be delayed and the grounds are much more vague. They may be delayed if there are reasonable grounds for believing that they will lead to interference with the gathering of information about the commission, preparation or instigation of acts of terrorism or because, by alerting someone, it will make it more difficult to prevent an act of terrorism or to secure the conviction of someone involved.[37]

It is far from clear how long these concessions may be delayed. PACE provides that they may be delayed for up to 36 hours.[38] But there is no similar statutory provision under the PTA. The police could therefore legally delay access to a solicitor or phoning a friend for the full period of a person's detention. The Codes of Practice, which do not have a statutory basis, do, however, provide that in no case should the delay go beyond 48 hours.[39] But no mention is made of detentions which occur at ports and airports. So even if the police follow the spirit rather than the letter of the law and observe the Codes of Practice, they can quite legally hold a person incommunicado at ports and airports for the full seven days.

There have never been any official statistics recording the length of time PTA detainees are kept incommunicado. In June 1991, the Home Secretary was asked to publish information on the extent to which people have been exercising their rights. He said the information was not available.[40] However, in the following month he was asked why the information was not available and whether he would make it policy to ensure that such information is made available in the future. He pointed out that it was not available because police forces do not in general make information from custody records available to anyone but the suspect or his or her legal representative. He then went on to note that a forthcoming study by the Home Office Research and Planning Unit had analysed the data for the period 22 March to 11 November 1990.[41] Of 214 people detained, 45 per cent requested that a friend be notified and 48 per cent asked to contact a solicitor. In only a handful of cases was the request delayed for over 36 hours. The figures are far from satisfactory as they tell us nothing about why, in a half of all cases, people did not make either request. Moreover, no information is presented on the number of requests which were delayed for less than 24 hours and between 24 and 36 hours. In addition, the numbers surveyed form only a proportion of all those detained in the period and it is unclear how representative the Home Office sample is of all those held.

Detention Conditions

The reviews of the PTA have made a number of recommendations designed to improve the conditions for people held under the Act. The Shackleton Report recommended that attention should be given to improving the standards of diet, exercise and comfort accorded to suspects.[42] The Jellicoe Report recorded that a number of the recommendations in the Shackleton Report concerning the detention of suspects had not been observed by all police forces. It therefore recommended that, subject to additional or alternative provisions relating to welfare, access to legal advice and the right not to be held incommunicado, all the provisions of the Codes of Practice (then in draft form), should apply to people held under the PTA. The report went further and specifically recommended that people arrested or detained in Britain should be supplied with clean bed linen, as well as mattress, blanket and pillow and that they should be offered a varied diet.[43]

The PACE Codes of Practice lay down a number of requirements concerning cells, washing facilities, clothing, meals and exercise. Most provisions are qualified by what may be reasonable, practicable or in the interests of safety or security. For example, 'as far as is practicable not more that one person shall be detained in a cell'.[44] The cell should be adequately heated, clean and ventilated. It must be adequately lit, subject to such dimming as is compatible with safety and security to allow persons detained overnight to sleep.[45] Blankets, mattresses, pillows and other bedding supplied should be of a reasonable standard and in a clean and sanitary condition.[46]

Access to toilet and washing facilities must be provided, but the Codes make no reference as to when this should be provided.[47] As the provisions stand, it would not be a breach of the Codes to deny a person access to washing facilities until just before their release on the seventh day of their detention. If a person's clothes are removed for investigation, for hygiene or health reasons or for cleaning, replacement clothing 'of a reasonable standard of comfort and cleanliness shall be provided'.[48]

The Codes note that at least two light meals and one main meal must be provided in any period of 24 hours. As far as practicable, the meals must offer a varied diet and meet any special dietary needs.[49] Brief outdoor exercise must be offered daily, but again only if it is practicable.[50] They specifically emphasise that the rules regarding bedding and a varied diet are particularly important in the case of a PTA detainee because they may well remain in police custody for some time.[51]

Interrogations

Prior to the introduction of the Codes of Practice, interrogations by the police were governed by the Judges' Rules. These were minimal. They required that the police kept a record of the interrogation and wrote down the suspect's statement, if one were made. The only restriction on the interrogation was that the police should not use oppressive behaviour and that any statement made by the suspect should be voluntary. As there was never any independent witness to most interrogations, these restrictions were of little consequence.

The Codes of Practice lay down a number of detailed procedures. They require that a person must normally be interviewed at a police station,[52] that 'an accurate record must be made of each interview',[53] and that no oppressive behaviour or threats are used to elicit answers.[54] The custody officer is responsible for delivering the detainee for questioning.[55] In any period of 24 hours there must be a break from questioning of at least eight hours.[56] Meal times must be recognised and there must be short breaks every two hours for refreshments.[57] All these breaks, however, can be ignored if there are grounds for believing that among other things, a break would 'otherwise prejudice the outcome of the investigation'.[58] With such a large qualification, the rules can easily be ignored. The situation is further exacerbated because there are no real sanctions for any breach of the Codes of Practice and this means that suspects are hardly better protected now than they were under the Judges' Rules and 'the police have little to lose even if it is proven that they have acted unlawfully'.[59]

Fingerprinting, Intimate and Strip Searches

The police may take a person's fingerprints provided either that they obtained his or her consent in writing, or an officer of at least the rank of superintendent authorises them to be taken. However, if someone has been charged with a recordable offence and has not yet had his or her fingerprints taken in the course of the investigation, their fingerprints may be taken.

The police also have considerable powers relating to searching people in custody. An intimate body search can only be authorised by a police officer of at least the rank of superintendent and only when there is reasonable suspicion that an article which can cause physical injury to a detained person has been concealed on them, or that the person has concealed a Class A drug.[60] An intimate search can only be carried out by a registered medical practitioner or a registered nurse unless a senior officer considers it impracticable.[61] Strip searches may take place when a custody officer considers it necessary to remove an article which the detained person should not be allowed to keep.[62]

Under the ordinary criminal law, if a person is subsequently not suspected of committing the offence, is given a police caution after not admitting to the offence or is cleared of the offence, the fingerprints must be destroyed together with any copies of them and the person may ask to be allowed to be a witness to the destruction of the fingerprints and copies. However, these provisions do not apply to someone who is arrested or detained under the PTA. In other words, people suspected of the most heinous crimes from murder to rape who are investigated under the ordinary law have the right to have their fingerprints and other samples destroyed. Yet an innocent person who is picked up under the PTA has no equivalent right.

Length of Detention

The power of arrest is accompanied by the power to detain for a specific period of time. Initially, this period must not exceed 48 hours.[63] However, the Secretary of State may extend this period for a further period not exceeding five days.[64] In England and Wales applications for extensions are filtered through the National Joint Unit at New Scotland Yard. There is now a standard form for applications, recording the name and circumstances of the detained person, the intelligence traces recorded against him or her, his or her criminal record (if any) and the reason for the application.

The application form is then submitted to the Home Office, whose officials advise the Secretary of State in person. If the Secretary of State is not available, authority may be given by one of the Ministers of State in the Home Office. In the event of a Minister not being available, the authority is granted by a senior official in the Home Office for the period until the Secretary of State is available. The police are told immediately of the decision and this is then confirmed in writing. Applications for extensions for suspects in Scotland are handled a little differently. They are made directly to the Scottish Office.[65]

The Colville Report summarised the various reasons for extensions from the previous reviews of the legislation. The following reasons were noted:

(1) Checking of fingerprints;
(2) Forensic tests;
(3) Checking the detainee's replies against intelligence;
(4) New lines of inquiry;
(5) Interrogation to identify accomplices;
(6) Correlating information obtained from one or more than one other detainee in the same case;
(7) Awaiting a decision by the DPP;
(8) Finding and consulting other witnesses;
(9) Identification parade;
(10) Checking an alibi;
(11) Translating documents;
(12) Obtaining an interpreter and then carrying out the necessary interviews with his or her assistance;

(13) Communications with foreign police forces, sometimes across time-zone and language difficulties;
(14) Evaluation of documents once translated and further investigated.

These reasons are not listed in the legislation, but they are noted in the Home Office circular to all Chief Police Officers.[66] The police have therefore been presented with a shopping list of possibilities for detaining a person who has already been in custody for two full days, for a further five days. It is significant that there is no list of reasons why a person *should not* be subject to extended detention. The orientation of the detention powers is to encourage extensive police incarceration and conversely, deny people their fundamental democratic right to freedom from arbitrary detention. As Ewing and Gearty put it: 'This is British law's black hole for civil liberties, and it is one into which hapless suspects may be quite lawfully sucked.'[67]

The detention powers have been condemned by the European Court of Human Rights, but the Government has chosen to ignore the judgment and derogate from the relevant provisions of the European Convention and the International Covenant on Civil and Political Rights. In *Brogan v United Kingdom*, the Court held that the detention of suspects under Section 12 of the PTA 1984, now Section 14 of the PTA 1989, constituted a breach of Article 5(3) of the European Convention on Human Rights because none of the suspects had been brought promptly before a judicial authority.[68] The Court did not recommend an acceptable period of detention before a magistrate or a judge reviews the case, but it considered that the shortest period experienced by one of the applicants – four days and six hours – breached the Convention.

Table 4.1 A notice of application for an extension to detention

---

PREVENTION OF TERRORISM (TEMPORARY PROVISIONS) ACT 1989

Notice of an Application for an Extension of Detention
To:

In accordance with *Section 14(5)/ Schedule 5 Paragraph 6(3) Prevention of Terrorism (Temporary Provisions) Act 1989, being a person who has been detained under Section 14(1)(a)(b)(c)*/Section 5 Paragraph 6(1)(a)(b)(c)* you are hereby informed that at ... hours on ... an application for an extension of your detention was made to the Secretary of State.

---

* Delete whichever is inappropriate

Almost a year after the Court gave its judgment, the Government announced that it still considered it necessary to detain terrorist suspects for up to seven days and rejected any suggestion of the introduction of a judicial review either by a magistrates court or a judge at some point in the procedure. The Government considered that the existing safeguards were satisfactory and in any event the decisions to detain suspects 'may be, and often are, taken on the basis of information, the nature of and source of which could not be revealed to a suspect or his [sic] legal adviser without serious risk to individuals assisting the police or the prospect of further valuable intelligence being lost'.[69]

The detainee must be given a notice explaining that an application for an extension to detention has been made to the Secretary of State. The current form is reproduced in Table 4.1.

Summary of the Differences between a PTA and a PACE Detention

The major differences between the law and procedures governing an arrest and detention under PACE and under the PTA are summarised in Table 4.2.

Table 4.2: Arrest and Detention: PACE and the PTA compared

Arrest

Police must have reasonable suspicion that a specific offence is being or has been committed [Sec. 24].	Police need not have reasonable suspicion of a specific offence under the PTA or that the person arrested is suspected of committing any offence. An arrest is typically only the first step in the investigation of a person's involvement in terrorism [Sec. 14(1) and Lynch70].

Detention

4 days.	7 days.

First Review

No later than 6 hours after the detention is first authorised [Sec. 40 (3)(a)].	As soon as practicable after the beginning of the investigation [Schd 3, sec. 1(2)(a) and sec. 3(2)(a)].

---

continued

Table 4.2 continued

Subsequent Reviews

9 hours and then intervals of no more than 9 hours. [Sec 40(3)(b)	12 hours and then intervals of no more than 12 hours [Schd. 3 sec. 1(2)(b) and sec 3(2)(b)].

24 hour point

Must be charged or released unless further detention is authorised by an officer of at least the rank of Superintendent [Sec. 42].	Must be charged or released unless further detention is authorised by an officer of at the least the rank of Inspector [Schd. 3, Sec. 4].

36 hour point

Must obtain a warrant for further detention from a Magistrates' Court [Sec. 43].	No review by Magistrates' Court. Case must be reviewed by an officer of at least the rank of Superintendent [Schd. 3 Sec. 4].

48 hour point

Must obtain another warrant if existing warrant has expired. [Sec 43]	Secretary of State may extend period of detention by a period or periods specified by him but not exceeding 5 days [Sec. 14(5)].

Concession to notify a friend or have access to a solicitor

May contact a friend, relative or other person known to them as soon as practicable. May be delayed for a serious arrestable offence and if authorised by an officer of at least the rank of superintendent. Cannot be delayed beyond 36 hours [Sec. 56 and 58].	May contact a friend, relative or other person known to them. May be delayed. No statutory limit on length of delay. COP limit delay for arrests to 48 hours. No limit under COP for detentions at ports and airports.[Schd. 3 sec. 7, COP, Code C, sec. 9].

Fingerprinting

Can only be taken if there are reasonable grounds for suspecting the involvement of the person in a criminal offence and the belief exists that fingerprints will tend to confirm the involvement [Sec. 61].	Can be taken to assist an officer in determining whether the person is or has been concerned in the commission, preparation or instigation of acts of terrorism, subject to an exclusion order, or reasonably suspected of an offence under the PTA [Sec 15 (10)].

Destruction of fingerprints

Must be destroyed if person is eliminated from police inquiries [Sec 64].	No requirement that the fingerprints are destroyed.

Equal Before the Law

Underlying all criminal law is the assumption that the law applies to everyone equally. This is no less true of the Prevention of Terrorism legislation. The basic problem is that men and women are not the same and, as so many feminists are pointing out, do not start as equals. This has been succinctly articulated by Tove Stang Dahl:

> As long as we live in a society where men and women follow different paths in life and have different living conditions, with different needs and potential, legal rules will necessarily affect men and women differently.[71]

When women are arrested under the PTA their needs in detention will be very different from those of men.[72] In addition, many women will be looking after children and other family members and the implications of their arrest and detention will therefore be very much greater than those for men. There is little acknowledgement of this reality. The major reviews of the legislation, the Home Office circulars and the Codes of Practice make no references to women or to children. Similarly, no distinction is made in the official statistics between men and women. For all these sources of information about the PTA, women and children do not exist.

In June 1991, the Secretary of State was asked to provide information on the number of women arrested under the PTA. He provided some information for the period from 1985.[73] At the same time he was asked to provide information on cases in which special arrangements for children had to be made as a result of their parents or guardians being examined or detained and the number of children taken into care as a consequence of the PTA. He replied that the information is not held centrally and could be obtained only at disproportionate costs.[74] Moreover, he did not guarantee that as a matter of policy the information would be collected in the future. The public will therefore continue to remain ignorant of the impact of this piece of legislation on the most vulnerable section of the population.

When a parent or guardian is arrested, the police have the power to remove children (without the authorisation of a magistrate) to a 'place of safety'.[75] Children subjected to Place of Safety Orders were not legally in the care of the local authority, but they became the responsibility of local authority Social Services and were typically removed from home.[76]

These procedures have now been superceded under the Children Act 1989.

The Use of Arrest Powers

The use of arrest powers other than at ports and airports has varied over the years, as can be seen from Figure 4.1. But the overall movement has been downwards. During the first five full years the Act was in force, from 1975 to 1979, the average number of people detained was 256 per annum. Over the five year period from 1 January 1987 to 31 December 1991, the average had dropped to 77 per year – less than a quarter of the initial rate.

The number of women detained for the period 1985 to 1990 is also shown in Figure 4.1. Out of 507 detentions, 64, or 13 per cent, involved women.

No information is provided on the outcome of inland arrests; outcome statistics are presented only for all detentions under the PTA and no distinction is made between arrests at ports and airports, and those inland. It is therefore impossible to assess accurately the impact of the PTA on the non-travelling or resident community. As there is no reason to assume that the outcome of detentions at ports and airports is likely to differ significantly from arrests inland, it is possible to apply the overall outcome rate to the arrest figures. On this basis, out of 2,308 arrests in the period from 1 November 1974 to the end of 1991, 1,984 people, or 86 per cent, would have been arrested and then released without any action being taken against them.

It is obvious from these figures that the principal use of the PTA powers of arrest, like the powers of detention at ports and airports, is to screen systematically sections of the population to gather intelligence. Although the arrest figures provide no information on which sections of the population are being screened, it is clear from other sources that it is mainly Irish people living in Britain or Irish visitors to Britain. There is nothing new in this conclusion: the Irish community in Britain has been complaining about the use of the arrest powers ever since the legislation was introduced.

After some major incident it is not uncommon for a large number of Irish people to be arrested, interrogated and then released. Unfortunately, the level of aggregation of the statistics – the figures are presented for quarterly periods only – prevents any systematic analysis of the extent of these swoops.

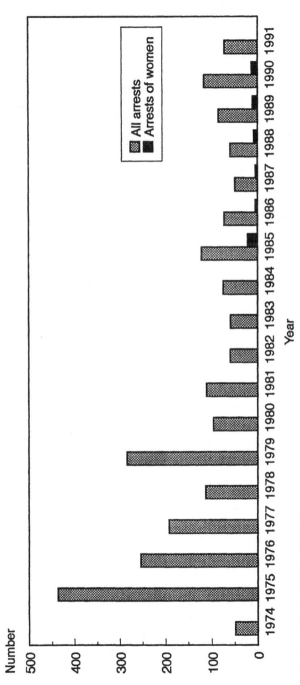

Figure 4.1 Number of Persons Arrested or Detained Other Than at Ports and Airports Under the PTA, 1974-1991 (showing gender for 1985-1990).

Source: Home Office Statistics

One of the biggest swoops occurred shortly after the PTA 74 became law following the Woolwich and Guildford bombings. Paul Hill, one of the Guildford Four, was the first person to be detained under the new legislation. Although the case is now firmly lodged in the public's mind as the Guildford Four, between 29 November and 5 December 1974, the period in which the four were arrested, there were reports that at least 76 people had been arrested. Only the Guildford Four were charged and convicted. Another set of arrests centred around Annie Maguire and her family involving another swoop in which more than 20 people were arrested.

From all the evidence it is clear that the police had very little to go on and were systematically arresting Irish people and then arresting their friends and acquaintances in one massive trawling operation. When talking about the eight people arrested when he was picked up, Paul Hill stated:

> There was nothing at all to link them to any offence: no explosives, no guns, no forensic evidence, no identification evidence. They had been arrested and charged simply because they were Irish and were linked to Paddy [Armstrong] and through Paddy to Gerry [Conlon] and me. Crucially, they had made no statements.[77]

Walker acknowledges that police swoops do take place, suggesting that 'everyone connected with a person against whom there is firm evidence may be arrested'.[78] But this is too charitable to the police. What emerges from the first use of these draconian powers is that there was no one against whom there was any firm evidence. The basis of suspicion was simply that they were Irish.

Although the number and size of police swoops have declined dramatically over the years, they are nevertheless still occurring.

The Use of Extended Powers of Detention

The use of extended powers of detention for those detained inland has fluctuated considerably as can be seen from Figure 4.2. In 1975 and 1979, 137 and 135 extensions respectively were granted. From these high figures there has been a steady decline.

Since 1984 more detailed information has been provided on the length of detentions beyond 48 hours but the information is not broken down by place of detention. One set of figures relates to *people* and shows how

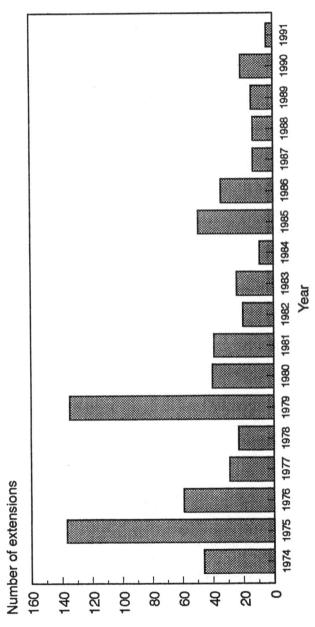

Figure 4.2 Number of Extensions to Detention Beyond 48 hours, 1974-1991.

Source: Home Office Statistics

long they have been detained. The information however relates only to those not charged or excluded. The figures show that the number of people detained for more than three days has declined from 13 per cent in 1984 to 10 per cent in 1991. The other set of figures relates to the number of *extensions*. In 1984, 65 per cent of all extensions exceeded three days. The proportion then dropped over the next five years and then rose again in 1990 to 48 per cent. In 1991 the proportion was the lowest ever recorded and stood at seven per cent. The extreme variation in the number of extensions granted to the police by the Executive is a key feature of the statistics. As no application for an extension had ever been rejected by the Home Office, it is clear that the Home Office does little or nothing to counter the extreme variability in the number of applications made by the police. A police decision to apply for an extension is likely to include political pressure to produce results as well as factors relating to the nature of the investigation as in 1985, for example, the year in which Patrick Magee was arrested and charged with the Brighton bombing when extensions were applied for and granted in nearly half of all detentions.

Outcome of Detentions

It was pointed out in Chapter 1 that of the 7,052 people detained under the PTA in connection with Northern Ireland affairs between 29 November 1974 and 31 December 1991, some 6,097 people were released without any action being taken against them. Of the rest, 197 were charged with offences under the PTA, 411 were charged under other legislation and 349 were excluded. The exclusion statistics will be considered in greater detail in Chapter 9. The aim here is to analyse the type of charges brought and the outcome of the proceedings.

The PTA, as we have shown elsewhere, introduced a number of new offences. Broadly speaking they fall into five main categories of offence: failure to comply with an exclusion order or helping a person to breach one; soliciting, receiving or giving money for either a proscribed organisation or for use in acts of terrorism; withholding information about acts of terrorism; failure to cooperate with an examination at a port; and being a member of or displaying support for a proscribed organisation. Over the years there have been some slight changes to these categories and the PTA 89 introduced a new set of offences, based on existing anti-drug legislation.

It is not possible to analyse the charges brought against people for activity associated solely with Northern Ireland affairs as the statistics include a small number of charges arising out of international terrorism. Of the 218 people who have been charged with offences under the PTA, 97 of the offences arose from the person's failure to cooperate at ports and airports. As those who are involved in political violence will presumably cooperate at ports and airports to avoid drawing attention to themselves, most refusals to cooperate are presumably because the person objects to the coerciveness of the legislation and the erosion of their civil liberties.

The next largest category of charges under the Act relates to support for a proscribed organisation. Sixty-eight have been charged with offences ranging from solicitoring or receiving money to displaying support. Fewer than 30 people have been charged with exclusion order offences and withholding information.

Figure 4.3 notes the outcome of all charges brought under the PTA. As can be seen, just over three quarters were found guilty. Of these, over half received non-custodial sentences and of those that were sent to prison, most received a sentence of one year or less. Of all offences under the PTA, the courts appear to take the view that support for a proscribed organisation is the most serious. Of the 35 prison sentences exceeding one year, 33 related to this category of offence.

Of the 426 people detained and charged with offences under other legislation, 64 were returned to Northern Ireland to be prosecuted. The rest were tried in Britain. The charges ranged from serious offences such as murder and attempted murder and causing explosions, to minor offences such as theft. In over a quarter of cases people were charged with offences such as rape or drunken driving, which appear to be totally unrelated to political violence. Yet they had been initially arrested or detained under the PTA.

Figure 4.4 shows the outcome of all charges brought under other legislation and dealt with in British courts. Thirteen per cent were not proceeded with, four per cent were awaiting trial, ten per cent were acquitted and 73 per cent were found guilty. Of those found guilty, some 42 per cent received non-custodial sentences, twelve per cent were sentenced to less than a year and 35 per cent to over five years in prison.

In the more recent period from 1 January 1989 to 31 December 1991, there have been over 60 incidents of political violence connected with Northern Ireland affairs in Britain. There have been 527 arrests and detentions in connection with political violence in Northern Ireland and international terrorism under the PTA. In the same period, however,

Figure 4.3 Persons Charged with Offences Under the PTA 1974-1991, shown by outcome.

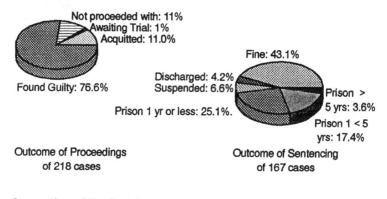

Not proceeded with: 11%
Awaiting Trial: 1%
Acquitted: 11.0%
Fine: 43.1%
Found Guilty: 76.6%
Discharged: 4.2%
Suspended: 6.6%
Prison > 5 yrs: 3.6%
Prison 1 yr or less: 25.1%.
Prison 1 < 5 yrs: 17.4%

Outcome of Proceedings
of 218 cases

Outcome of Sentencing
of 167 cases

Source: Home Office Statistics.

Figure 4.4: Persons Charged with other Offences after being detained under the PTA, 1974-1991 shown by outcome.

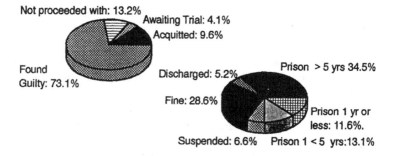

Not proceeded with: 13.2%
Awaiting Trial: 4.1%
Acquitted: 9.6%
Prison > 5 yrs 34.5%
Found Guilty: 73.1%
Discharged: 5.2%
Fine: 28.6%
Prison 1 yr or less: 11.6%.
Suspended: 6.6%   Prison 1 < 5 yrs:13.1%

Outcome of Proceedings
of 362 cases

Outcome of Sentencing
of 266 cases

Source: Home Office Statistics.

there have been only 13 convictions in Britain leading to sentences of more than five years for both types of terrorism.

Conclusions

The introduction of the PTA established a dual system of criminal justice in Britain: one for people drawn into the criminal justice process under the PTA and another for those being dealt with under the ordinary criminal law. The focus in this chapter has been on describing the arrest and detention powers under the PTA and comparing them with those under PACE. Although the emphasis was on law and procedures, the two systems also differ in terms of the culture and atmosphere which surround the detaining and custody of the suspects. These aspects are intangible but, as will be seen from later chapters, the level of security is often intense, the pressure on the police to produce results greater and detention regimes also differ qualitatively from those for ordinary decent criminals. Thus the dual system must not only be seen in terms of the differences in law, but also in terms of the broader social context.

The two systems have very different objectives. The principal aim of the ordinary criminal justice system is to take some formal action against those suspected of being involved in crime. This may involve charging the person or giving them a formal caution after the offence has been admitted.[79] The main objective of the PTA is to gather intelligence.

All the evidence from the official statistics suggests that the police have systematically used the arrest powers to screen certain sections of the population. The main target of these operations has been the Irish community living in Britain. In the same way as the travelling Irish have become a suspect community under the port powers, the resident Irish have become a suspect community through the use of the powers of arrest. The use of the powers of arrest differs little from that used by the army in Northern Ireland under the Emergency Provisions Acts, where the main Catholic areas have been systematically screened since the start of the troubles.[80]

Although there has been a substantial reduction in the number of people being drawn into the prevention of terrorism net, there has been little change in the ratio of those charged to those detained. For every ten people detained, nine are likely to be charged with no offence whatsoever. The pursuit of a prosecution is not and never has been the prime objective of the PTA.

Many people will argue that intelligence gathering must be the prime object of the powers of arrest as this will be the only way to defeat political violence. This is far too simple. It is possible that the trawling or screening operations do bring in some valuable information. But this information must be balanced against the information which is not obtained voluntarily from the Irish community because the legislation and its use are seen as oppressive and discriminatory. Moreover, the argument takes no account of the number of people who may be encouraged to turn away from constitutional politics to political violence as a direct result of their experiences of the PTA or their perception of the law as oppressive. If any lesson is to be learnt from the last 20 years in Northern Ireland it is that repressive legislation and the wide-scale infringement of civil liberties, far from preventing political violence, play an important role in maintaining and sustaining it.

The use of the powers of arrest to screen sections of the population may help to reassure the public that something is being done to catch the perpetrators of the bombings and other incidents. To this extent, the PTA may have an important expressive function. But this function is probably less effective today, following the miscarriages of justice, than it was in the aftermath of the Birmingham and other bombings in the 1970s.

While the prime objective of the PTA is intelligence gathering, it is important to emphasise that in some cases the objective will be to secure a conviction. In a few cases people will be arrested because the police have a very strong suspicion of their involvement and their aim will be to obtain a confession. Indeed, the whole detention and interrogation regime under the PTA, as will be shown in Chapters 7 and 8, is designed to make the trained and hardened terrorist speak rather than exercise their right to remain silent. The intense pressure to which all detainees are subject – irrespective of whether the objective is to gather intelligence or secure a conviction – is therefore a product of the what the authorities consider to be necessary to crack the trained terrorist.

Finally, arrest and detention under the PTA constitute an effective abrogation of the rule of law. Police officers can arrest anyone without giving any specific justification and without fear of being called to account and, moreover, they can legally hold anyone incommunicado for up to seven days without any reference to an independent judicial authority. It is now commonplace to argue that the situation has been transformed since the introduction of the PACE Codes of Practice to cover PTA detentions. But as will be shown in later chapters, they have not fundamentally altered the disparity of power between the police and the detainee. The police themselves carry out the supervisory and management tasks required under the Codes: there is no independent supervision or control of police practices.

5   Arrest and Detention under the PTA: Two Case Studies

Introduction

This chapter presents detailed descriptions of two women's experience of being arrested and detained under the PTA. The first was held for three days and 17 hours in Paddington Green police station and her seven year old daughter was taken into care. The second was held for over 15 hours. While they were detained their homes were extensively searched and large quantities of their property was taken away by the police. They were subsequently released without any action being taken against them.

Both cases illustrate the way in which totally innocent people come under suspicion. This can occur in many different ways as we shall show in the next chapter. In the first case, Sally became a suspect because her husband, from whom she had been estranged for seven years, was suspected of offences and she and her seven year old daughter had recently spent some time with him. In the second case the reason is more complicated. In 1980 Teresa, who was born in Ireland, and her husband, gave a young lad a lift when they were on holiday in Portugal. His name was Gerry and it turned out that he was Irish. In 1988 he was arrested in Germany and charged with firearms offences. He was acquitted. After he was arrested the Hertfordshire Special Branch visited the couple and asked them various questions about the hitchhiker, who had noted their names and address in his address book. They thought that this was the end of the matter. It was not. On the 4 February 1991 – some six weeks before the Queen was due to open a new terminal at Stansted airport, where they both worked – they were arrested by the Essex police at their home. The Essex Special Branch had presumably carried out a security check, using the Police National Computer, on all employees at the airport prior to the Queen's visit and had come across a record of the couple noting details of either their interview with the Hertfordshire Special Branch in 1988 or the fact that the names Teresa and Don had been on a letter sent to a prisoner in Crumlin jail in Belfast.

A senior officer in the Essex police had presumably then ordered that they be arrested and their house extensively searched.

The two cases are atypical in some respects. To begin with, most arrests under the PTA are of men not women. Moreover, Sally is English and not Irish, a single parent and university educated, with a well-paid professional job. These characteristics no doubt explain her different treatment under the PTA from that of most of the other men and women in the study who were held at Paddington Green. Similarly Teresa, though Irish, is married to an Englishman and most of her friends in England are English, not Irish.

In other respects, however, the cases are fairly typical. In the first place, they illustrate the coerciveness of policing; in neither case were the 'suspects' given the opportunity to help the police with their concerns voluntarily. Secondly, they provide a comprehensive picture of the feelings and emotions which are experienced during and after an arrest, detention and house search. They show how the whole process adds up to an horrific and terrifying ordeal in which people feel totally powerless compared with the combined power of the police and various other actors, such as solicitors, doctors, and social workers. Thirdly, and of considerable importance, the cases illustrate the routineness of the work for the police and other professionals, who are playing their part in a large modern policing bureaucracy. In this and other bureaucratic processes human beings lose their distinctiveness and become 'suspects' or 'clients'. As Bauman has so powerfully argued, 'dehumanisation is inextricably related to the most essential, rationalising tendency of modern bureaucracy'.[1] Once dehumanised, people can be viewed with ethical indifference and moral questions are of no concern to those carrying out their tasks. They are only doing their job. As violence has become increasingly concentrated under state control, moral responsibility is replaced by a technical responsibility.[2]

Case 1: Sally's Experience

Saturday 6.00 a.m.

At 6 o'clock in the morning there was a knock at the door and of course Emma and I were both still in bed. I've got quite a complicated burglar alarm, which doesn't take that long to switch off but I obviously need to switch it off before I could open the door. In the time I was doing that they were already shouting that they were going to bash the door down. So it wasn't more than a minute, two minutes. I said, 'Hang on'. I think they'd shouted, 'We're police officers', and I just said, 'Hang on' and by the time I was attempting to shut off the alarm they were shouting very loudly they were going to bash the door down. There were three men and two women, one of whom I later saw at Paddington Green, who I think was the officer in charge of that particular aspect of the case. But he didn't interview me and he was the one who spoke to me here.

I asked if I could get dressed and the female officer came up stairs with me. And then – it's very, very hazy – but very soon after that they told me that I was being taken to the station. I said, 'My daughter's upstairs, can I make a telephone call to a friend for my daughter?' They said, 'No. You cannot use the phone', and I said, 'Can I leave her with my neighbour?' They said, 'No, we've made provision for her', and I said, 'What do you mean?' and they said, 'She'll come with us.' I then went upstairs and tried to calm her down because she was obviously still sleepy and I think dazed by all the people in the house making lots of noise.

One of the male officers came upstairs and told me to pack a bag for her for three days. I was just stunned – but I wasn't arguing. I've thought about this since and I think probably a lot of people in the same situation argue, and I think it's probably because I was aware of who they were, I was aware of their powers and having heard a lot about what it's like when you're arrested under the PTA I knew there was little point in doing anything.

I think by this point I was very shaky and the female officer was following me around. She came into the bedroom when I put clothes on and I said to her, 'Are you a social worker?', that's what I assumed she was, and she said no she wasn't. I don't think she was a Special Branch officer. I think she was just an ordinary plain clothes woman officer, and she seemed a bit concerned about what I was being put through. When I said, 'Why are they saying three days?', she said something to me like 'It's going to take a long time to go through this place'. I said, 'What do you mean?' and she said, 'Well, we don't often come to a place with so many books for a start', and I'm thinking, what in the world is she talking about?

Anyway, I suppose about half an hour later when I had packed this bag, what was paramount in my mind was that I should not scare Emma. I didn't want her to panic and I was constantly saying to her, 'It's okay', and I said to her, 'These men have come because we've had burglaries and they want to look through the place and we're going to have to go to the police station.' At this point I thought we were going

together. Then I was told she was being taken on her own. I still thought
we were going to end up in the same building together. I just thought
I was being taken down to the local police station, Paddington Green
had not come into my head.

They just kept saying she would be all right. I think I kept saying that
if I could phone a friend, she could stay with a friend. They kept saying,
'Stop worrying about her, we've made arrangements'. And at this
point a uniformed police woman appeared at the door. She had
obviously been waiting in a car outside and Emma was just taken off
with her.

I stood at the door and saw Emma being taken away and I think that
the thing that affected me most of all was that I completely lost control
as a parent. I think that's the thing that through the whole four days really
got to me. I could deal with it from my own point of view but the fact
that they took away my rights as a parent to control my child's destiny
makes me a bit tearful.

So I suppose I left here about 15 minutes later with this plain clothes
policewoman. I couldn't tell you who was driving the car. They were
male. There were about three other men left here when we left. They
had actually said I was being arrested under the Prevention of Terrorism
Act.

When we were in the police station we went through the whole thing
about fingerprints and photographs and the forensic tests but I wasn't
strip-searched. I was telling myself this is a sociological observation, just
take all this, this is interesting. I really thought I was going to be there
for a few hours and I almost cracked a joke. I almost said when this guy
was doing the forensic test under the fingernails I nearly said, 'Oh I'm
glad I haven't been playing cards'. It was just because I couldn't believe
they were going to keep me there for very long.

When I first got to the police station, before the tests and photographs,
a separate officer who didn't seem to be a branch officer took details
like name, date of birth, all that sort of thing and he asked me if I had
a solicitor. I knew her address, but I didn't have a telephone number
and they actually went up there and got her, so she was there immediately. I was lucky she hadn't gone away for the weekend.

The cell was slightly bigger than this room, bigger than the room we
were interviewed in, about 14 x 14, a built-in bed in one corner,
wooden, with a very thin hard mattress covered in thick plastic with a
pillow kind of built into it, shaped like a lilo. There was one dirty blanket.
Twice I asked for blankets to be changed because they smelt of vomit
and I was told the first time that they were clean blankets. I just said that

I can't sleep in them, they smell, and they actually went and got me some more. Oh, and one time they smelt of urine as well. They looked clean, they looked like they had gone through a cleaning process, but they obviously had been so filthy to start off with that the smell hadn't gone. But twice I asked them to change the blankets and they did, they put up slight objections, but they did bring me some more.

I tore the lining out of my coat to put over the pillow so that my face wasn't on the plastic and I slept under my coat with the blanket on top so that I wasn't really touching the blanket. There wasn't anything else in the cell, apart from a toilet. There wasn't a table or a chair.

The toilet was clean but it was in a fairly exposed position. Because I was checked on all the time I was in the cell – somebody was peering through the window every hour. There was this feeling of vulnerability if you did want to use it. You couldn't actually get any privacy, although nobody did actually look in while I was using it.

While we're on the subject of me being looked at, the worst thing was being checked every hour through the night. I'm a light sleeper and they just woke me up every hour and at one point half way through the night I sat up and said, 'Do you have to do this, you're waking me up?' The woman said, 'Yes, we check that you're okay'.

I could hear the keys unlocking the door in the corridor, then I could hear the footsteps down the corridor – everything echoes because there's nothing soft – then the hatch was slid back and they just looked in. The light wasn't kept on all the time and so I'm not quite sure how they managed to see that I was okay, given that the light was off. They actually allowed me to decide when I wanted the light off. They turned it off, but I could ring and say, 'I want to go to sleep now, could you turn the light off?' These are all those things that I realise that other people didn't have the benefit of, when I've listened to what other people have gone through.

I don't recall much of what was asked during the first interview. It was probably all about the whereabouts of her father, when I'd left him, why I'd visited him, and what we'd done. I think it was mainly about those sorts of things. We had spent two weeks with him over Christmas. I remember realising that it all sounded very odd because here I am saying, 'Yes, I don't have a relationship with this man, I left him for domestic reasons seven years ago but I went on holiday with him last week.' It sounded lunatic but it was the truth. I could see why they were frowning and several times during the interviews they kept coming back to my relationship with him and saying, 'This is a relationship that has been going on for all these years and he does confide in you, doesn't he?'

They were unable to accept that I was attempting a civilised friendship with the father of my daughter and the fact that he was living elsewhere and she was going there regularly. I wanted to see where she was going. I realised it all sounded very ludicrous and perhaps a little bit suspicious. At the interview, which must have lasted about two and a half hours, they said they were keeping me overnight and that's when I really did break down.

I kept saying what about my daughter, where is she? They said that she's with a foster parent, she's okay. That's all they told me. And I was in a real state. At 8 o'clock it was bedtime and I'm just imagining what a seven year old is feeling being taken away from her mother with a total stranger. It was awful. I can't really describe how I felt. And then that was the night I was woken up every hour.

I was checked by a doctor when I first got there. I had completely forgotten that. He looked very carefully at my body, presumably to make sure that I didn't have any marks on me, or that if I did have marks on me I couldn't then say later 'they did it'. He didn't do a medical. He took my blood pressure, he took a few details about medication that I might be taking and then he asked me to strip off to my underclothes. And then he just looked – there was a female police officer there, there wasn't a nurse, and he explained what he was doing.

I was allowed to wash on Saturday but I didn't have anything to wash with. It wasn't until the Monday morning that friends actually sent in some toiletries. There was a small bar of soap. The wash basin was along the corridor. It was a small room, about this size again, smaller than this, with two shower cubicles which had no curtains.

I suppose I should really explain this because I've talked to another friend who was arrested at the same time. She was held for four days and what I didn't realise – I've been brought up in a fairly uninhibited family so getting into a shower with a female police officer standing there watching me didn't bother me one bit but for her, who was brought up as a Roman Catholic, it was dreadful, it was one of the worst things for her, having to strip off in front of another person and being watched. It didn't bother me but obviously its something that's very important in terms of people's privacy and how they can be affected by things. So I was allowed a shower, it was very uncomfortable given that it was lukewarm, but it was clean. I can't remember about cleaning my teeth, because I didn't have a toothbrush. I can't remember whether they provided me with one or not. I don't think they did because I think I would have been very suspicious about using somebody else's toothbrush. I don't think my teeth got cleaned that night or in the morning.

Sunday

On the Sunday morning I was dreadful. I was shaking, I was walking, I really was in a terrible state. I don't think they got the doctor because of that. I think the doctor came as a routine. He was quite concerned – he wasn't a police doctor. I saw two different doctors while I was there and they came from a surgery nearby. I assumed he wasn't a police doctor. I don't know what is and what isn't a police doctor but he was quite concerned when I sat up. He said, 'You don't look very well', and I said, 'Well, I haven't slept'. No, I didn't say that, I said, 'I was woken up every hour', and he looked at the police officer and said, 'Why?' I then explained, rather than let her say something. I said, 'Well, I was told I had to be checked on every hour and I'm a very light sleeper and that's why I've just not had any sleep.' He said, 'Well, we'll give you some sleeping tablets for the following night', which he did, but they weren't strong enough. So in the middle of Sunday night I was ringing the bell for more sleeping tablets and they got another doctor from the same practice to come out in the middle of the night and he prescribed me something stronger.

After seeing the doctor first thing on Sunday morning, I was in my cell for probably half an hour to an hour before another two hour interview. The same two officers interviewed me every time. There were only two in the room, a man and a woman, plain clothes. I think we did something like a two hour interview in the morning and a two hour interview in the afternoon on Sunday. When I think about it now I can't possibly imagine what we could have been talking about for all that length of time, but I realised by this time that they had gone through all my personal books. Stripping off in a shower in front of another woman doesn't bother me at all, but what really, really bothered me was that they had read my journal. I write it – it's partly a personal therapist because I can't afford a proper one – but it is extremely personal stuff and I realised they'd read it. I've found it quite difficult since to write any more in it. I've kind of blocked it off.

I hadn't had it for very long. It's only since I left Emma's father so there was very little about him in it. It goes back to about 1982, no, '83, and it is all completely personal stuff. It's not day to day stuff, it's in my head. But I realised they'd been through all of that and also my telephone book, which I've had for years. They must have thought they had got hold of something really special, because I used to work in a press office. There were all kinds of telephone numbers in there, every newspaper and every TV channel and people like Tony Benn. It doesn't look like a personal directory, lots of political and charitable organisations. They had photocopies of that in front of them and they would occasionally pick out the odd one and say, 'Why have you got this one in your address book? Why have you got that?' Then mysteriously they would say, 'Have you ever done any charitable work?' My engagement diaries had also been photocopied and that was the worst intrusion of me personally, knowing that they've still got copies of them as well. I think the Sunday interviews centred mainly on that sort of stuff.

I don't think they were trying to break me down. They were just trying to get more information from me. If they were trying to break me down in any way they were doing it by using Emma. Over the three days, the female officer, who was the one who really got under my skin because they seemed not to be taking what according to the TV is the usual line of 'one soft, one hard', but she seemed to be taking both of those roles. So she would be incredibly hard in the interviews, accusing me of lying, shouting at me: 'That's not what you said yesterday', confusing me like that, and then after the interview, in my cell, she would come in and say, 'Sally, you've not eaten anything, would you like me to get you a take-away? Would you like vinegar on your chips?' She was taking the mother role and the interrogator role and confusing me like hell. Because I was so scared, when she was being kind to me I was warming to it. I was almost confiding in her about how I was feeling. She was also bringing me odd pieces of information about Emma and, on the surface she seemed to be concerned and wanting me to be reassured that Emma was okay. But she was saying things like, 'Well, we have a little report that she won't eat anything until she sees her mother.'

It was not the first time that Emma was mentioned. I think it must have been on the Saturday night, when I was obviously quite grief stricken about her first night being somewhere strange. I must have indicated this and – I'm trying to think of the officer's name, an Irish name, Mary somebody – anyway she said, 'Would you like me to find out how she is?'

I said yes and that I want her to know that I'm okay. Then I said 'Do you think you could tell her?' I said, 'I didn't want her to know I'd been arrested, do you think you could tell her I'm in hospital?' She said yes she would do that. She came back half an hour later and said she had conveyed a message that I was in hospital. She did do it because Emma did think I was in hospital because I've since told her that I wasn't. It was then on the Sunday night that I got the bit about, 'Well, she's okay but she won't eat, she's refusing to eat until she sees you'. I don't remember them saying anything more like that. When I think about it, they did genuinely seem to be concerned about that aspect of my problem. It's just that I can't believe they were really concerned, because of the law. I think I was held incommunicado for 48 hours, so after the 48 hours were up, it was then possible for friends to know where I was and where Emma was, so they then allowed a friend to get the details. I gave them a friend's telephone number and said, 'Please phone her, she will get Emma wherever she is', and they did do that. So my friend got a phone call at school to say that Emma was in care and this was the place to go and she went round and got her. And that was on the Monday night. Emma was then with a friend.

She was in an absolutely desperate state when she was picked up. She had obviously spent two extremely terrified days. Having talked to friends who are social workers, what I should have done was find out from the duty social worker where she was and, just for Emma's benefit, gone round with and thanked the woman. I'm sure the woman was a very nice foster lady, that's not really the point. But I should have cleared it up in our heads by going round there and saying, 'Well, you had my daughter for two days and I just want to say thanks for taking care of her' in order for Emma to feel that it was really okay to be there. You see, she won't talk about it, she won't ever talk about it. All she ever said was there was a Sikh boy in the house. It was a black family and there was a Sikh boy who was also being fostered and that's all she said. She watched television for most of the time. She won't tell me anything more. She's repressed it, locked it away. It'll come out I think.

The Social Services Department colluded in it all. They should have found out if any members of the family or friends could have taken her before she was sent to a foster parent. It may have been that social services were not told the background or that they were given the wrong information on purpose.

Monday

Monday was the worst day of all because it was the Monday afternoon that I began to think that they weren't going to let me go. There were a number of things that made me feel like this. First of all my solicitor, who knew my estranged husband, began to realise that her personal relationship was too close for her to be able to deal with the case properly and I suppose for professional reasons she was also a bit concerned. So on the Sunday night she went away telling me she was going to find

me another solicitor to take on the case. Also, she was doing this over
the weekend, on a personal basis, and she wasn't sure whether her firm
was going to allow her to come back on the Monday morning anyway.
She had just started with a new firm of solicitors.

She found me somebody else who I felt was quite unhelpful to me,
because on the Monday lunchtime he said, 'You've got to stop answering
their questions'. At this point I was answering everything completely
on the grounds that I had nothing to hide. I was therefore going to
answer all their questions. He said, 'You've got to stop answering all
their questions', and I said, 'What do you mean?' He said, 'You've got
to start saying "no comment"', but I said, 'That's ridiculous. They're
going to think there's something very suspicious about what I know',
and he said, 'They're going to charge you anyway and all you're doing
is giving them a lot of information that they can use against you, that
they may want to use against you'. I said, 'What do you mean, they're
going to charge me?' I said, 'Do you mean with withholding evidence',
and he said, 'Yes, well, that and conspiracy'. I just thought, this is unbelievable, this is my solicitor telling me that they're going to charge me
with conspiracy. I then went back into the cell. I will talk about
exercise later, but when they were taking me out to exercise on the
Monday they took me down a different route, down a different
corridor. Sitting on a bench was a guy with fairly long hair and a
beard. I knew, I absolutely knew, he had been following me prior to
my arrest. As I was taken down the corridor he stared at me and I knew,
it just suddenly clicked, 'Good god, they've been tailing me'. Everything
seemed to point to the fact that they thought I was somebody really big.
Whilst I was walking round this exercise yard – it wasn't an exercise
yard, it was a car-park – I kept thinking, he knows I went into a call
box, he knows I made a phone call from a call box. There's nothing
illegal about making a phone call from a call box but they made me think
that somehow that connected me with being part of a conspiracy.
And I'm thinking, they're going to think, why didn't I go home and
use my own phone. That's because I knew it was tapped. It was all going
through my head, all this nonsense.

It was the only time they took me a different way. They took me past
the cells where they obviously held other people. I went through two
locked doors. It was just the ordinary Paddington Green cells where a
couple of times during the night I had heard a lot of noise coming from
these cells, obviously a few drunks or whatever. That's why I was in a
terrible state on the Monday. There were just all these things going
through my head, of things I had done that are perfectly legal. Ordinary

things which people do. Yet I thought they were going to charge me with conspiracy for having driven down this particular road at this particular time.

The exercise, going back to that, was absolutely incredible. I was handcuffed to a female officer and taken out into the car-park of Paddington Green police station. It has on two sides of it the actual police station, which has got to be five, six stories high. The third side is the building where some of them live, which is a tower block. On the fourth side of this rectangle are these huge gates, 60 foot high. I'm handcuffed and I'm thinking how in the world would I get out anyway? And why are they treating me like this? I presume they are just regulations that they follow. But it's – being handcuffed when you're innocent. I suppose being handcuffed when you're guilty might be quite bad, but I couldn't put it all together in my head, it all seemed surreal. I think I only had exercise twice in four days for about ten minutes each time.

I do recall one or two things that were asked in interviews that seemed so ludicrous I couldn't believe it. I think it was the Sunday night, they asked me about Pill. I'm thinking, I don't know what the hell they were talking about. They left me to stew on it. It was the male interrogator, he sort of grinned and smiled and said, 'Oh well, we'll have to take that up tomorrow won't we?' For hours I kept thinking, 'What the hell are they talking about?' The following day they had photocopies of my diary, my previous year's diary. They actually had left my current diary in the house. They hadn't picked that one up. They had got my two previous years but they hadn't got my current diary which I thought was quite silly of them. Then it suddenly clicked. There were three entries on consecutive weeks, on Thursdays, which just said, 'Pill and Anne, Pill Tonya and then Pill and then my name.' It clicked that this was taking a group of nine year olds to Pill High School for a cookery lesson. It just had gone completely out of my head. They thought it was funny as well when I explained what it was. Three different classes on three different weeks. I remember that because it was so ludicrous. There was so much of that sort of thing, picking up on little things that meant nothing. That's one of the major things that I remember from Monday.

They asked me specifically about a place in London. Had I ever been there, what did I know about it. They asked me about a number of names, most of whom I couldn't help them with. Someone's girlfriend: I didn't even know he had a girlfriend. So they asked me that sort of specific thing but they didn't ask me about any actual incidents, because I suppose the thing is nothing actually had happened. That was perhaps another reason why my treatment was fairly low-key, nobody was dead,

I hadn't been arrested after some huge explosion, so obviously their emotions weren't as keyed up as they would have been after something like that. They asked me a lot of details about how and why I went abroad, and then I suppose it was mainly about other people. Who I knew, how I'd known them, where I'd known them from, that sort of thing.

Nobody actually came to see me. A close friend, who my solicitor had then got in touch with, came to the police station with a nightdress and toiletries and a few books. I was allowed those. I was continually asking for a radio and they wouldn't let me have a radio. And that I couldn't understand. I couldn't understand how listening to Radio 4 would be different to reading a book. Monday, I was in a dreadful state because this was the time when the officer came in very concerned that I hadn't eaten. All I had been eating for those three days was cornflakes and drinking tea and I wasn't eating many of the cornflakes. This is when she kept offering me a take-away. She did in fact go out and get me some fish and chips. I think on the Monday we had three interviews. I think there was an early evening one as well. But I don't recall. I think on the Monday night I just took the sleeping tablets very early and knocked myself out.

They got me to this stage where I honestly thought I was going to be there for ever. I sat in the cell on Monday afternoon and started planning what I was going to do. It makes me feel quite good about myself that I can be so positive. I was actually thinking I would have to do a maths degree, I've got to fill up the time. It sounds ridiculous now but this is what I was thinking. I'm going to have to do one because they're not going to let me out.

Despite how dreadful it was, I know that they didn't treat me in the way they treated, for instance, Annie Maguire, having listened to her. I think it is partly to do with the lapse of time and with the way things have been changing. They now know that they have to be more careful, but it's also because I'm not Irish and I'm articulate and I think they have to be very careful. I'm convinced, in comparison with Annie Maguire, I got kid glove treatment.

Tuesday

Tuesday I had one interview in the morning, this is when we cleared up the thing about the cookery lessons. On the Tuesday afternoon – my solicitor at this point was still saying that I should be saying 'no comment' – the female officer came into the cell and said, 'We think we might be able to let you go home'. I obviously responded to this – 'When?' She said, 'you would have to make a signed statement'. I didn't know the legal standing of this signed statement. It seemed to me that this was what I had been doing through all these interviews and I think I said, 'Well, isn't that what we've been doing, I've been signing these bits of paper and you've been writing down everything that I've said'. That's part of the reason why it took so long I think. They wrote down every single word, even when I was saying, 'Oh, I can't quite remember'. They wrote down every single word verbatim. I had to read back through it and sign it.

They thought I was very odd that I kept correcting their grammar. The teacher coming out in me! You need a full stop there, stupid! She said to me this signed statement was different. I did have the where-withal to say I would like to talk to my solicitor about it. She said, 'Oh, we'll ring him'. But he didn't come to the station and I've since been told that he should have been there when I made the signed statement. But this was held out like a little carrot – if you do this for us, we'll let you go. It seemed to me I wasn't going to be doing anything different from what I had been doing for the previous four days. She said it would be like a summary, because I now know that they could use that in court. Anyway, it took an awfully long time. They finally said to me around 2 or 3 in the afternoon that I would be going home that evening. I didn't actually get here until 11.30 that night, because I then went into a different interview room. I was let out of the area where the cells were, the locked-up area, and taken into a much more comfortable office which was adjacent to their main office. I was allowed to make a phone call. They allowed me to ring Carol, who had Emma, and I told her that I would be home that night. Then we started doing the signed statement, which took a good two and a half hours to write out. They went through all my property, bags and bags of it. I couldn't believe that they'd taken my clothes and everything was there in this office. We went through all that and that came home with me in plastic bags. The same two officers brought me home.

Tuesday 11.30 p.m.: Returning Home

They took me on Saturday morning and I got home on Tuesday at 11.30 in the evening. So it was four days and three nights that I spent there.

And that is, I'm told, within the legal limits the European Court has allowed.

I have a feeling too, that part of the reason I was kept there was to give them time to go through this flat completely. I was told on the Tuesday afternoon, when she came and said we could probably let you go, she said, 'Your flat's being cleaned at the moment'. I said, 'What do you mean?' She said, 'Well, the finger printing material.' I've seen that – I've had a number of burglaries – I said, 'Well, I don't care about that, I can go now, I'll clear it up.' She said, 'Oh, you can't imagine the amount, it'll be all over every wall and every single surface.' I still now occasionally find fingerprinting material in the back of the cupboard or something that. They just must have gone through the whole place. I opened an old shoulderbag a couple of weeks ago and took out a wallet I hadn't used for years and ended up with silver fingerprinting material.

My next door neighbour didn't even know it was going on. It's amazing, isn't it. A couple of people upstairs noticed it was going on and asked the milkman to stop the milk. I've got fairly thoughtful neighbours who noticed something was going on and wouldn't think any worse of me.

There was considerable damage done and I've actually made a claim. They took up all the carpet and despite the fact that my carpets are pretty poor quality, they did actually tear them in the corners when they ripped them up. It was pretty cheap foam backed carpet and as they took it up all the foam disintegrated. They took up the new carpet in the bedroom and didn't lay that properly so when I'm walking on it I can feel gaps where the underlay doesn't meet and they tore that as well. There's a lot more than this. Let me think – lampshades, all the pink lampshades were covered in grey fingerprinting material. One lamp was broken. They took the back of the wardrobe out. Upstairs I've got fitted wardrobes that go right along the wall and there is a gap between the back of the wardrobe and the intervening wall. The partition wall had only recently been built. When I moved in the only partition was the wardrobe so there was no soundproofing. I therefore built the breeze block wall the other side and it was obvious this was new. They were very interested in why this wall had been built, and in fact took out the back of the wardrobe and that was very difficult to repair. I ended up claiming £1,200 and they've met the claim. There was virtually no query about it at all. They sent the loss adjuster and all he said was, because I'd claimed for replacements for the carpet he said he could only give me what the carpets were worth, which was virtually nothing as they were so old. I'm out of pocket if I want to replace my carpets with carpets that aren't torn.

I didn't see Emma when I got home. I didn't want to because I knew she'd be asleep, so my friend Carol kept her there and brought her round the following morning. I felt that was better for her as I didn't want any further disruption at 11.30 p.m. If I had come home earlier, like I was expecting to, I would have been able to see her. I saw her the following morning, which was quite an emotional meeting but it took me a long time to actually come round to talking to her about what had happened. I knew I had to.

Our meeting was difficult. I suppose what I just wanted to keep doing was holding her and reassuring myself that we were back together again. But at the same time knowing I didn't want to make her feel that there was something extra-special about it. I was constantly trying to think that I don't want her to be upset any more than she's been upset but of course she's gone through the worst of it and I now know what I should have done was really talk through it with her. All she kept saying was 'I don't want to talk about it'. I occasionally brought it up and said, 'What was the place like, what was the woman called, how did you feel and what did you do?' All she said was 'I don't want to talk about it', in a very emotional way – there was anger there.

Sometime after my release I said that I thought it might be a good idea if we went round to see the woman she stayed with, because I've never thanked her for looking after her. There was no response and when I asked her, 'What do you think about that?' she said, 'Oh, I don't know'. I could tell she didn't want to think about it in any way. On the one hand it appears that she's very resilient and she's dealt with it well but I think it's all there in the back of her head and one of the things that has happened over the last year is that I notice her being much more insecure about her friendships. She's very desperate to keep friends and be with people. She seems to have lost a certain self-confidence, whether that would have happened anyway I don't know. It's just the way she's grown up and it feels like it's much more apparent. Even her teacher has mentioned her insecurity in her friendships within the class. Other girls just shrug it off – girls can be quite nasty to each other, but she can get desperately upset about it. She did cry quite a bit. I think she cries a lot more now than she used to do. It's hard to pin-point it but I just feel there is a definite decrease in her sense of security and that's with me as well.

I've tried very very hard to keep it all secret from those people who I thought would not understand, because from a political point of

view they might have a different outlook. Maybe that's the only reason
why I would keep it from someone. Because I've done that, I've had
a sort of schizophrenic existence and I think what's happened is that I've
buried it in certain circumstances and I've accumulated a great amount
of stress. I was advised when I came out of Paddington Green that I
should get some therapy. I couldn't afford it so I investigated cheaper
versions. I just didn't ever do it. I was told by my solicitor that there
was somebody at the Maudsley who actually did work on people who
had been incarcerated. I didn't go to the Maudsley because a number
of people who were more radical in their therapy said, 'Don't go near
the Maudsley'. So I've never had any therapy. What I'm actually doing
at the moment is I'm making investigations with a friend who's an
acupuncturist to have some treatment to deal with what I think is accumulated stress. Because I go through times when for short periods I just
feel remarkably ill and I think I must be getting 'flu and then it goes
away again. I will go through nights when I don't sleep. I suppose I also
have become generally less happy than I was. Until this happened I never
sat down or went to bed and thought, 'Well, if I don't wake up in the
morning this would all go away and it wouldn't matter'. Two years ago
this would not have been the kind of thought that ever would have gone
through my mind. It just is occasionally that you think, 'I can't deal with
it any more. I just won't wake up'. Maybe lots of people have those
feelings, its just quite unusual for me. It's mainly been hard at work
because the work environment is very closed and I kept it from
everybody. I said I was in hospital for those four days.

My solicitor who is the friend, phoned work and said I was in
hospital. But I suppose if she hadn't been a close friend, if she had just
been a solicitor, I might not have been able to get away with that. Emma
didn't go to school, obviously, on Monday; she did go to the school
on Tuesday. Carol took her to school on Tuesday. And of course
everyone wanted to know how I was. But she just managed to say very
little. They wanted to send me flowers and to know which ward I was
in. Carol said, 'Oh I can't remember' and left it. But they still think I
was in hospital, so I've kept it entirely secret from them, except for one
very close friend.

My mother doesn't know about my detention. It would kill her, it
would just destroy her. She's not sure, because I never confirmed it, but
she was told that I was arrested, because the police visited my aunt and
uncle. They told them that I had been arrested and that information was
then conveyed to my mother. When she said it to me I just said, 'Oh,
they just asked me a few questions'. But my mother was interviewed

twice, not by Special Branch but by the CID. Obviously they were very polite and a different kettle of fish, it wasn't Special Branch, well, I assume it wasn't.

Case 2: Teresa's Experience

Monday 6.30 a.m.

My husband had gone down for the paper at 6.30 a.m. The door bell went and it was one of the Hertfordshire police who had interviewed us in 1988. I found out afterwards that they had been watching the house all night. My friend found out from the kids down the road; they had heard people talking. The policeman came in and I said, 'What is up Paul?' and he said, 'A couple of officers want to talk to you'. He never told me it was the Essex police or anything. So, I said, 'About Gerry?' He said, 'Oh I don't know'. He was lying. Anyway, I made him a cup of tea and we were chatting away when the door bell went again. Now in my room you can see into the hall from where I was sitting next to Paul chatting. My husband answered the door and I could see a crowd of police coming in with a policewoman. I said, 'What's wrong?' There were more than two. So when they came in I said: 'Bloody Hell! There are five!' One of them said, 'No, four because I am going'. I realised that he was the other Hertfordshire guy who came with Paul. So I now had four Essex police officers standing there. Two of them turned to my husband and said, 'We are arresting you under the Prevention of Terrorism Act'. I'm not kidding you; I am glad I was sitting down because I could feel my stomach going down to my feet. The Birmingham 6 flashed through my mind. This is how innocent people are picked up. Up to then I had thought that the police didn't pick up people who are completely innocent.

They took my husband away and I didn't have the sense to ask where they were taking him. This left two police officers and this Special Branch woman – Susan. She then asked me for a cup of tea and referred to me by my first name which I thought was odd. My mind was all in a twirl, but afterwards I realised why. She had worked up the other terminal at Stansted Airport for a few months. I had never seen her, but she had obviously seen me. I was friendly with the Special Branch up there and I regularly chatted with them.

Anyway, I made them a cup of tea and we were sitting there talking about the Gulf War and everything. I had to wait for the searchers to come. So I asked her did she come in unmarked cars because I was worried about the neighbours and she said, 'Yes'. The doorbell went again and this guy came in with a case. He then asked me if I had money in the house. Now I wondered why the police should be concerned with my few bob, like. I said I couldn't remember. 'Have you large amounts of money in the house?' The penny dropped then. I said, 'No. I wasn't gun-running today'. He wanted me to show him around the house because he was going to take it over. I objected at first and said I wasn't going to leave him to search my house. He said that I would be going away to Harlow Police Station. I said I wasn't going to leave him alone in the house, he could plant something. He said, 'I shan't!' He got annoyed like. I said, 'How do I know?' He then said, 'It might take me the whole day to search here. It might take me two days, three days'. I said, 'This is my own home!'

Anyway I showed him around the house and pointed out the ladder to the loft. I said that he wouldn't find anything. I was then frisked by the policewoman. I then had to go to the toilet and the woman said: 'You will leave the door open won't you Teresa? You won't lock the door will you?' So I went to the toilet. When I went down, I was frisked again. My husband wasn't strip-searched, he wasn't frisked. He wasn't Irish of course.

I wasn't arrested in my house but I was under house arrest. I wasn't allowed to telephone. When I went into the kitchen to make her a cup of tea, I looked at the clock and I wondered whether my boy was still at work. I thought that I could give him a ring and tell him what was happening. She said: 'I'd rather you didn't'. As it happened my son had already left. I said: 'Listen, if I want to use that phone I would use that phone'. She just looked at me. This was the week of all the snow and the week when Downing Street was attacked by mortars. They should have been watching Mr Major and not my little house. They might have caught someone then.

I was taken off to Harlow about 9 o'clock. When I left the house, there were cars everywhere. I was then walked down the street and across the road. When I turned the corner there was a police van full of police in uniform. Two neighbours told me afterwards that they had guns. Now I don't know and Special Branch denied it when I asked them. There was another car coming down with the blue light flashing and I had to walk right across that place to the far side where they had parked their car, in front of all the neighbours. The milkman came along later and saw them take piles of stuff out of my house. He said to my husband the next day: 'Thank god you are alive, I thought that there had been a murder in your house.' I was all embarrassed because I thought the neighbours would think that I had stolen from the shop or something.

When I got to Harlow Police Station I was formally arrested and I was then checked in. I was put in this room and a doctor came. She examined me after I had stripped but only to my underwear. She examined my heart and took my blood pressure. I said to her, 'I am innocent'. She didn't speak to me. She just looked at me. They have to examine you again when you leave and, that night, she examined me again and then she said, 'Good luck!' You feel terrible because you feel she thinks you are a criminal.

I was then taken down to the cells. I was shocked; it was a terrible place. There was a sink in the corridor between two cells and there was a fellow shaving at the sink. I was wondering what he was thinking. Was he thinking that I was a criminal like him? You feel embarrassed as you are not like him. But he could have been innocent too; I am prejudging him! At the end of the corridor there was a shower unit, with frosted glass. It was in direct view of a policeman at the top. Now I wasn't going to have a shower in there because there was no curtain. Somebody could easily see you. Fortunately I didn't have to.

I said, 'You're not putting me in a cell are you?' She said, 'I'm afraid so'. I went in and she got me blankets. They treated me well. The police matron kept on coming up and asking if I was all right. I had a cup of tea. Oh yes, there were only two cells for women. In the first one the toilet was blocked and I had to come out. I was put in the second, which had a heating problem. It was freezing.

When I was checked in I was given a piece of paper telling me my rights. But you don't read that stuff. I just stuffed it in my pocket and I didn't sign for the bit of paper. I am a greenhorn. I was cute enough, however, to ask for a lawyer, but I didn't know the name of one. The only solicitor I knew was when I bought the house. 'Do you know one?' I was asked. Now my sister's son was lifted sometime ago and they had a solicitor. I didn't know his number. So I thought if I told them my sister knew the name of a solicitor they would phone her and it would tip off the family where we were.

He came back later and said that he had rung the solicitor and he said that the solicitor didn't deal with prevention of terrorism cases. I said, 'What do I do now?' He said, 'Do you want the duty solicitor?' I said, 'Yes'. I then had to wait until the duty solicitor came before I was interrogated. In the meantime I was taken down and mug-shot and finger-printed.

I was then put back in the cell. When the solicitor came I said: 'I'm innocent.' I then realised how stupid it sounded and said, 'I suppose everyone says that', and he said, 'Yes'. I said, 'I really am'. It was then that he pointed out that if I lived in Hertfordshire why was I being interviewed by Essex police. I said, 'What do you mean?' He said, 'How is it that the Hertfordshire police have nothing to do with it?' Then it dawned on me that it must be something to do with Stansted Airport. I said that I hadn't done anything. In my mind you see was the fact that we had picked up a hitchhiker. I told him about that. I never connected with the Queen's visit.

I was then taken away for interrogation. They asked about my family tree. The thing that stuck in my mind was the bigotry of it. The guy who was interrogating me told me I was a Catholic. I said I wasn't a Catholic. He then said, 'You were born a Catholic'. I said, 'No one is born anything. You are what your parents decide you are and true, my parents did inflict Catholicism on me. But it wasn't my religion'. He said, 'I'm flummoxed'. I said, 'You would be'. He asked me about my father who was born in 1884. He asked me about my brothers. I was frightened then. So I thought that I had better let him know that my family is very pro-English. I did it subtly. So with the first brother – my half-brother really because my father was married twice – I said he served in the war. I had to let them know that I didn't come from a republican family. I didn't tell him, but my husband told them upstairs, that my other brother was killed in the war. Then they wanted to know about all my other brothers and their lives. I had to tell them their names and dates of birth, how many children they had. The same with the sisters, but they were more interested in my brothers. All the way down. I told them about my son. If they thought I was really a terrorist why didn't they arrest my boy in Harlow as well; he is 31 now? I also have three sisters and my mother living around here and they didn't touch them. This made me think that it had to be connected with the airport.

That interrogation was the mild one. The solicitor had sat through it without saying a word. I got no advice; he just kept writing. They now wanted to break for lunch. I said, 'Keep going'. I was stupid really. I was so nice. I thought I have nothing to lose, my life is an open book. I was then taken away for lunch and brought back in the afternoon.

After lunch the duty solicitor had to go off but before he went he told me that I wouldn't be here tonight. So he is telling me that I was innocent. Yet I was still in there. His assistant then came instead. I wasn't sure if she was qualified or not but she was very nice. When I was asked to sign the statement, I asked her to read it. She didn't advise me against.

I had another set of interviews in the afternoon. It then went into serious stuff. This is the interesting bit. Four names were mentioned. 'Did I know anyone living in Harlow?' I said, 'No'. They asked me about these four names. Now only one of them had an Irish sound. I said, 'Get on, you are making those names up'. So he said, 'Yeah, that is all I have time for'. He called one of them William. I said that if he is William they would call him Liam if he was Irish. Then they asked me if I knew anyone in Northern Ireland. I said, 'No, apart from Gerry'. 'Have you written to anyone in Northern Ireland?' I said, 'Only Gerry and no one else'. I said, 'I don't know anyone'. 'Have you ever written to anyone in prison in Northern Ireland?' I said, 'No'. I said, 'I have just told you no'. He then said have I ever sent anything electrical to Northern Ireland and I said, 'No'. By now I had had enough. There is an old Irish rebel song the Dubliners used to sing. So I said:

'I would get out of here if I had a couple of sticks of gelignite and an old alarm clock'.

He said, 'Yeah, yeah'. I said, 'I have just told you. All I sent were photographs to Gerry'. He said, 'All right'.

I don't know how long I was interrogated for: I lost track of time. Anyway you know that under the PTA they don't tape interviews. Well there was a twin-deck tape recorder in the room. The Special Branch guy said that they weren't using the tape recorder because the tapes have a habit of going astray.

I was taken back down to the cell. I was given more blankets but I couldn't put them up near my face. This is a handicap for a woman; they think terrible things about who might have used them. By now it was getting dark. I could tell by looking through that thick glass in the top of the cell that it was getting dark. Some years ago I suffered an attack of anxiety and I could feel it coming on again. Oh my God, I thought. I am that freezing. I was waiting there all that time. In the meantime they had been through my wallet and things like that. The policewoman had come down on one occasion with a receipt from a china shop. On the receipt was written 'Glass Blower' and the price. She said, 'What is that?' 'Oh' I said, 'that is for a little metal man'. She said, 'What?' I said, 'A little metal man'. I then explained that it was a little ornament for a friend. She then said, 'Are you going to America because they have found the receipt and tickets and everything'. I said, 'Yes, we are going to New York and we will be there on the 17 March'. I told her the dates that we would be away.

She came back later and I said, 'Will I be here tonight?' I can't fault her. She felt that she couldn't say too much but she said, 'No'. When the door opened at 6 o'clock, I said, 'Was I going home now'. The guy said, 'Not for the moment, when they have finished searching your house. I am just the change over the shift'. I said, 'It is freezing in here' and he said, 'It is'. He asked the police matron why it was so cold and she said that she didn't know. There was cold air coming in under the bed. I was asked if I wanted any more blankets and I said, 'No'. I was feeling terrible anxiety again as I was locked in. I tried to sleep a little. Time means nothing to you. It is like a bad dream. Then sometime later the policewoman came back and said, 'Right, out you come'. I said, 'Am I going home?' and she said, 'No, you have to see the doctor'. So I went up and the doctor examined me. The policewoman then told me that I would be going home because they had nearly finished searching my house. As I passed my husband's cell, I shouted in, 'It won't be long now'. At 10 o'clock they came and released me.

When I got up to the desk where they check you in, my husband was there and he was talking to this policemen who years ago used to be a milkman with my husband. I said, 'Oh you have stopped taking bottles of milk to harass people?' He said he didn't harass anybody.

The Detective Inspector who was in charge of the operation was there. I said that I was going to go and see Gerry Collins because of this. And he said: 'Who is Gerry Collins?' Here is the brain of the Essex again, you see. My husband then tells me in front of them, that someone in the Harlow area had written a letter to someone in Crumlin Road signed Teresa and Don. That is what they obviously were on about with me. Well I said, 'Well I have news for you. They don't call my husband by that name in Ireland, but Gordie'. And the ex-milkman said, 'Yes, that is right'. I then said to this guy that we had only picked the lad up because he was a hitchhiker. What if I had picked up Jack the Ripper or I may have said the Yorkshire Ripper, I can't remember. He said, 'Well he is worse that the Ripper'. The boy hadn't even stood trial and they thought he was worse than the Ripper.

Oh yes, I forgot to say, they said that I needn't tell anybody at work what had happened. Don't tell anybody from work! The Special Branch were from work and they had gone up to the airport while we were inside, asked for the locker keys and had gone through our lockers. They went through my husband's stuff and they went into my desk in my office, shut the door, and all my friends were outside. What did my friends think?

We were then driven back home. When I came in I was so delighted and I laughed. And the policewoman said: 'I can't understand you Teresa. You have been through a terrible ordeal and you are still smiling.' You see she was sympathetic and, as I said, she would have known about me. I said, 'Of course, I am delighted to be home'.

The house was very tidy. The books were tidier than when I left them. One room had been very untidy because we were decorating and I was worried about it when they were going through my house. To a man that is nothing but to a woman it is terrible. Reading my diary was bad. But there were other things, the personal things that they went through.

They opened my post and my son's post. They took away our bank statements. Nothing they don't now know about me. They know more about me than I know myself. That is the galling bit. You are not dignified any more. I am still working at the airport and you see these uniformed people and you think, are these the ones that went through my little home? That is the most awful thing. You just don't know. To a woman that is much worse than to a man.

Tuesday

On the Tuesday my husband broke down when his employers came round to take away his pass. I wasn't there. He was suspended immediately and there was a letter waiting for him when he got back that night. I rang my manager, the branch manager when I got home. He was wonderful, he called them the biggest so and sos. He called them everything. I was already being made redundant at the end of March because of the change and because of what happened to me, I never got the chance to get a good job after that. I had a good job to start with. How could I go for an interview with that hanging over my head. I can't go for a job. You know you are innocent, but you can't go for a good job.

Wednesday

On the Wednesday, I talked to my friend's husband and I said that I had been arrested. He said, 'You were arrested, why?' As soon as I started telling him, I burst out crying. Now I am not accustomed to the bladder near my eyes, but the tears were just pouring. I have never known anything like it. Tears just came all morning. As I went about

my work, the tears just kept coming. Then I got a phone call from this
guy in the police. Could he come and bring some of our stuff back? They
never asked to take it. But they asked to bring it back! He brought back
our passports. He handed the passports to my husband and said, 'There
you are, you can go to New York now mate'. So what was that telling
us?

I saw in one of the plastic bags a newspaper with IRA on it. He said,
'We were going to ask you about that'. When they got to it, they handed
me the middle page of the *Daily Mail* with IRA on it. I opened it and
realised immediately that they had got it out of my desk at work. At
that time, the *Daily Mail* was running a series on Margaret and Townsend
and my mate wanted the stories. She wasn't on shift at the time and I
had left it on my desk to give it to her when she came on shift. The
back of the centre page had something on the IRA. I didn't even read
it. See what they can hang you for!

They told my husband that they had taken a round of ammunition
out of the house. The penny then dropped. You don't mean the small
bullet case in my jewellery box? They called it a round for ammunition
which I thought was a bandoleer. I said that is an empty shell. Someone
gave to me once. It was so cute that I saved it in my jewellery box. He
said that they had to send it away to forensics. It came back in two halves.
I thought that they had broken it. That is how much I know about guns.

They took a book on the guerrilla days in Ireland by Tom Barry
written in 1920. I hadn't read it, but I *have* now. Tom and I now have
one enemy in common – the Essex, but he knew how to deal with them!
There was a book on Bernadette Devlin. I still haven't read that one.
They took away a tape with 'Irish' written on it. That meant Irish music.
They took away a tape that had 'French' on it, but it was really Glen
Campbell. My diaries were one of the last things they brought back. I
asked if they had found Gerry's name because I had his address in one
of my diaries. They took away the cinefilms of our holidays.

They wanted my mind, they wanted every person I knew. They knew
there were no arms. They wanted my mind. They wanted to know
everything about this Irish person, my contacts, everyone I knew.

Weeks Later

Over time my stuff gradually came back. The diaries were the second
last thing to be returned. Towards the end of March. I then got a phone
call from the guy in charge, he said, 'Do I need all those wires?' Now

I had worked for an electronic's factory from home and we had to put circuits together and I had a whole lot of little wires about 4 inches long, which I had to solder. He said, 'Did I want them back?' I said, 'You took them, I want them back – every one of them'. He said, 'You were so nice Teresa'. I said, 'But I am not nice now'.

We learnt later that they had kept two Polaroid pictures of us, which we demanded back, once we had found out. The two pictures were then delivered to Stansted. Two of the guys from there, one whom we knew, came up. He walked in and you could tell he was embarrassed. He gave me the photographs, ignoring Don. This showed that I was the victim of the raid because I was Irish. He came up to me and said, 'There you are, it is nothing to do with me'. But it was the Irish person who was terrorised. I had a go at the other fellow for not telling me that he worked at the airport. I said, 'You are devious'. He said, 'I am not devious. I just didn't say'. I had a good go at him. Anyway I kept the photographs.

One of them said that we had made a complaint. Now we had not made a complaint. How can I go to the Gestapo to make a complaint against a Stormtrooper? There is no point in making a complaint to the police through the police. So the only time we have protested was when we wrote to our MP. Don sent a copy of our letter to the police. It was only a copy. That is when we received a letter back from the police saying that a senior officer would be coming to visit us to investigate the complaint.

When the senior officer came round about the complaint I made him a cup of tea and I said: 'You make a burglar look like a noble creature'. He said, 'I think the best way to conduct this is for you to ask me questions and I will answer them'. So what was the first question I should ask? 'Why?' 'Oh! I am not at liberty to say so'. I said, 'You are wasting your time then. You sent a letter which had said that no evidence had been found.' 'Oh let me tell you', he said, 'that is a standard letter which is sent out to everybody.' I said, 'You didn't even apologise'. He said, 'Let me take this opportunity now to apologise to you'. I said, 'Will you go out and tell my neighbours that'. He laughed, embarrassed. I said, 'I will put a proposition to you and I will tell you something else. I am going to tell the world what you have done to me. I will go to my grave telling everyone, because I am not going to let you get away with it. You see him (pointing to my husband) he will lie down and let you walk all over him, but he is English. But I won't.'

It is only in the last six months that I have been able to let it lie. All the time in your mind you are trying to ask why. Now I am more settled and I see a reason and the reason is that they just came here as though it was normal to them. My husband could forgive anyone, but I can't. I am Celtic and now I have a hatred in me. I watch the police at work and if they break the law, I record it. I followed a copper speeding in a car and I overtook him and shouted at him, 'speed limit'. I tried to slow him down. He overtook me but I kept up with him. I have seen them get into a car legless and drive away. I have seen them hound one of their own. I am telling you about the Essex police, because these are my enemy.

I was terrorised. All my friends are English and they were very good. One of them, a week after my arrest, came up with a box of chocolates. I was sitting there telling her what had happened. She noticed that I kept on looking out of the front window. She asked me was I expecting someone, because I kept on looking out of the window. It dawned on me that I was doing it. You know, I kept looking out, worried that a car would draw up and they would be coming to take me away again. Her and I cried together that afternoon. She cried with me when she realised what I was suffering.

You are absolutely terrorised and all that kept coming to my mind was Germany in the 1930s. You are powerless, you are defenceless. You have no defence. It was only by getting involved in the anti-PTA campaign that I have gained strength. The fight comes back. You see I never got justice. An apology in the beginning would have done it, but nothing will do it now. I feel an anger which has grown into a hatred. I hate them, I hate them. For a while I didn't even speak to them but I now smile at them. I am going to be as devious as those bastards. I laugh at them. You give me the first opportunity and I will be just as devious as them.

I was speaking to one the other night, the one who first approached me. He said to me, 'So many new jobs lately'. I said, 'Thanks to the Essex police', and he said, 'We are not all bad, some of us are nice'. I said, 'Wasn't there some nice Stormtroopers?' He said, 'There were'. I said, 'There couldn't have been. If you were nice you couldn't ever do that to an innocent person. In Nuremberg they said they were only doing a job, they were only doing their duty. The judges then said, "What about your conscience?"' I turned to the policemen and said, 'What about your conscience, Fred? Does it bother you?'

6 Arrests: People's Experiences

Introduction

The last chapter presented two case studies of people's experiences of being arrested and detained under the PTA. In this chapter a number of people's experiences of being arrested in different situations are described. Some were arrested at home, others on the street and one at work. A number of the arrests took place in front of spouses, partners and children. Most involved the removal of a large quantity of material from people's homes. When an arrest takes place, the police may or may not inform the media. If the media are informed then the police typically provide other details about the case on which a story can then be constructed. The role of the media is therefore critical and examples are given at the end of the chapter describing how PTA cases are reported.

Profile of the Cases

In the study some 43 people were arrested inland. Table 6.1 notes various details on the people involved and other characteristics of the arrest and detention. Of those arrested 31 were men and 12 were women. Nearly half were Irish Catholics living in England.

Thirty were arrested at home – typically very early in the morning. Ten were arrested on the street, one of whom was arrested outside a prison after visiting a prisoner. In addition, two were arrested in a police station after going there voluntarily.

The reasons why these people were arrested can only be guessed. Some appear to have been arrested as part of mass screening operations. These operations, although declining, have been fairly common over the years and typically occur after a major arms or explosives find, or some major incident. Others were arrested because they were connected, however remotely, to someone who had been charged. A number were arrested because the authorities had decided to exclude them. Some of the people were already well-known to the authorities because they were already attending trials or visiting relatives in prison. Others were arrested after a member of the public had reported something suspicious.

Twenty-nine were subsequently released, seven excluded and seven were charged. Thus some action was taken against one-third of all those arrested. The type of cases examined in this study are therefore untypical of all those arrested under the PTA because typically around 14 per cent of all those arrested are charged or excluded. But it is important to note that of the seven who were charged, one had the charges dropped, five were acquitted and one was convicted of breaking an exclusion order. This means that *not one was convicted in a criminal court of a substantive offence.* In this sense, the sample of cases is more typical of all people arrested than it may at first appear.

Table 6.1 Sex, origin, place of arrest, outcome and average length of detention of those arrested inland.

	Arrested
Sex	
Male	31
Female	12
Origin	
Northern Ireland Catholic visiting Britain	9
Irish people from Republic visiting Britain	6
Irish Catholics living in England	20
English living in Britain	5
Northern Ireland Protestants living in England	3
Place of arrest	
Home	30
Street	10
Work	1
Police station	2
Outcome	
Released	29
Excluded	7
Charged	7
Average length of detention: 80 hours	
Totals	43

Arrests at Home

In recent years the police appear to have developed a uniform policy when carrying out arrests at home. Typically, they are carried out in a carefully planned operation, using a number police officers in the early hours of the morning between 5 o'clock and 7 o'clock, when people are at their most vulnerable. Although the level of suspicion and types of offences for which people are sought may vary greatly, nevertheless all house arrests now appear to be carried out in the same manner.

Many of the 30 people who were arrested at home provided graphic descriptions of their experiences. In at least five of the cases considerable force was used. These arrests always involved a large number of policemen who used force to gain entry, some of whom were armed. All five people, however, were subsequently released without being either charged or being served with an exclusion order.

> I was woken up at 5 o'clock by armed members of the SPG plus plain clothes members of the Special Branch and Anti-Terrorist Squad. They didn't actually introduce themselves but I assumed that the uniformed police were SPG because they were wearing jack-boots and they had guns ... When they arrived they smashed the windows and the front door and just ran up the stairs into my room and poked a gun into my temple while I was asleep and just told me not to move – to freeze and to take my hands out from under the covers very slowly and put them on my head. Then the person who I assumed to be the leader of the operation (a plainclothesman) just informed me that I was being arrested under Section 12, I think it was, of the PTA and did I understand? I said, 'No', but it didn't matter. (373M/81, 120 hours, released)

In another case the person had returned home in the early hours of the morning and was concerned about the person with whom he shared a house, because he had been arrested for shoplifting that morning.

> I went to bed and the next thing I heard was the door being hammered with sledge hammers two or three times. I got up, got to the top of the landing and just then the door flew open and I stood back and looked down the stairs. The police were standing in the hall and a guy came up the stairs, pushed my face and threw me back into the bedroom and told me to lie face down. What I was thinking at

this time was that it was all about [my friend's] shoplifting ... At no point did they say who they were, Special Branch – PTA – though that's who I assumed they were. Not until we were leaving some hours later did they say something along the lines of 'Tell him what the crack is. I presume you know we're Special Branch and you're being arrested under the Prevention of Terrorism Act.' They did not mention what section. (401M/81, 10 hours, released)

Some people are raided on more than one occasion. In 1979 a man was visited one Sunday morning by two men dressed in jeans and anorak jackets and they asked him questions about what he had done the previous week. They identified themselves very clearly as police officers and stayed for about half an hour. Two days later at 6 o'clock in the morning the bell went and he looked out and saw the place 'swarming' with police. They had a warrant and he let them in. Two years later they made another raid using considerable force.

... at six o'clock they were in ... They didn't knock or anything, just broke in the main door ... I was up to go to work in the bathroom and when they banged at the door I told them to hang on but before I realised it they were in – with a hammer and they'd broken it. At that time I wasn't woken up but I thought I was dreaming! Next thing I was out of the bathroom and the door to my bedroom opened and there were uniformed police – I had a gun to the back of the neck – they threw me on the bed and then threw me against the wall. This kind of thing had never, never, never happened to me before. (399M/81, 10 hours, released).

In 1985 at about 7 a.m. two young men were chatting together watching TV. This is what happened next.

I was in the kitchen getting matches to put the fire on when there was a knock at the door. 'Who is it?' 'Open up please.' 'Who is it?' Sledge-hammer and glass and then the door came off. I had a mortice, two latches, the Yale and the chair jammed up against the handle – so they did it quite a few times ... So they came in. First, a Detective Sergeant with a gun ... He saw me just standing there – I was half dressed – so before he reached me he put the gun away. The other people came in and they put their guns away. (371M/85, 36 hours, released)

Other house arrests did not involve force and the police made their entry after showing a warrant. The police in the following four cases were not visibly armed, but typically there was a large number of them and hence the experience was nonetheless frightening.

The police came to the house at about 6 a.m. ... When they rang the bell I looked out from upstairs and saw some people standing on the path – they weren't wearing uniforms or anything. I asked, 'What is it?' and they said, 'Police – we've got a warrant', I can't remember the exact words ... I made them show me the piece of paper but all I could tell you now is that it definitely had my name on it. My hand was shaking as I held it. I couldn't concentrate on it, I don't know what it said but it certainly wasn't informative. (392F/79, 30 hours, released)

At approximately 8 a.m. two plainclothes police officers arrived and, after showing me their ID and a warrant – which I saw briefly – they entered the house ... The Sergeant opened the back door and six or seven more plainclothes police officers entered the house, including one woman police officer also in plain clothes. (189M/84, 7 days, released)

I was arrested at around 6 a.m. The police knocked at the door which I went down and answered. They showed me a warrant and they rushed upstairs. There must have been 20. There was also a vanload in the street behind the house. I was told that I was being arrested under the PTA but I don't remember when. The police did not identify themselves as being either Special Branch or Anti-Terrorist. They just told me to get dressed because I was going to the Police Station. (414M/85, 7 days, charged and acquitted)

It was about 6 a.m. when I heard a knock on the front door. I went down and opened the door and there were a couple of uniformed and plain clothes police standing there. They didn't identify themselves. The first thing they said was, 'Is ... here?' I said, 'Yes, that's me.' They said, 'You come with us', and brought me into the living room. The uniformed police stayed with me and the others went upstairs. (419M/86, 7 days, excluded)

In a number of cases the police were able to enter the house without the person hearing them.

I share my flat with a friend and we have separate bedrooms. In the early hours I was awoken by the sound of my bedroom door being smashed open. The police entered, led by someone whom I later found out was from the Anti-Terrorist Squad. About four to six uniformed SPG members and about three to four anti-terrorist branch officers were in the flat. I jumped out of bed and the police officer said something like 'Okay you cunt' and told me to stand with my hands up against the wall. As I was facing the wall I think they searched me with some electronic instrument but I am not sure. I stood like this for about five minutes and then I was allowed to put on pants and trousers. (205M/83, 6 days, charged)

At 6.30 a.m. I awoke to find a man, in his late twenties/early thirties, of medium height and with a short but full beard, entering my bedroom. He was waving a piece of paper which he claimed was a search warrant issued under the PTA. (147M/84, 25 hours, released)

In some cases the arrests were accompanied by various actions which must have alerted the whole neighbourhood as to what was happening. In one case:

... they'd got a tripod outside in the road taking photographs of the outside of the building and at the same time the police cordoned off the estate and the lights were switched off, the electricity was switched off. Out here there were four armed police. No way we were likely to run for it, certainly they were well organised. (399M/81, 4 days, released)

The police justify the use of dawn raids by pointing out that the house may be full of armed and dangerous terrorists: hence the timing of the raids and the use of a large number of police officers, some of whom are armed. The objective is to create surprise, reduce the possibility of escape and minimise the threat to the lives of the police officers. This may be a valid justification in a few cases. But the actual objective in the majority of cases is very different. The dawn raids form part of a system of detention and interrogation that is designed to extort not only intelligence but also confessions. They ensure that people arrive at the police station tired, hungry, demoralised, anxious and suggestible.

As has been shown, the majority of arrests under the PTA are carried out for intelligence gathering and most of those arrested are subsequently released without charge. These facts have been known for many years, yet nothing has been done to control police discretion in carrying out the arrests. Neither does it seem that magistrates, through the issue of warrants, provide any independent control over searches. Consequently many people are subject to terrifying ordeals as a direct result of a failure of the system to control dawn raids. In this sense, the Prevention of Terrorism Acts produce their own terror and state officials are responsible for carrying it out.

Arrests on the Streets

The circumstances of those arrested on the street varied considerably. In some cases people are arrested because something appears suspicious. For example, a couple, who were returning to Ireland after a week's honeymoon in England, were arrested in Wales.

> We stopped in Port Talbot and parked the car coming up to a pedestrian crossing. I had parked where I shouldn't have been parked right enough. But there was a car parked right behind us and right in front of us. A policewoman had seen Baker Car Hire on the car, I suppose, and our cases were on the back seat of it as well, so she suspected we weren't up to much because there were parked cars behind as well as in front of us. There were no tickets on any of them. But she was standing in a little alleyway when we came back. She asked us our names and where we were from and where we were going. She was only new at her job and she tried to get some of the guards from up the barracks – the barracks were only just up the road from us[1]... They held us then. They said they were arresting us on suspicion for a bomb attack after being in Winchester the day before – or Warchester. (570M&F/89, 5 hours, released)

In other cases people are arrested on the street as part of a planned operation. In one case, a woman was returning home to Ireland and was approaching the coach station.

> I was walking along with my suitcase and a man came up behind me and called my name. I turned round and he tapped me on the shoulder and he showed me a card and he said, 'I arrest you under the Special Terrorism Act', and he took my suitcase off me and there was another lady with him, so he said, 'Would you mind moving over beside this building?' So we walked over, the three of us. He radioed

for the car to come round ... The car came along and another
woman jumped out and they put me into the car and put my suitcase
in the back of the car, so when I got into the car they told me to put
my hands up at the back of the two back seats, there was two men
and two women, and then I took them down and they told me to
put them back up again so I put them back up and about a couple
of minutes later I took my arms back down and they gave my arms
a wee shove and I just looked at them and they never said anything
more to me. (505F/84, 2 days, released)

In some cases the arrest was a particularly terrifying experience. In
1986 a man was wandering down the road to his local pub with ten or
so friends when they were arrested.

Just as we got near the crossroads outside the pub we were surrounded
by people who later turned out to be police. You would have
thought that they had arrived by helicopter the way they sprung on
us ... They were dressed in combat jackets, wigs and sunglasses and
all sorts of clothes for disguises. I got a bit frightened at this point and
I said to the man I wanted to see his ID. He showed me his ID with
his thumb over it. It just said something like Constabulary or police
... They didn't say anything about arresting me under the PTA. In
fact they said nothing until I asked for the ID. I knew what I was being
arrested for if they were police but I initially thought that they were
a loyalist gang, especially when I saw a combat jacket and all the gear
lying in the back of the car. There was very little room in the car with
all the gear. One of them pointed his gun at me in the car. I felt that
he was more or less telling me that he could do anything to me.
(425M/86, 3 days, charged, convicted and fined)

In the same year, a man was over in England visiting his brother in
prison. He had just left the prison.

When I came out of the prison they were just waiting at the door.
I was arrested ... by three plain clothes detectives outside the prison.
They told me that I was being arrested under the PTA. I was put in
a car and driven to Paddington Green police station. (418M/86, 7
days, excluded)

In November 1990 the police carried out a mass arrest operation in
London and detained at least nine people. Two were released without

charge, four were excluded and three were charged with conspiring to cause explosions. Charges against two of these people have since been dropped. Two of the arrests took place on the street after a night out. One of those arrested described her terrifying experience.

> We left the pub at about 12.30. We walked down to the National [dance hall] and up the steps. A bouncer said, 'Sorry, we're not letting any more in, it's already crowded.' We thought damn, turned and walked down the stairs and stood on the pavement. We were basically saying 'Cheerio' to each other. Then out of nowhere, various plainclothes detectives pounced on us from behind and threw us up against the wall of the National. We were spread against the wall. There was an officer behind each of us pinning us to the wall. All they said was: 'Don't move, don't say a word. Put your hands up against the wall', and they spread-eagled our legs. They told us not to turn around ... One of them grabbed me by the throat and dragged me into one of the black marias that had appeared from nowhere. (800F/90, 39 hours, released)

In five cases in the study, people were arrested in planned operations either in restaurants or just outside as they left.

In one case three people were just about to order a meal in a Kentucky Fried Chicken restaurant when they were arrested. They had been in London for a week attending the committal hearings of a relative at Lambeth Court, where they had experienced numerous searches going in and out.

> I was just lifted straight up off the floor. The other two were up at the counter to order a meal and the place was fairly full. And I said, 'Look, you get the meal and I'll get the seat.' And I was half way down, I had spotted a seat, and I was lifted straight off the floor. I was run out of the Kentucky and I was thrown up against the police van and I always remember one of them saying, 'Make sure he is not armed. Make sure he is not armed'. I was spread-eagled and searched and put into the car between two. I ended up right in the middle with two Special Branch men one on either side of me. (521M/88, 96 hours, released)

The second member of the party described her experiences.

I turned around and these men had him by each arm and he was being taken out of the door of the restaurant. And before I got time to even think I looked and there was this big guy standing by me and he had me by the arm and he said to me: 'I'm arresting you under the Prevention of Terrorism Act'. I said, 'My god, you're joking me', and he said, 'No, come on, I'm taking you outside'. So I didn't even get time to see what happened to our friend, we were just taken out. I was put into a car. (522F/88 115 hours, excluded)

Three businessmen had a similar experience after enjoying an evening out in a local restaurant. Two of the party had flown over from Ireland and had been met by an English colleague at Heathrow who had then driven them to their hotel where they had checked in. Later they all went out to the restaurant. They noticed that the service was particularly slow and the bill took a long time in arriving. The driver then left at about 00.40 a.m. to pick up his car leaving the other two to put on their jackets. This is what happened next.

I left the premises and turned towards my car, it was parked about 25 yards from the door. I saw a police motorcyclist approaching me, he appeared to be dazed, not walking steady, so I naturally turned towards him. He then turned me round, told me to place my hands on the window sill in front of me and informed me that I was being arrested under the Prevention of Terrorism Act and anything I said may be used in evidence against me. He then instructed me to lay face down on the floor where he searched me, handcuffed me (passing the comment that I had large wrists and he would try not to hurt me). He then asked me if I had anything on my person 'which could hurt him'. I said no and that somebody was making a bloody big mistake ... From my position on the ground, I saw the other two come out of the restaurant, they were both apprehended and I believe that one of them was made to lie on the floor and the other up against the wall. It was quite difficult to see exactly what happened, lying face down on the ground. After a few minutes I was asked to stand up and the motorcycle policeman assisted me. He apologised for my shirt and trousers getting dirty, I said that's OK, I'll send you the cleaning bill. I told him that the handcuffs were extremely uncomfortable and tight, and also that somebody had made a very big mistake, at which he replied, 'I hope so sir'. I was then taken to a waiting police car, and it was then that I realised that there were police marksmen with rifles and spotlights pointing at us all over the place.

There were police everywhere, the street was cordoned off. I assume that every road which ran into the street was also blocked. (801M/91, 5 hours, released)

He and the others were then taken to the police station and when his handcuffs were eventually removed his hand was turning blue and he had a ridge the width of a cuff approximately ⅛ inch deep. They told the police who they were and the nature of their business. Eventually, they were released from custody at 5.40 a.m. and taken back to their hotel. They were informed that they had been arrested because someone sitting in the restaurant had overheard two Irishmen and one Englishman talking about the IRA – something which they had not done. They had, however, talked about the visit of one of the party to Colombia eighteen months earlier, while having a drink in the hotel bar before leaving for the restaurant. During the conversation they had discussed a number of bomb attacks and shootings which had taken place in Colombia. They assumed that this conversation had been overheard and reported to the police.

Arrests at Other Places

In two cases people were arrested at an unemployment office. These arrests clearly involved close cooperation between the Special Branch and Department of Social Security officials, involving the exchange of confidential information and the notification of the person's presence in the office. They illustrate the way in which various state agencies work together in policing.

What happened was that I went to the unemployment place and they told me to come back the next day and I went back the next day. When I got back the Special Branch were sitting there. The man who brought me in says, 'Box number 5' and I went into box number 5. One of them was sitting behind the desk and the other one come in behind and just said, 'Special Branch. You're under arrest'. I couldn't do anything, they just arrested me and that was it. (267F/79, 7 days, exclusion)

In another case a man from Northern Ireland came over to Britain to seek work. Initially he had signed on and then one day as he came out of the Social Security office he was arrested. (509M/89, 6 days, charged but dropped, excluded)

While arrests at home can have a considerable impact on relationships with neighbours, arrests at work can not only have a similar impact but can also lead to people losing their jobs. There was only one case in the study in which the arrest was carried out at the person's place of work.

> I was taken from work. They came into the yard, identified me ... and then I was taken away. There were three or four police officers if I remember rightly ... I was operating at the time, my work place, the office, is at street level and adjacent to a garage and they'd actually reversed the car into the garage, and came in and took me out there straight into the car and hardly anything was said. I said, 'What the hell is all this about?' And so this fellow says, 'It's to do with the bombing, see.' So it was just a question of just getting into the car. There was nothing said on the way to the station apart from the fact that they'd radioed ahead to their mates at Paddington Green outside to expect us. (311M/81, 2 days, released)

The Impact on Third Parties

Adults

When a person is arrested in a house, everyone who lives in it then comes under suspicion. In one particular case, the flatmate, who was a nurse and who had been on night-duty, arrived home.

> Immediately they grabbed hold of her – as soon as she put her key in the door. They physically dragged her up the stairs. They took her into her bedroom and systematically went through all her belongings like diaries and postcards and Christmas cards and things like that. It was terrible what they did to her – she didn't even know what the PTA was. They arrested her and held her for 48 hours. (374F/81, 5 days, released)

In another case, when the police went to the house to arrest the father, who was at work, the son was arrested.

> They got several armed police up and down the stairways, like Kojaks, you know – probably watch too much TV – and they'd gone

in there with dogs, broke the door down, arrested my other son from his bed, and for absolutely no reason other than they were going to take somebody, it seems to me, I mean the kid's never been in trouble before, never been in trouble since.

Moreover, they appeared to have shown little concern for the man's wife, who was eight months pregnant at the time.

They had held my wife prisoner in her own home, and it was fairly obvious to anybody – and these people claim to be reasonably civilised people, these police – and it was fairly obvious, and I'd told them anyhow, that she was within a week or two, a couple of weeks, of giving birth, and it was a complicated birth, and they still held her, they still kept the dogs in the house ... And what really annoyed me was the fact that apart from the fact they'd arrested my young son, my wife was in a very late state of pregnancy and they showed a callous disregard for her situation, and that really got me. I thought well, you people are claiming that you're opposed to anybody else being violent and here you are being violent yourselves. (311M/81, 2 days, released)

Children

Children are particularly vulnerable when either one or both their parents are arrested. In the case study presented in Chapter 5, we described how a mother was arrested and how her child was put into care with a stranger when she could have been looked after by a family friend.

In a number of other house arrests children were present and the police appeared to show no great concern. In one case it was not clear who eventually looked after the children. But the mother was arrested and taken to Paddington Green after leaving food for them.

I didn't leave for an hour and a half partly because they were searching the house and partly because they let me have a shower, leave the kids food out and take some clothes ... The children were much younger then; they were only about nine and ten. They were still asleep when we left at about 7.30 a.m. If anyone had been up that early no one would have known I was being taken away by the police. There were about four or five of them, including the policewoman. They were all in plain clothes and we left in unmarked cars. (392F/79, 30 hours, released)

In another case the children were still in bed when the police broke into the house.

A number [of police] went straight up to the bedroom where the children, ten years old, a 13 year old and a four month old, were still in bed. There was some argument over the children and my wife became very upset when the police wanted to take the baby out of the crib in order to search it. I tried to keep her calm as I was concerned that the police would arrest her and take the children into care. Fortunately, my neighbour came and took the children next door. They were upset and crying. (189M/84, 7 days, released)

In a third case a woman tried to make arrangements for someone to look after the children.

I suggested that I would go next door and ask my neighbour or use her phone to get my sister to come over. They wouldn't let me do that, nor would they let me tell anyone where I was going. They radioed another car to pick me up. A WPC came and she stayed with the children until my sister arrived. (417F/85, 12 hours, released)

In a number of these cases the police may not have known that there were children in the house. However, in one case during the mass arrests in London in 1990 they clearly knew that there were children in the house, because the person they wished to arrest was baby-sitting for the mother whom they had already arrested in the early hours of the morning. They also knew that the children would already be in a distraught state because their mother was not at home. Yet none of this information appears to have influenced their determination to arrest the baby-sitter in front of the children. The children's mother tells what happened.

He was just going up the stairs to the toilet or something, and as he got three-quarters up the stairs, the front door just went BANG. They just burst open the door and they left a great hole in the wall. And he turned round and as soon as they banged the door a few ran up the stairs and held him by the hair, pulled him down the stairs and brought him into the sitting room where the kids were watching television. The twins are four and Kerry will be six at Christmas. Initially he started resisting arrest but he'd seen that the kids were roaring and crying so he then stopped, you know, for their sake. They took him out and went off in a car. A WPC took the three of them upstairs to get them dressed. And said to Maeve, 'Where's all your kids' clothes?' And Maeve got all the clothes out and the three children dressed themselves. So I said, 'Were you crying?' She said, 'Oh I wasn't crying Mummy', but she'd make out that she wasn't, but she said, 'The other two kept crying and crying, Mummy, for you'. (791F/91, 39 hours, released)

Search of Premises

The police make much use of their powers of search under the PTA. In all cases when people were arrested or questioned at home a search of the house ensued. The searches varied in intensity. In two cases in 1981 the searches were comprehensive and caused considerable damage.

They then proceeded to wreck the place basically. They took all the floorboards up, took door knobs off, handles off chests of drawers, you know, stupid things like that. They put torches under the floor boards, they had dogs in as well and searched places I didn't even know that I had! Up in the attic, on the roof. Most of the time they took me with them but not all the time. They were searching the house for about five hours. (373M/81, 5 days, released)

... when I did eventually get out the place had been wrecked, they actually laid siege to the house ... and they went through the whole place with a fine toothcomb. (311M/81, 2 days, released)

In a number of cases they used dogs to help with the search.

There was a dog with them, and the dog sniffed round the house but the only thing they found was the cat and it got quite excited, it appeared to be far more interested in the cat than in anything else. (392F/79, 30 hours, released)

They had sniffer dogs. My brother was going through the same thing in his room. And at no time at all could I speak to him ... They were searching all over upstairs and down here again – I couldn't come and check them and my brother couldn't come and check so they just had a free hand to do whatever they liked. They were still here when they took us off to Paddington Green. (399M/81, 4 days, released)

They stayed in the house along with me for three hours – searched my belongings, tearing floorboards up, they stayed in the house, from what the neighbours told me, for about six or seven hours and they were in the attic, they took up floorboards, they looked behind fireplaces, they took down shelves, generally did a thorough search of the house. They had sniffer dogs as well – two sniffer dogs. (401M/81, 10 hours, released)

In other cases, the search seemed to have been less intensive and with a particular interest in documents and personal letters and files.

After searching the kitchen they went back upstairs and searched my bedroom, paying particular attention to my filing cabinets and wardrobe. Throughout the course of the ensuing search, which lasted for about an hour and a half, I commuted between the different rooms, observing the progress of the search. From time to time the police officers, who had refused both to reveal their names, units or stations, punctuated their search with a 'running interrogation' concerning particular items they had come across ... He (the officer leading the search) seemed to be particularly interested in my press cuttings and other literature, files covering the defence and intelligence fields in which, as a journalist ... I have made my speciality. (147M/84, 25 hours, released)

Children and Searches

Children's property is no less likely than adult's property to give rise to suspicion, as the following case shows.

The police were about half an hour in the children's room, taking their radio and toys apart, some of which they took away. All Christmas cards were taken off the walls, a lot of which were from Ireland, and the Christmas tree was taken out of its barrel. They took all the clothes out of the cupboards and anything that was put back was just thrown in. The furniture was moved around and all the fitted carpets were pulled up, ripping the one in the bathroom. Only one floorboard was taken up, which was already loose from the time the central heating had been put in. There was quite a lot of damage done but when I complained I was told that I would have to see a solicitor. (189M/84, 7 days, released)

In many of these cases the search of the premises was thorough and the searches often continued after the occupants had been arrested and taken to the police station. Although the details of arrest and searches have been presented in separate sections, it would be wrong to conceive of them as unrelated processes. In some cases, for example in the case studies presented in Chapter 5, the principal purpose of the arrest appears to have been to carry out a search of the premises. On occasions this is carried out without arresting the occupants. In one case a women had her flat searched.

At about 7.50 p.m. I was alone in the flat. I had just come out of the shower. I was wearing a pair of tracksuit bottoms and a T-shirt. My hair was wet. I came into the kitchen and took my evening meal out of the oven. I had it cooking prior to having a shower. I put the plate of food on the table. The television was on and the programme, *EastEnders*, was being screened. I had barely taken a mouthful of food when I heard a loud noise. It was obvious to me that the door of the flat had been burst open. I was rigid with fear and couldn't move from where I was sitting for what seemed like two minutes. I thought it was burglars. Eventually I stood up and moved to look down the hall. As I looked down there were men walking towards me. One was hefty of build and bearded; he was pointing a gun at me and shouted, 'Freeze'. I think there were about six men and they were all wearing plain clothes. They were all well dressed – most, I think, were wearing suits. The hefty bearded man told me to go to the bathroom. I was told to put my hands on the wall. The man told me to do this twice. He put the small silver gun close to my head (the gun was little longer than a hand in size). The other men went into the kitchen and I could hear the cupboard doors being banged loudly. Only the man with the gun remained with me. I do not know if any of the other men had guns as my eyes were fixed on the man holding the gun which was pointed at me. None of the men told me they were police at this stage. (726F/90, search only)

Her flatmate described her experience on returning home:

I got off the bus about 8.30 and as I approached the door, which is a street door, I noticed that it was smashed, the glass was on the pavement and I walked into – I was really frightened when I saw this – so I walked into the adjoining shop and asked them what happened and just at that moment I was tapped on the shoulder and this identification was pushed into my face and he said, 'It's the police'. So I was escorted into my flat. The place was just full of plain clothes men and I walked towards my bedroom and I heard noises. The door was closed and I heard noises inside and I asked what was happening and I was so much in shock that I couldn't think straight, all I could do was just ask what was happening. They said, 'There's a dog in there'. And I said, 'A dog in my bedroom?' and he said, 'Yes' and I said, 'Just a dog?' and he said, sarcastically I presume now, 'A dog handler'.

I went into the kitchen and I was just surrounded the whole time, the whole body space, everything, was invaded, so I asked what was happening and one of them said, 'We're searching the flat', and I asked had they a warrant and he said yes. So I told him that he was invading my space and my privacy and I told him it was a social rape and he said, 'That's a very emotive statement', and I just stood there and he asked me would I be willing to talk about my friends and I said no I wasn't. I would talk to them if there was a solicitor present but I didn't want to talk to him because I didn't trust him. (582F/90, search only)

After two hours of searching they left the house. Before they left one of the women asked the police to secure the front door which they had smashed. This request was refused. She then phoned the local police station pointing out that two women lived in the flat and that their safety was in jeopardy. The only response was to ask her if she would like to make a complaint.

Material Removed

Most of the searches involved the removal of a large quantity of material from the houses. This mainly covered books, documents and other papers and further supports the contention that many arrests and house searches are primarily used to gather intelligence information.

They took lots of stuff away – binbags full of newspapers, articles, things that I'd written down, diaries, address books, even novels of a political nature – Solzhenitsyn, they took that away. I did however get all the things back. (373M/81, 5 days, released)

They took a lot of stuff away in plastic bags. I'd a lot of pamphlets on their use of plastic bullets. And stuff that had been happening, like H-Block and what have you. That sort of stuff was all taken away. It was stuff that had been printed. Publicly available, and yet they took the whole lot away. Family photographs were all dusted down for fingerprints, any sort of Delftware, plates and saucers, were fingerprinted. It was just absurd. (311M/81, 2 days, released)

My briefcase and two filing cabinets were emptied and the contents put in a plastic bag, labelled and taken away together with the empty filing cabinets. I had maybe 2,000 leaflets, pamphlets and booklets and other political material dating back to 1968. (189M/84, 7 days, released)

They took things away from the house in plastic bags such as papers, etc. which just belonged to me. They also took packets of weed killer. I did get all my belongings back but the only thing which I have found missing is my passport. (419M/86, 7 days, excluded)

The Journey to the Police Station

The intense security which surrounded many of the arrests and searches was maintained throughout all the subsequent stages. The working assumption was that hardened and dangerous terrorists had been arrested. The journey to the police station was no exception and those arrested were often driven at fast speed in a convoy of police vehicles, all with blue lights flashing. The police station itself was often surrounded by armed police.

I was told to get some gear and some washing gear. When we went down the stairs I was handcuffed to a plain clothes [officer] and my brother the same. The neighbours must have seen us. They put us in the back of the van and off we went, siren blaring. I couldn't understand it at all – the big fish type of thing you know – I mean Paddington Green in ten minutes! (399M/81, 96 hours, released)

They took us away in a van – a cavalcade of motorbikes and sirens drove us to Paddington Green. (373M/81, 96 hours, released)

I was escorted to the Bridewell with one outrider in front and one behind, both with lights flashing. With all this treatment I was beginning to wonder what the police would charge me with. (189M/84, 80 hours, released)

These journeys have an important symbolic function. They draw attention to the fact that law and order appear to be being upheld and the public's safety is maintained. As one person put it:

I think that it's just that they like to give the impression that they're doing something, collecting information, keeping people at night for no reason. (399M/81, 96 hours, released)

The importance of the function is not altered by the fact that the majority of those arrested are neither charged with any criminal offence nor excluded.

Notification of Arrest

When someone goes missing after being arrested or detained under the PTA, they can be held incommunicado for 48 hours without being allowed to contact a friend or relative. This can obviously cause considerable anxiety. There have been a number of examples over the years of people phoning police stations to inquire whether or not a friend or relative is being detained and the police have lied to them. In one case in 1985, the detainee's father rang Paddington Green after his son had been held for over 24 hours and was told that he was not being detained (372M/85, 36 hours, released). In a more recent case, the police lied to the detainee's solicitor and the Irish Embassy and again denied that the named person was being held.[2]

Media Coverage of PTA Arrests

The majority of arrests and detentions do not appear to be reported in the press or on radio or television. In a search of *The Times,* the *Guardian* and the *Independent* on a computer database, there were reports of 66 people being detained under the PTA from 1 January 1988 to 31 December 1990. In the same period the Home Office statistics recorded that 332 people had been detained under the PTA in connection with Northern Ireland affairs. In other words, less than one fifth of all detentions appear to be reported. Much of the activity surrounding the PTA does not, therefore, become public knowledge.

Although only a proportion of all arrests are reported, some receive a great deal of inaccurate, sensational and prejudicial coverage and these reports can have a very detrimental impact not only for those who are subsequently charged but also for those who are subsequently released without charge; the prejudicial reporting may lose them friends or a job because many people believe that people would not be arrested unless the police have some firm evidence against them. There are numerous examples of sensational and inaccurate reporting.

In October 1989 five Irish men were arrested in a dawn raid in Cheltenham. Some of the headlines in the tabloid press (13 October 1989) were as follows:

Thatcher Bomb Gang Arrested (*Daily Express*),
5 Seized at Hotel in IRA Hunt (*Sun*),
Five Irishmen Held as Cops swoop on Hotel (*Daily Mirror*),
Five Quizzed in Terror Plot Fears (*Daily Mail*).

As can be seen, there are a number of key words – bomb gang, IRA hunt, Irishmen, terror plot – which all carry particular emotive meanings and associations. In the body of the stories, some of these themes were developed and new 'facts' were introduced. The *Daily Express*, for example, which carried the story on its front page and maintained that the police believed that the men 'are linked to a new bomb plot to kill the prime minister', recorded that the men were interested in a future Tory Party conference to be held in Cheltenham the following year; the conference was to take place a week after the Cheltenham Gold Cup meeting when thousands of Irish people come over from Ireland; and they had been arrested by armed police with sniffer dogs.

The broadsheet press also carried the story.

5 Irishmen Arrested in Hotel Raid (The *Daily Telegraph*),
Irishmen Arrested in Hotel Raid (The *Independent*),
Arrest of Five Irishmen 'Not Linked to March Tory meeting',
(The *Guardian*).

All these headlines were much more low keyed and did not talk about plots, gangs or the IRA. However, all the headlines noted the fact that the five arrested were Irishmen. The important question is why this item of information is deemed to be important? When reporting other types of arrests in the United Kingdom, it is not common practice to say that five Welshmen or five Englishmen were arrested. The item of information is significant only within the context of the PTA and the assumption that it is mainly Irish people who are involved in terrorism.

In this case, as in so many others, all five men were subsequently released without charge, but only a few papers carried the story of their release. The men, who had been working on a building site for a company from County Down, all returned immediately to Northern Ireland. As a result, work on the project was disrupted and the company lost money.

It appears to be fairly common practice for the broadsheet press and the TV news reports to use the word terror or terrorism in the main heading describing an arrest under the PTA. Some typical headlines are as follows: **Several Held under Terror Act** (The *Guardian*, 3 April 1991), **Four Held under Terrorism Act**, (The *Guardian*, 26 October 1990), **Two Arrested in Terrorism Inquiry**, (The *Daily Telegraph*, 19 August 1989), **Two Held in Terror Raid**, (The *Daily Telegraph*, 4 April 1989). In other cases the headlines go further and link the arrests to some other 'facts' such as some reference to the IRA or some specific incident. **Six Arrested after Raid on 'IRA Safe Houses'** (*The Times*, 12 November 1990), **Six Arrested over IRA Bomb Attacks** (The *Guardian*, 5 June 1990), **Two Held in Hunt for IRA Bombers**, (The *Independent*, 11 May 1989).

All these reports appeared immediately after the arrests and before the police had made any decision about what should happen to those detained. They are very prejudicial because they imply that the person arrested is in some way connected to the IRA. As some of the people were subsequently charged, the headlines may have prevented a fair trial. As Lord Ellenborough said in 1811:

> If anything is more important in the administration of justice, it is that jurymen should come to the trial of those persons on whose guilt or innocence they have to decide, with minds pure and unprejudiced. Is it possible that they should do so, after reading for weeks and months before *ex parte* statements of the evidence of the accused, which the latter had no opportunity to disprove or controvert? [3]

This point is best illustrated by the reporting in the Winchester 3 case. Three Irish people were arrested under the PTA on Sunday 30 August 1987. The arrests were reported on the following day on both ITN and BBC TV news reports. The next day the news was linking the arrests with an IRA attempt to assassinate the Secretary of State for Northern Ireland, Tom King.

> New evidence held by the Special Branch officers tonight makes them suspect that they have thwarted an IRA attempt to assassinate the Northern Ireland Secretary of State Tom King. It comes after two days of questioning three people found in the grounds of King's house and held under the PTA. The police are looking for another woman. (BBC Nine o'clock News, 1 September, 1987)

The report was not only inaccurate – two people and not three were arrested in the grounds of King's house – but it also constructed a case against them containing three elements: (a) there was a plot; (b) the plot had the aim of assassinating Tom King; and (c) that it was organised by the IRA. Further elements to the story were added throughout the week, including a possible attack on the forthcoming Conservative Party Conference. The press, as can be seen from Figure 6.1, carried similar stories.

At the time of the reports, none of the three had been charged with any offence and in fact no charges were made until a week after their arrest.

Another feature of the reporting throughout this and other PTA cases is the media's focus on security. All the news reports of the first court appearance of the Winchester 3 focused on the security. The BBC TV Six o'clock News began with Sue Lawley.

> Three people have appeared before a special magistrates' court at Chippenham in Wiltshire, charged with conspiring to murder the Northern Ireland Secretary, Tom King. The hearing took place in the local police station where the three, two men and a women, have been held since their arrest eight days ago. Our Home Affairs Correspondent, Bill Hamilton, reports: 'From early morning armed officers moved into the little Wiltshire Market town, where the police station had been turned into a temporary court room. Police dogs made several circuits of the building and every piece of waste ground was systematically checked. An hour before the hearing scores of police vehicles lined the front of the improvised court house, with men drafted in from all over the country. Neighbouring householders trained their own cameras on all the activity, while police marksmen kept a constant look-out from roof tops. Everyone entering the building was subjected to an electronic body search. The

Figure 6.1 Press coverage following the arrest of the Winchester 3

court room itself being the police canteen, with lunch tables being turned into desks for the magistrate and solicitors.

The report then provided details on the names and addresses and the charges against the three.

Many of the TV reports showed pictures of the tight security which included the arrival of the three in a prison van flanked by motorcycle outriders and police cars in front and behind. Shots also showed police marksmen on the roofs of surrounding buildings. These are images now commonplace in PTA cases.

The police play a central role in the reporting of PTA arrests. They decide whether any particular arrest should be reported and they control the amount of information given to the press. They also decide whether to let the press know that a suspect is being moved from one police station to another under heavy security so that they can be at the scene to take pictures. The police therefore play a crucial gate keeping role in the supply of information to the public.

They also, through their symbiotic relationship with the media, play a key part in the construction of the case. This is particularly important in those cases in which the person is subsequently charged with conspiracy. The essential characteristic of a conspiracy charge is that the person need not have committed any substantive criminal offence. Conspiracy, however, carries the same penalty as the actual commission of the crime alleged to have been planned. At the same time, the burden of proof is shifted onto the defendants to prove that they were not part of the alleged conspiracy. In this context, what is reported in the media becomes crucial because news stories can play a part in supporting and reinforcing speculative leaps from a number of circumstantial pieces of evidence.

In the Winchester 3 case the crucial leap was from the nationality of the three to the inference that there was a conspiracy to murder by an Irish terrorist organisation. The conspiracy, however, was constructed, as we have seen, by the press and the media. Without exception every news story claimed that there was an IRA plot to murder Tom King. While some of the reports prefixed plot with the word alleged, nevertheless the key circumstantial evidence as well as the inference had already been established.

Despite a massive search by the police which included the police using metal detectors – a shot which HTV then used on a number of occasions to provide continuity when subsequently reporting the story – the police found no guns, no ammunition, no explosives and no evidence linking the three defendants with violence or the IRA. The three, however, were subsequently convicted of conspiring to murder Tom King and 'conspiring with persons unknown to murder persons unknown'. On 28 October 1988 they were sentenced to 25 years imprisonment on each count, the sentences to run concurrently. On 28 April 1990 all the convictions against the three were quashed, not because of prejudicial reporting at the time of their arrest and trial, but as a result of an interview given by Tom King during the trial. He had announced, on the very day that the defendants had informed the court that they would be using their right to remain silent, that the right of silence would be restricted in Northern Ireland. He subsequently gave an interview to explain the new policy and it was this that was considered prejudicial.

Although the convictions were quashed, the three were nevertheless served with exclusion orders. Their release from prison received widespread coverage and some of the media, like the Executive, still believed that they were associated with terrorism or the IRA. **'IRA Three' are Freed by Appeal Court**, (*The Times*, 28 April 1990), **Terrorism Case Three Freed over King Interview** (The *Daily Telegraph*, 28 April 1990). Other reports avoided words which made links with terrorism or the IRA. **Winchester Three Convictions Quashed** (*Financial Times*, 28 April 1990), **Court of Appeal Frees Three over King Interview**, (The *Independent*, 28 April 1990).

From a broader perspective, the way in which the media report PTA cases is important at a number of different levels. To begin with, it forms another element of power which is generally mobilised against the individual who is detained. Adverse publicity further exacerbates the ordeal of those in custody and increases the stress which is associated with arrest and detention. Secondly, as we have pointed out, it can affect how people are viewed by neighbours, friends and employers when they are released, or prejudice a trial if they are charged. Thirdly, the sensational reporting of PTA cases affects the whole of the Irish community and can incite racial hatred. The constant use of essentially prejudicial terms such as terrorists, terrorism, bombers, IRA – often linked with some reference to Irish people – creates and sustains the idea that hundreds of Irish people are terrorists or involved in political violence and perpetuates the impression that the whole of the Irish community is suspect. These points are often reinforced by the failure of the media both to give the same coverage to the release of PTA suspects as they give to the arrests and the failure to report regularly that 86 per cent of all the people arrested under the Acts have been released without any action being taken against them.

Conclusions

Since the introduction of the PTA in 1974, 2,308 people have been arrested inland. Of these it is estimated that 1,984 have been released without any action being taken against them. This chapter has presented a small sample of these people's experiences and it has shown how men, women and children have suffered terrifying ordeals. Moreover, houses have been wrecked and large quantities of personal possessions have been closely examined and taken away. The impact that these experiences have had on people's lives is dealt with in Chapter 11.

In many cases the ordeal is made unnecessarily terrifying by the amount of force which is used. In carrying out an arrest the police are allowed to use only an amount of force which is proportionate to the threat posed. But in a number of cases the force used was clearly disproportionate. For example, in the case of those arrested after regularly attending hearings in a Magistrate's Court or the person arrested outside the prison, the police knew all about these people's movements. Yet they were not arrested inside these buildings but on the streets by armed police in full view of the public. Similarly, the amount of armed force used in some of the house arrests and searches appears to have been unnecessary. In some cases, the ordeal was made more terrifying and threatening because it involved armed male officers breaking into all-female households.

These forms of violent entry and arrest serve a number of different functions.[4] In the first place, the arrests on the street help to reinforce a 'cowboy' image of the police as people who venture into a public space to apprehend violent and dangerous men and women. Clearly, the element of surprise is necessary in some arrests for the safety of both the police and the public. But in many of these cases the police were posed with no threat, particularly in those cases where the authorities knew all about the people's movements. Secondly, these very public arrests, in which a large number of police officers are deployed, some of whom are armed, draw attention to the dangers of terrorism and the threat which it poses. Public fears may therefore be increased. But at the same time, the public is reassured when terrorists are seen to be arrested. In a complex set of relationships, the questionable legality of much of the police action may therefore be legitimated as a direct result of the practices themselves.

The media, by reporting some of the arrests, also help reassure the public that terrorists are being captured. As has already been pointed out, the same amount of coverage will only very rarely be given to the release of those arrested. At the same time, as we have seen, the media sometimes play an important role in constructing a case against those arrested, even before action has been taken against them.

Finally, these types of arrest play a crucial role in making those arrested more amenable to subsequent police interrogation. The arrest is therefore the first step in a carefully constructed process in which, in the words of the Diplock Commission, 'the aim is to build up an atmosphere in which the initial desire to remain silent is replaced by an urge to confide in the questioner'.[5]

From a broader perspective, all the evidence suggests that the principal object of a high proportion of the arrests is either to gather intelligence or to screen the Irish community, rather than start proceedings against the suspect. In other cases it is clear that the objective is simply to harass certain members of the Irish community living in Britain. A police culture has therefore grown up around the PTA, in which the police know they can more or less behave as they wish. They can control who is visited, arrested and detained in the knowledge that none of their decisions is open to public scrutiny – few of those arrested or detained are dealt with formally in a public hearing. Even those who are subsequently excluded are not entitled to a public hearing: their cases are decided by the Home Secretary.

7   In Custody: People's Experiences

Introduction

The aim of this chapter is to describe what people experience as they are taken into police custody, the physical conditions under which they are held and the detention regimes to which they are subject. All three elements will produce some form of stress in the detainee. Although these three aspects of the custody experience are treated separately for the purposes of presenting people's experiences, in practice all three elements combine to have a profoundly adverse affect on most people's physical and psychological wellbeing.

Chapter 4 described the legal differences between a PTA detention and a detention under the ordinary criminal law. One key difference is the length of time a person can be detained – four days under the ordinary criminal law and seven days under the PTA. But apart from the differences in law, there are other significant differences for both the police and the detainee. The security surrounding a PTA detention will normally be considerably greater than a detention under the ordinary criminal law, except for a very serious crime. This heightened level of security will affect the whole atmosphere of the police station and increase the tension. In addition, because public concern about terrorism is generally greater than for ordinary crime, the police will be under increased pressure to produce results whether this is in terms of gathering good quality information or obtaining confessions.

From the viewpoint of the detainee there are also significant differences. Firstly, the opprobrium associated with being detained under the PTA is often considerably greater than being detained under the ordinary criminal law. Secondly, there is what can be best described as the 'injustice effect', following the widespread publicity given to the Birmingham 6, Guildford 4, the Maguire 7 and Judith Ward. Thus 18 people, most of them Irish, have now been convicted for crimes which they did not commit. As a result, the assertion that 'if you are innocent then you have nothing to fear' is a hollow platitude. All the evidence of the last 20 years suggests that Irish people do have much to fear if they are drawn into the British criminal justice system. As a result of these factors, a PTA detainee, on entering custody, will have a very different set of attitudes and emotions than those detained under the ordinary criminal law.

The experience will be further compounded for women. Custody is predominantly a male environment. Most of the personnel are men and, most importantly, men play the key role in interrogations. The whole culture of custody is masculine where toughness, aggression, bravado and competitiveness are dominant features. It is inevitable that in such a climate women will at best feel sexually vulnerable and, at worst, terrified.[1]

Being taken into police custody happens in one of two ways. Either the person is arrested and then taken directly to the police station which authorised the arrest or they are examined at a port or airport and then subsequently taken into police custody. Some 43 persons in this study entered custody through the direct route and 54 by the indirect route. Sometimes people are moved to another police station following a period of detention at the police station to which they had initially been taken.

The 97 people who were detained in police custody in this study were held in 30 different police stations in England, Scotland and Wales. Nearly 60 per cent of all the detentions, however, took place in just three police stations: Paddington Green (24), Stranraer (21) and the Liverpool Bridewell (13).

Initiation into Custody

When a person is taken into custody, the police go through a range of procedures which involves recording the person's name and taking their fingerprints and photograph. Less often it can also involve taking swabs and sometimes strip-searching. To the police these procedures are routine and form part of their everyday work. They have been carefully refined over many years to meet various requirements such as creating an official record of the person, preventing the person from harming themselves while in custody and, most important of all, to continue the pressure which has already been applied at the point of arrest. Keeping up the pressure means that suspects are more likely to confide in the police than remain silent, irrespective of whether they are suspected of actual involvement in terrorism or are simply wanted for questioning.

At another level the routine procedures can be seen as an initiation ritual; part of a broader process of criminalisation in which certain sections of the population are separated out from the rest and labelled as criminals, or, in this study, as terrorists. This experience is likely to have a profound effect on a person's self-identity and self-confidence when they are stripped of their belongings and then photographed as a suspect. These processes are common to the initiation into many 'total institutions' and Goffman has described them as 'mortification processes' because the self is systematically, if often unintentionally, mortified through a series of debasements, degradations and humiliations.[2]

Recording Details and Taking Away Belongings

The first thing that happens to anyone entering custody is having their details noted down by a police officer (now called a custody officer) and for their personal belongings to be taken away, including anything which they might use to damage themselves. This always includes taking away a person's watch. This action is an essential part of the detention regime and is designed to increase the sense of isolation and disorientation, as we will show in more detail below.

… all my personal possessions were removed; including my watch, driving licence and money. My shoes, tie and supporter's scarf were also taken. (252M/83, 23 hours, released)

After my details were taken, my laces and belt were taken off, my pockets were emptied and my personal belongings were removed. I was locked in a cell. My luggage was taken away as well. It was a couple of hours later when they first came back. (421M/87, 72 hours, excluded)

Everything was taken from me, including my zipper-boots, coat, belt, rings, watch and my St Christopher medallion. I was put into a cell wearing my own shirt, jumper and trousers. (189M/84, 80 hours, released)

The significance of these practices varies between individuals and depends on the manner in which the procedures are carried out. Again, men and women's reactions are likely to be very different. All the custody officers in the study were men, a factor which increased the women's sexual vulnerability. This was often compounded by actions which would not apply to men. For example, one woman had to take off her shoes and tights and place them outside the cell (417F/85, 12 hours, released). Another had the bow of her blouse cut off and taken away (415F/85, 10 hours, released). In another, a woman who was arrested after a night socialising in a local pub, was prevented by the male custody officer from using the toilet for four hours:

> Then I got up again and went over to this female sergeant, or whatever, I wouldn't know if they were sergeants or what, I said, 'Look I'm desperate to go to the toilet'. It must have been about two o'clock then and she said, 'Oh I'm sorry, you can't use the toilet'. I said, 'Look I'm desperate to go to the toilet. If you don't let me use the toilet I'll either wet myself or wee or over the floor'. She says, 'Well, if you want to do that well go ahead but you'll clean it up'. So I stood up again and I said, 'Look I know our basic rights and you ARE entitled to use the toilet'. She says, 'I'm sorry you can't use the toilet you'll just have to wait till you get booked in'. So eventually I was getting up, prancing up and down the reception area going, 'I'm desperate to go to the toilet', and they just never took a blind bit of notice. And then they were constantly taking the other fellas away and as I said, it was five o'clock when the detective then came over and says, 'Right you can now get booked in, Carol'. And I said, 'Does that mean I can now use the toilet?' and he started laughing, 'Yes you'll be able to use the toilet in a minute'. And that was the time that I was booked in. (791F/90, 39 hours, released)

Fingerprinting and Photographing

Everyone in the study was fingerprinted and photographed. However the number and type of prints taken and also the number of photographs, varied. There was also considerable variation in the number of times people went through these procedures during their detention. Typically, the procedure for taking photographs involved the person holding a plaque in front of them stating their name, address and height.

> When I arrived at the Liverpool Bridewell I was first photographed and then I was fingerprinted. Either that night or the following morning two other specialists took forensic tests – clippings off my

fingernails, swabs of my hands, and I had to spit into a small tube. (260M/85, 68 hours, charged)

In some cases numerous photographs and a wide range of different types of prints are taken.

During questioning I was taken to a different room where I had a total of 21 photographs taken from three different angles and three sets of my fingerprints taken, palm prints and prints of the tips of my fingers and wrists. During this the two police officers were laughing and joking amongst themselves. One remarked that they knew people handled explosives with the tips of their fingers and that was why they were taking these types of prints. I was also told they were taking three sets of everything – for Scotland Yard, the RUC and themselves – and that they had had to take more photographs because the camera had not been sitting right the first time. They also took a record of my height, my complexion and the colour of my eyes and hair. Overall, these two police officers gave me the impression that they were not well-trained and were inexperienced. They told me where my fingerprints and everything were going. They seemed like two novices and in comparison with the RUC it was like sitting with two infants that might burst into tears at any moment. (257M/85, 5 hours, released)

They took all our belongings, our money. The thing I thought strange about it was the way they took our fingerprints. They took five copies of our fingerprints. Now I've had my fingerprints taken here in Belfast but never the way they did it. They did it with the tips of the fingers, the sides of the fingers, they took a knuckle imprint and they took a palm print. They insisted that I signed for them, which I refused to do. I refused to sign for anything at all. (201M/85, 31 hours, released)

The taking of swabs was less common but it was reported as having taken place in a number of cases in the study.

… they took swabs and specimens from under my fingernails for tests and I got really frightened because there were so many rumours in the past about various people having been picked up in London all day. (272F/81, 24 hours, released)

A number of people objected to their fingerprints or swabs being taken, but all eventually gave in to various different forms of police pressure. In one case:

> That evening I was taken out of the cell to be fingerprinted and photographed. When I refused I was told I could not refuse, that I had no rights whatsoever under the PTA. My fingerprints, palm prints and prints of the side of my hand were then taken and I was photographed. During this time the police asked me questions on a casual basis. (252M/83, 48 hours, released)

In another case:

> The Chief Constable also said that they wanted to take fingerprints and swabs. I said that I didn't want a swab taken and he replied that whether I wanted them taken or not that they were going to take swabs because they have the power. He left the cell for about 10 minutes and when he came back there was a crowd of them at the door. About four or five uniformed officers, another plain clothes officer and the Chief. When they said they were coming to take me I said, 'That's OK' and didn't put up a fight. (421M/87, 72 hours, excluded)

If the purpose of fingerprinting and taking swabs was simply to create a record and to produce samples for forensic testing, then one set would be sufficient. But when a person is moved from one police station to another, it appears to be normal practice to produce another set. This provides further support for the view that these procedures go beyond bureaucratic requirements (because of course prints or photographs could simply be passed on from one police station to another) and form part of a broader process of criminalisation.

> I was fingerprinted and photographed two or three different times. They actually brought me down to photograph me and the officer who was doing the photographing said nothing again. The other officer said that he was sick of looking at me but they brought me back again. They took a side view, front view, every angle. There was also a card in front of me. I was in the fingerprinting room a long time. I was photographed and fingerprinted again on the Monday after I had been charged and transferred to the criminal wing because I was an ordinary prisoner so to speak. During the time I was held under

the PTA I was I think photographed and fingerprinted three or four times. (425M/86, 48 hours, charged)

In some cases the police take swabs and remove items of hair. In one case in the study a police doctor removed 'a great clump of hair' from the head of a woman who was pregnant, as well as a sample of pubic hair 'which was really degrading'. (397F/85, 96 hours, released) It is hard to comprehend what circumstances would ethically justify this sort of thoroughly intrusive and degrading practice other than in a rape case. If the police used the sample in an attempt to establish a relationship between her and someone else, it reflects the extent to which the police are prepared to go in their fight against terrorism. The woman was eventually released without charge after four days of detention.

The fear that a person might suffer the same fate as the Birmingham 6 or the Guildford 4 was never very far away from many people's minds as they went through these routine procedures. That fear is well-illustrated by a number of cases below.

My finger prints were taken. They were the first things to be done. And photographs. A policeman took them, he was a coloured man, he might have been Indian or something like that, really really tall. We weren't long in the station at this time and I was trembling and shaking and he said to me, 'Are you nervous?' and I said, 'I am yes'. And he said, 'What are you nervous about?' and I said, 'Wouldn't you be nervous if you were in this position?' He said, 'You're thinking about the Birmingham 6 aren't you?' and I said, 'Yes I am'. He said, 'Look, what police force conducted that investigation? It was Birmingham, wasn't it? It wasn't us.' As if to say, 'You're okay with us'. But they take everything, your fingers, your hands, sides of your hands, everything. And I got my photographs taken, just sat on the chair and the camera was somewhere over here and they took my photograph. But we had been staying in a flat, and the guy we were staying with had lots of videos, the Maguires – and we had been watching this and we had been seeing the re-enactment of the tests and the scraping of the nails and then god, here was I sitting in Cannon Row police station getting the very same thing done and my nerves were just really really gone. Thinking – they took swabs – thinking 'Holy God, I'm gone, if they can do it to one they can do it to anybody they like.' Then my hair was cut, they took a bit of my hair, they did the hand swab where they take a bit of cotton wool and tweezers and dip it into some solution and they run it along your hand

and each swab of cotton wool is put into a different little bottle and it's labelled and marked. Your nails are scraped and your hand is put onto white tissue or something like that and they scrape your nails. I would love to be able to put into words how terrifying it was, to go through it. (522F/88, 115 hours, excluded)

What frightened me most was when they took the swabs particularly since the first time I was arrested under the PTA this was never done. I kept asking when the results of the swabs would be ready and all they would say was, why are you worried? I said no I wasn't worried but there had been TV programmes showing that playing cards can bring up nitroglycerine. I am a painter by trade and because I have my tools with me the police asked whether I had handled any substances recently or solvents. I said no, that I had handled the tools. I got really paranoid because it was fairly easy to pick up traces of some solvents and was afraid if the officers come back and said that they had found traces of some solvent on me that they would take it that I had been handling explosives. Their attitude was if you have nothing to hide then you have nothing to worry about. (421M/87, 72 hours, excluded)

Some people manage, despite the stress, to retain a sense of humour. One student who was asked, 'Do you handle explosives during the course of your work?' retorted, 'No, but I do have a set of playing cards' (371M/85, 36 hours, released).

Fingerprints and other samples, as we pointed out in Chapter 4, are not destroyed when people are released after being detained or arrested under the PTA. They are however destroyed when people are arrested and then released without charge under the ordinary criminal law. But this distinction has caused considerable confusion, even among the British authorities. In 1985 an Irish national who had been stopped and examined at a port and then subsequently detained in the local police station, wrote to the Minister of Foreign Affairs in Dublin to complain about her 28-hour detention ordeal. She particularly asked the Department to investigate the possibility of her fingerprints and photographs either being destroyed or returned to her. In his response the Minister included a copy of a letter from the British authorities, which stated that the detention was necessary, including the need to keep her incommunicado, and pointed out that 'permanent records of fingerprints are only [sic] kept of persons who have been convicted'. The British authorities subsequently wrote back pointing out that they had given incorrect information and that records are retained of all persons detained under the PTA, and that they had written to the National Identification Bureau to seek confirmation that the fingerprints had not been destroyed (508F/85, 28 hours, released).

Strip-searching

Strip-searching of women in police and prison custody has aroused considerable controversy in recent years.[3] It does not appear to be a routine procedure on entry into police custody and is used only in some cases. Some men in the study were strip-searched.

> In Paddington Green station I was again strip-searched in the presence of three male officers, the two that had been present when I was strip-searched at the airport and another senior officer who was also a member of the Special Branch ... on both occasions I was not kept naked for any undue length of time. (246M/79, 196 hours, excluded)

> They stripped off all my clothes and searched them before giving me them back to put on again. (418M/86, 48 hours, excluded)

> I was then escorted to a cell where I was made to take off my coat and shoes. These were thrown on the ground outside the cell. I was not to have any of them until my release. I was then frisked and told to take my trousers down. The private parts of my body were inspected. I was then locked up. (253M/83, 48 hours, released)

Women, without exception, found strip-searching to be a most degrading and humiliating procedure. Here is one description of the process.

> I was strip-searched after I had given all my details to the custody sergeant and asked for a solicitor and told I couldn't have one. You hear so much about strip-searching, but it's something you would have to go through to really realise how humiliating it is. These two policewomen came in and they put, I think everything was in sealed bags, and they took out this big white sheet and they laid it on the floor and I was told to stand on the sheet and take off everything. Each item I took off went into a bag and was labelled, like 'left shoe' 'right shoe' 'left sock', 'right sock'. I was just left standing with nothing on,

with no clothes on. I was then given this white boiler suit, this paper thing, and I was told to put that on and step off the sheet. The sheet was then folded up and that was put into a bag and that was labelled. So obviously all this was stuff that was going to be forensically tested. I had no underwear, couldn't have access to my clothes, they eventually gave me a pair of jeans and a T-shirt. But I had no underwear and it's not very nice a woman going round in a T-shirt and no underwear. So I kept the white boiler suit on under the T-shirt to give myself a bit of cover, so I kept that on the whole time. (522F/88, 115 hours, excluded)

In another case a young woman who had been visiting her father (who was on remand) was arrested by plain clothes officers on the streets of London and then taken to Paddington Green. She was not only strip-searched but was also subject to an intimate body search of her anal passage. She had a period at the time.

One of the women then said, 'We are going to strip-search you, we want you to take all your clothes off'. So I started taking my clothes off and they started searching all my clothes. I said that I had taken my period that morning and I had a piece of toilet roll on and I handed it to the girl and I said, 'Are you actually going to search the toilet roll that was stained' so she took the toilet roll. I had no cloak or anything. I had nothing round me. I was standing stark naked.

So after they went through my clothes they handed me back my bra and she said to me, 'Would you like a sanitary towel', and I said, 'Yes'. She went and got me a couple of them and I put my pants and the sanitary towel on and my clothes, my jeans and T-shirt which I was wearing and the woman said to me that I was going to have to go down and see the doctor. They brought me to the doctor in a different room and the doctor said, 'I am the doctor and I want to examine you'. I can't remember whether he said his name, and I can't remember his name, anyway I am no good on names. He examined my ears, my throat. I had my bra and my jeans off me – he said, 'You need your pants off you, I am going to examine your back passage'. He said, 'Lean over to the side', and there was one of the women detectives with me in the room. He said, 'Bring your legs right up so I can examine you.' I was on a couch. I was again stark naked.

He put his finger in my back passage and he pressed up very hard and I told him it was sore. He took his fingers down and took the glove off him and threw it away and took the woman to the side and said something to her. I don't know what he said. He said, 'Put your clothes back on you' so I put my clothes, my jeans and all, on me again and they brought me back to the room which I was in. (505F/84, 24 hours, released)

If the police were asked to comment on this incident, it would no doubt be described in terms of a terrorist suspect being arrested and subject to an intimate body search by a medical practitioner and it would be justified on the basis of the fight against terrorism. However, from the perspective of the woman involved, the incident shares a number of characteristics of a rape. A woman one minute is free and going home and the next is accosted by complete strangers, taken to a place and held in captivity against her will. She is stripped and then has a another complete stranger force his finger up her anal passage.

Racism in the Processing of Suspects

A number of people observed that the form which was used to record fingerprints had 'Irish Suspect' written on the top.

There they went through the fingerprints in triplicate. Palms, side of the hands, I've got a scar there (on the side of right hand). There was a piece of paper with 'Irish Suspect' written in red ink all over it. (373M/81, 196 hours, released)

On the fingerprint form the words 'Irish Suspect' were printed in red. I was then photographed and I was medically examined. (205M/83, 196 hours, released)

Another suspect, held in a different police station, described an identical procedure.

'Irish Suspect' was written in red letters across the top of the form. (420M/83, 196 hours, released)

It is difficult to judge how widespread this practice may be among the police because few people get the opportunity to look at what is written on the fingerprint form. In two cases in the early 1980s the people detained reported having to hold a plaque, with the words 'Irish Suspect', when being photographed. This does suggest that for some

time at least, the police used 'Irish Suspect' as a useful label to categorise
all those detained under the PTA in connection with Northern Ireland
affairs.

This is clearly a racist practice and reflects the way the police think
about the policing of political violence in connection with Northern
Ireland affairs. It adds weight to the view that all Irish people are automatically seen as suspects. The racism was aptly summed up by one
person who reported having to hold a sign with 'Irish Suspect' written
on it.

> The first time they take you in they question you and they finger-
> print you and they photograph you and they've got this hideous sign
> which they hang in front which says 'Irish Suspect', you know.
> When I came out, with my Celtish sort of humour, I saw the funny
> side of it, because it's really asking the question '*Irish* Suspect? or Irish
> *Suspect?*' And I couldn't help putting it down in writing and asking
> 'Irish Suspect Who?' (or What?). (311M/81, 72 hours, released)

The stress stemming from the initiation procedures coupled with being
defined as member of a suspect group is then further increased by the
physical conditions of the suspect's environment.

Detention Conditions

Chapter 4 noted that the official reviews have drawn attention from time
to time to the poor conditions under which PTA detainees are held and
they have made recommendations for improvements. The aim here is
not to assess what has happened to these various recommendations, but
to describe how people experienced the conditions.

The Cells

Paddington Green is the most important police station as far as the PTA
is concerned. It was built in the early 1960s and was officially opened
in 1973. Most terrorist suspects who are arrested in the Metropolitan
Police area are taken there for interrogation. The feeling of being
detained in Paddington Green was captured by one person who was
arrested in 1981.

It's a purpose built jail, it's not just by accident. It's been there about 12 years. They were thinking well ahead, you know. I'm making the point that the British Government is not onto anything by accident when it comes to the working class and the whole thing is to isolate a person and to see what effect that has on a person. I'm sure it's very scary for a person who's not politically minded, suddenly to be lifted from their work or home and think, 'Jesus Christ, what's happened?' And there's no contact with the outside world, absolutely no contact with the outside world. What happens is, you're taken along this long corridor, they open – even the corridor is blocked off in effect in three sections, because they take you through one steel door and then they lock that door behind you, take you on further down, as far down as you can possibly go, almost down to where they have, I believe, a rest room, then they open another steel door, they unlock that, take you through, lock it behind you, and then you're locked in a cell. The whole thing is to not only demoralise you but to really emphasise that you're on your own, you're in hostile surroundings. I think it's very important that anyone else – unfortunately there will be other people who realise that that's what awaits them, so that when they are going through it, they will hopefully have read your report. It's probably not so scary if you are aware of it, if you're mentally prepared for it. (311M/81, 72 hours, released)

In 1988 another person described their experiences in a similarly graphic style.

It is a strange sort of thing. You don't know what you are doing. Why am I sitting here? Why am I sitting in this room with a clean blanket, with no windows, no clocks or anything like that, a little hole in the ceiling where you can vaguely tell if it is night or day? It is disconcerting to be sitting here not knowing the time of day, or what on earth is going on. (900M/88, 7 days, charged and acquitted)

There were a number of comprehensive descriptions of the cells in Paddington Green.

The cells themselves were six feet under the ground, I believe they said afterwards. The cell height was about nine foot and the way the light worked is that they have a reflector – what bit of light there is comes through these things. The electric light in my cell was on all the time so unless you saw someone with a watch you had no idea what the time was at all. There was a bench over the radiator with a plastic cover on it and no blanket, no pillowcases, no pillow, nothing. There was no window as such, just square glass. (311M/81, 72 hours, released)

It was underground and a little bit larger than this room – about 9 x 9 – just a barren bench with a few dirty old blankets. A white light was on all the time – 24 hours a day, and a fan heater which was extremely noisy was also left on 24 hours a day, that was all part of the pressure. There was no window either. I didn't know if it was night or day. (373M/81, 196 hours, released)

The cell was very small. There was just a wooden bench with a mattress, a pillow and a blanket. There was a window up at the very top. It was very hard to sleep. There was a light on outside the door which shone into the cell 24 hours. (419M/86, 196 hours, excluded)

The noise was a problem for some:

A lot of the time there was noise like a generator – it stopped and then it started again. (371M/85, 36 hours, released)

While some had no complaints about the cleanliness of the cell, most found them dirty. 'The cell was filthy' (397F/85, 4 days, released). 'I was put in a really disgusting cell' (419M/86, 7 days, excluded) were typical comments. Others remarked about the cells either being too hot in summer or too cold in winter.

It was really hot, you couldn't sleep because it was so hot. You had to take your shirt off. (373M/81, 168 hours, released)

It was really hot weather and these cells were underground so the heat in them was fierce. I was left there until about 11 a.m. The cell was really hot and there was no ventilation. The only air you seemed to get was through gaps in the door. (419M/86, 168 hours, excluded)

The cells at Paddington Green have toilets in them which flush from inside the cell.

The cell was large, comprising a toilet and no wash-basin. The toilet didn't work. I rang the bell numerous times and occasionally someone

would flush it for you. You see they had a button on the inside that
you could flush it with but it didn't work. They had one on the outside
as well. They didn't have toilet paper either. I asked for some when
I got breakfast in the morning but they didn't bring any. (401M/81,
7 days, released)

Another, with a wry sense of humour, described the facilities in
glowing terms:

There was a toilet in the cell which flushed from the inside and there
was toilet paper. All the luxuries from home. (419M/86, 7 days,
excluded)

The condition of the bed linen varied. 'I had a mattress and a pillow
and a couple of blankets which seemed to be clean enough. There was
no smell off them.' (418M/86, 2 days, excluded). This contrasted with
the experience of the woman described in the full case study in Chapter
5 and also with a number of other people's experiences.

At night I was given a dirty pillow and one blanket – these were
removed during the day. (246M/79, 168 hours, excluded)

The bedding is non-existent. There's a plank type of bed and a
wafer thin sort of foam covering on it and one grey blanket and the
thing that substituted for a pillow was blood-stained and it certainly
wasn't my blood ... Whether that was a deliberate thing or whether
someone had actually suffered I don't know, or it could well be
something to frighten you. It could be a tactic to psychologically
unbalance the person taken in there. (311M/81, 3 days, released)

Stranraer police station is used for all those people detained when
embarking from the boat either at Cairnryan or Stranraer itself. Most
people in the sample found the cell conditions unsatisfactory.

They put us in separate cells. Mine was absolutely filthy, with open
windows. I was given an old dirty rubber mattress to lie on but I wasn't
given any blankets with the result that I couldn't sleep all night due
to the cold. The following morning I began coughing up mouthfuls
of blood. This I believe was due to gunshot wounds I received two
years ago which punctured my lung. (185M/78, 7 days, excluded)

The cell had a wooden construction about two and a half feet wide and one foot off the floor, and a wooden effort that was supposed to be a pillow. I was given a rubber mattress about two inches thick to carry in and a blanket – and that was it. There was a toilet which the police flushed from the outside – I had to bang the cell door when I wanted to use the toilet to ask for some toilet paper. I was always given a few pieces although I did ask for a roll. The window was high up in the cell, it had bars and glass and I could see whether it was day or night. The light was a circular heavy-duty glass thing that as far as I can remember was turned off late at night. I slept off and on. It was May and very warm. (250M/79, 7 days, excluded, later lifted)

We were given three blue plastic mattresses between the four of us, and one blanket each. We were not given any pillows or sheets and there was nowhere to put the mattresses except on the asphalt-type floor. The cell had a toilet in the corner but there was no toilet paper. There was one ordinary light bulb, that was left on all the time, and a window high up on the wall with bars and a frame for glass – but the glass had been knocked out at some stage and not replaced. The cell had no heating and was very, very cold. (252M/83, 23 hours, released)

A gate separated these two cells from the others in the block. I had to carry a mattress from a storeroom to the cell – which was about 10 by 12 feet, painted blue with a black door. The mattress smelt and there was nowhere to put it except the floor. I was given one dark-coloured blanket that had a hole in the middle. Although I was told I would get the other blanket I asked for in a minute I never received it – nor did I get any sheets or a pillow. There was a toilet in the cell and a wash-hand basin just outside. The window was very small and up level with the ceiling. It had bars and wire and was open to the outside. When I repeatedly asked to have the light switched off it was just rapidly switched off and on and then left on all the time. The cell was freezing cold – I did not see any form of heating and although I was told it did exist, it was not turned on when I asked. (243M/83, 168 hours, excluded)

The cells were very dirty, the mattress was dirty, the blankets were dirty. The condition of the cell overall was very poor. (201M/85, 31 hours, released)

Liverpool Bridewell was constructed by French prisoners of war for their own incarceration during the Napoleonic Wars. According to the Jellicoe Report it is 'a forbidding building'. But despite its appearance, the Review considered that the inside was 'considerably less depressing than its outer appearance suggests'.[4]

Following the Shackleton Report, three cells were set aside in Liverpool Bridewell for the custody of people held under the PTA 1976. The Jellicoe Report described the conditions for PTA suspects in these cells in glowing terms.

All the cells in the Bridewell possess their own WC (this is not uncommon), a small, translucent external window, and a good mattress, blanket and pillow; persons held under the 1976 Act are in addition supplied with bed linen (almost unique on the mainland, but standard practice in Northern Ireland police offices[sic]), and a more varied diet is provided for them.[5]

This official view of conditions in Liverpool Bridewell, however, contrasts with the experiences of those who have been detained there under the PTA over the last decade. Here are three of many similar descriptions of the conditions.

The place was diabolical – the whole place is medieval, absolutely medieval. One policeman told me that it had been there from the days of slavery; that it was built during the time of the Napoleonic Wars and slaves used to be brought in chains from the Liverpool docks ... the cell just had grey walls with a wee arched window away up at the ceiling. There was a wooden bunk with a mattress on it and two old blankets and that was it – it's medieval. There was a toilet. I wouldn't say it was dirty but there was an old smell off a place like that – and I could hear the drunks and all coming in – yelling, bawling and squealing. (255M/83, 7 days, excluded)

The cells were two floors up at the end of the block, Nos 23, 24 and 25. One cell at either end with a centre piece where there was toilet and washing facilities. Initially, I was put in cell No. 25, the one on the right-hand side walking down the corridor. The cell had a window which had been painted over and no natural light could get through. The toilet was not flushing and there was a small piece of toilet paper on the end of a roll. There was a bed with very hard bedding – of the type that made the timber beneath seem softer. I have neck trouble so I took it off and lay on the bench. It was filthy anyway. I was given a blanket which had cigarette burns and was covered with brown stuff as if it had been messed in – you just could not have had it over you. There was a pillow-case which was absolutely filthy and made me feel ill. I did not use it at all. There was cold air blowing through the vents. It was very cold. I could not understand this because the interrogation room had been really warm, as had the rest of the station. The cells however, were really cold, freezing. The light was left on full all the time. When I asked to have it switched off or dimmed this was refused and no explanation was given. With the light on and the cold air blowing in I did not sleep much – although I did sleep on and off. (189M/84, 70 hours, released)

Another suspect in the following year was not placed in the cells on the second floor but was put down below. His experience was as follows:

I was put in a cell – if you could call it a cell: a dungeon, because that's what it was, a dungeon. It was just unimaginable. The cell was about 13 feet long and about six or seven feet broad with a wooden bench, a toilet at the far end, old green walls and a very weak lightbulb buried in the ceiling which you could not get near and which did not get turned off. It is unbelievable. It is really nineteenth century. The window was blacked out, painted out – you couldn't see out, there was no natural lighting at all, nothing. I was given two blankets. There was just this wooden bench about two and a half feet wide, no mattress. (259M/85, 7 days, charged, later dropped)

The conditions were little different in all the other police stations to which people in the study were taken. Cells were often filthy, with no natural light. The bed linen was seldom clean. Birmingham police station was described as follows.

I was taken to a cell which was the last one on a corridor on the first floor. The only source of daylight in the cell was a spy-hole in the opposite door. The cell walls were painted black to eye level, cream from there to the ceiling. There was a long wooden bench two feet wide each side of the door. A mattress was laid on one bench with blankets and pillow but no sheets. If I turned over in my sleep the mattress would fall to the floor. There was no other furniture. The toilet was at the end of the cell opposite the door; there were no washing facilities. I was treated to silent hostility by prison officers, except for one woman who, when she came on duty on Sunday night, whispered that my daughter had just been on TV talking about me and warned me not to tell anyone else what she had told me. (182F/85, 4 days, charged)

The description of Blackpool police station in the same year was little different.

The conditions of the cell were terrible. There was a bench along the wall and no mattress, only a dirty blanket and no pillow. I asked for another blanket and a pillow but I was not given them. There was a toilet in the cell which flushed from the outside. They would flush it when asked. There was no toilet paper and I didn't ask for any as they would only laugh at you. The food was chronic especially at Blackpool. I didn't eat anything during those first few days. The light was on 24 hours and I couldn't sleep. I felt terrible. (414M/85, 168 hours, charged)

Kilburn and Manchester police stations were no better.

The cell was about three feet wide and seven feet long. There was no natural lighting, just this frosted glass which meant you couldn't see in and you couldn't see out. There was no heating at all and I was freezing. The mattress was a wee plastic thing on a wooden bench. The blankets were stinking and there was no pillow. There was a toilet in the cell. It flushed from the inside. I had toilet paper. It was stinking too. The whole cell was filthy and dirty. (422M/87, 168 hours, excluded)

The cell was stinking and it was very small. There was excrement lying on the floor and the smell was awful. When I was first put in the cell I just wanted to lay down but there wasn't even a mattress there. After trying to sleep on the bare floor I banged on the door and said I needed a mattress or something to sleep on. So eventually they threw me a mattress and one blanket. I didn't have a pillow. There was a toilet in the cell which flushed from the inside but which was filthy. I had to ask for toilet paper which they gave me. The temperature in the cell was humid and there was an irritating humming noise which seemed to be coming from the boiler. There was no window in the cell. The light was on, I think it probably was on all night although

I'm not sure because I eventually fell asleep from exhaustion. Throughout my detention, I had no difficulty in sleeping because I was tired and because I had nothing to do. (421M/87, 72 hours, excluded)

The cell conditions were horrific, it was like being in a condemned cell. One blanket, no mattress and the cell was freezing. The light was on all night. There was no toilet paper and the toilet was blocked. I flushed the toilet and it started to overflow. It was revolting but none of the officers wanted to know. The next day they blamed me for having blocked it myself and that I had put a blanket down it. Basic facilities were completely denied to me. On the Monday morning I didn't get any breakfast. When they brought me into the interview room I told them that I hadn't got any breakfast and they said that they would investigate it. They said later that I was not being picked on not getting any breakfast because everybody in that particular bit had got no breakfast and they just made the feeble excuse. (425M/86, 48 hours, charged)

Food

The food was a constant source of complaint in most English police stations but there were positive comments about the food in two Scottish police stations, Stranraer – where it was thought that the food was purchased in the local cafe – and Galloway police station. The food in Paddington Green appears to have been consistently bad for a number of years.

I refused to eat the food after about two days. I was very frightened, in a bit of a nervous state because I was convinced that they were going to frame us up and charge us – because of the way they were carrying on – they thought this was cut and dried so I lost my appetite. The food was atrocious anyway, it was cold and the dessert and lunch were all on the same plate so you had custard with steak and kidney pie, so I didn't eat it. They did give me a pint of milk every day – that was all I had for about 5 days. (373M/81, 7 days, released)

Breakfast the next morning was disgusting even by the standards of previous meals. I was retching so badly that I thought I would throw up while I was eating it. (372M/85, 36 hours, released)

The food was rotten. The tea was usually cold when I got it. I know that they brought it from other stations on some occasions. I did eat some of it because you do get hungry. The uniformed police put the food through the door. They weren't abusive, just handed me the food and said nothing to me. (419M/86, 7 days, excluded)

At Ealing police station in 1980 a person received only sandwiches for every meal because it was a Bank Holiday. In addition he complained that the police spat in his food.

There were a lot of uniformed police in the police station who were giving a lot of hassle – kicking the doors, shouting, and spitting in the food and all, but there was no violence used against me. (303M/85, 7 days, charged, dropped)

The food in Liverpool Bridewell was regarded as no better than the cell conditions.

I didn't like the food – I don't like beans and toast for my breakfast, maybe the English do but I don't. I hate beans in the morning but I ate it because there was nothing else to eat. (255M/83, 7 days, excluded)

The grub was ugh – beefburger, mashed potatoes, peas and cold rice. The police that brought me my food even told me they didn't know how I was going to eat it. The food was really bad. (259M/85, 7 days, charged, later dropped)

Half the time it was cold and the same stuff for every meal. I picked through it but if it was being served up at home I wouldn't eat it. But when you're in custody you get hungry. (491M/86, 7 days, excluded)

From people's experiences in this study the conditions under which PTA detainees are held have changed little over the decade. The cells are still often dirty, the toilet out of order or smelly, the bed linen invariably filthy and the food in many places very poor.

Detention Regimes

The aim of any police detention regime is to create an environment in which the maximum pressure is put on individuals to talk. The importance of constructing the right environment was recognised by the Diplock Commission when considering the type of techniques required to deal with terrorism in Northern Ireland in 1972. It recommended that interrogation should be designed 'to build up an atmosphere in which the initial desire to remain silent is replaced by an urge to confide in the questioner'.[6]

Physical violence and torture have often been characteristics of detention regimes in many countries throughout the world. In Northern Ireland, following the introduction of internment in 1971, there were allegations against the security forces of torture and brutality in the treatment of many of those arrested. The Committee of Inquiry set up to investigate the allegations confirmed that 'interrogation in depth' had taken place, and that this involved placing black hoods over suspects' heads, exposing them to continuous and monotonous noise, making them stand legs with their apart and hands raised against a wall for continuous periods of six to seven hours at a time, and finally depriving them of food and sleep.[7] These interrogation methods were subsequently declared to be illegal by the European Commission on Human Rights and the European Court of Human Rights.[8] In 1977 two special interrogation centres were built in Northern Ireland and shortly after they opened there were allegations that beatings and other techniques were part of the detention regimes. In May 1978 the Government set up an inquiry which confirmed that assaults had taken place.[9] Allegations of ill-treatment in Castlereagh continue to be made. In November 1991 Amnesty International and the Committee for the Administration of Justice in Northern Ireland submitted evidence of maltreatment to the United Nations Committee Against Torture. In a dossier compiled by Northern Ireland solicitors, 238 out of a total of 268 clients detained under the PTA from June 1989 to November 1991 alleged that they had been ill-treated.[10] In Britain, it is now clear that those convicted of the Birmingham and Guildford bombings were also physically assaulted over many days, leading to their false confessions.

All these cases illustrate the point that it is mistaken to contrapose the rule of law to arbitrary violence and the abuse of power. The law is an integral part of the repressive order and the organisation of violence.[11]

The evidence from this study suggests that the systematic use of physical violence is rarely part of detention regimes in Britain. Only three people reported the use of violence. In one case a person had their face slapped, another had their hair pulled and in another case the interrogating officer slapped his hand hard on the table. Direct physical violence appears, therefore, to be a thing of the past. The principal form of pressure is psychological. In effect, there has been a shift from a focus on the body to a focus on the mind.

There are a number of well-known techniques to increase the psychological pressure on detainees. These include general discomfort, deprivation of sleep, food, exercise and washing facilities, isolation and threats to personal integrity. It is impossible from our data to assess how far all these factors are deliberately used in any police station; some may occur unintentionally. For example, there may be no deliberate strategy to deny people their sleep or exercise but people may be deprived of them because of the conditions. There is some evidence to suggest, however, that most of the techniques have been used to a greater or lesser extent in Paddington Green. This is not surprising as it is the main holding centre for detainees under the PTA.

We have already noted people's discomfort in relation to the physical conditions. We will now turn to the other elements of the regime.

Deprivation of Time-keeping Mechanisms

One of the standard techniques is to deny the detainee any knowledge of the time. Watches, as we have seen, are therefore taken away on entry into custody. In Paddington Green even the clock in the interrogation room was observed by one detainee to have been taped over (311M/81, 3 days, released). Many of the cells have no natural light, thus preventing any knowledge of the time from outside indicators. In the more specially designed holding centres such as Paddington Green, or where cells have been specially adapted, the lighting is controlled from the outside by a dimmer switch, permitting total control of the type of light in the cell.

> The cell was very large, yellow walls, dull door. There was no natural light. The only source of light was bottle glass. You couldn't see through it. You couldn't even tell whether it was day or night ... The light was turned off for about half an hour in the night and then it was turned on brighter. I didn't ask to have it put off. (371M/85, 36 hours, released)

Detainees used a variety of methods to resist being deprived of their knowledge of time. Some made a mark on the wall to count the days. Others tried to keep track of the time by when the meals arrived.

I kept note of the days by meals. I was fed regularly and received cups of tea and drinks of water. On a couple of occasions I was told I couldn't have tea until they had talked to me a bit more. (205M/83, 6 days, released)

Deprivation of Sleep

Another technique is to deny people their sleep. People under stress find it difficult to sleep, but there is evidence to suggest that in a number of cases there was a deliberate strategy to interrupt people's sleep: for example, keeping the light on or making an excessive number of checks, which involve sliding back the hatch on the cell door.

… and just from time to time they have a look through the door or deliberately wake you up during the night – that's another tactic they use. You're trying to get a kip and they come in – 'Are you all right?' I mean they know very well that you're all right but it's just so as to annoy you – keep you awake, you know. If you were to complain to someone, they would say, 'Yes, but we're just concerned for you', but it's not that at all, of course. (311M/81, 3 days, released)

I was not cold but obviously you could not regulate the heating yourself so you just had to suffer what the police considered to be an acceptable temperature. During the night you were inspected through a wee flap in the door. I did not sleep the best under these conditions – I was never in what you would call a deep sleep. I just had intermittent naps. I suppose you could say I was quite tired and felt rather poorly most of the time. (245M/79, 7 days, excluded)

I didn't sleep very well that night – fitfully. When I was sleeping I was sweating and then when I woke up I was freezing and my clothes were all damp and clinging to me so that made me feel even colder if you understand; sweating one minute and freezing the next. I was just given one blanket. (272M/81, 24 hours, released)

A number of people complained about how difficult it was to sleep because the cell light would be kept on all day.

The cell light was kept on 24 hours a day. There was a shutter six inches by nine inches and at intervals somebody would look through the gap and sometimes ask me if I was okay. I could tell whether it was day or night because there was opaque glass in the top of the cell. (205M/83, 6 days, released)

Deprivation of Food

We have already described the generally poor quality of the food. Whether this is deliberate or simply a feature of police custody it is hard to tell. But there is evidence that people are deliberately deprived of food by making it totally inedible, principally by putting both courses on the same plate. As a result:

I couldn't eat the food. I did try but the first time I ate it I was sick. It was cold and a lot of the time where they'd put it on the plate it so spilled into other things like you had custard in baked beans. (397F/85, 4 days, released)

Deprivation of Washing and Other Facilities

Most detainees were not permitted to wash for as much as two days into their detention period. It appeared to be part of the overall programme to pressurise people.

I was only allowed to wash once – on the third day – and I was not given a change of clothing; although I was offered the clean pair of socks I had brought with me, expecting to be staying in England only the one night. (255M/83, 7 days, excluded)

At no point was I allowed to wash. There were washing facilities which I saw other prisoners using when I went out to get a drink of water but I wasn't allowed to use them. Because the place was stinking I didn't take my clothes off. Eventually I didn't even bother to ask about washing facilities because I felt if they were going to let me wash then they would come and tell me. I didn't see why I should have to bang on a cell and say I want to get washed when they knew that I desperately needed a wash. I felt I should be given an opportunity to get washed rather than have to fight for it. So they never offered and I never asked. (421M/87, 3 days, excluded)

Women were more affected by the lack of facilities than men.

> I had not slept much the previous night and was feeling pretty hung-over and wanted a bath after my journey. There was, however, no wash-stand in the cell and I was repeatedly refused washing facilities until just before I was released when I was allowed to have a bath. Fortunately I did not need any sanitary protection during my detention. Not being able to wash or comb your hair, or do the other little things that give you confidence in everyday life, has an importance when you are being interviewed. (165F/83, 31 hours, released)

> I wasn't allowed a wash for two days. I didn't get a chance for a wash; I didn't see anybody, I rang the bell a few times but it still wasn't working then. I didn't ask at the interviews. (397F/85, 4 days, released)

> There was no wash-basin in the cell, just the toilet. I remember now I was brought down to a room on a few occasions, it was like a doctor's room, it was where actually they took forensics, and I was allowed to brush my teeth and wash my hands and face. After how many days that was, it's hard to remember. (522F/88, 115 hours, excluded)

The detention regimes appear to make no allowance for women with periods. We have already seen the humiliating and degrading experiences of one woman who was strip-searched while having her period. In another case, a group of three women were detained at around 6.45 p.m. while getting off the boat at Stranraer. One of them had started a period while on board and had had no chance to get protection once off the boat. She did not receive sanitary towels until late that night and then had to pay for them. The following afternoon she was bleeding heavily and her clothes were stained. By night time she was haemor-rhaging and had bad stomach cramps and the other two women requested a doctor for her. The doctor came very late that night and told her that if she got worse she would have to be moved to hospital. She was given painkillers and more sanitary towels. At no time in her 44 hours of detention was she allowed to wash or given any privacy to change her towels. (512F/85, 44 hours, released)

Deprivation of Privacy

Many of the above deprivations also involved gross infringements of people's privacy. People were not allowed to wash in private. In most cases a police officer was present and in some cases the sink appeared to be in a public corridor. There appeared to be little privacy when using the toilet; some had to asked for toilet paper; others felt that they could be seen when someone looked in through the hatch in the cell door. Often the toilet could only be flushed from the outside. Those who were strip-searched suffered considerable loss of privacy which was further compounded if they had their clothes taken away for forensic testing. In two cases in the study, the detainees were given paper suits to wear.

Deprivation of privacy is a key element in the whole detention and interrogation strategy: it demoralises and depersonalises the detainee. It is a common feature of all mortification processes.

Deprivation of Exercise

Most detainees were allowed little or no exercise during their time in custody. One case study in Chapter 5 described the limited exercise facilities in Paddington Green. It was no better in other police stations.

> One policeman in particular asked when he first came if I wanted to be taken around the yard – there was a whole furore; apparently you're not allowed into the yard but he didn't know this. I don't know whether you're allowed exercise or not but I was in the cell for seven days and I had no exercise. The only time I left the cell was when I was taken to the interview room. (255M/83, 7 days, excluded)

> After four days the uniformed officers ended up taking me out and walking me round the yard. They gave me half an hour's exercise. I was handcuffed. I asked them why was I being exercised and what was the crack ... The officer said that exercise of prisoners every day was compulsory under some new law. The uniformed police were not hostile to me although they weren't sympathetic to me. (422M/87, 5 days, excluded)

Isolation

One of the most standard techniques in any detention regime is to isolate totally the detainee from the outside world. This not only causes various levels of distress but, perhaps more importantly, it increases the detainees' intimacy with and dependency on their captors. The expectation is that this will increase their willingness to talk.

As we saw in Chapter 4, the law permits a PTA detainee to be held in custody for up to seven days and they can be totally isolated from any contact with the outside world for the first two days of this period, having no right to contact a solicitor or to inform a friend of their detention. The police describe this isolation as being incommunicado. The impact of feeling incommunicado was graphically described by one person:

> I straight away asked for a solicitor. I was told that under the PTA I was being held incommunicado for 48 hours. I couldn't see a solicitor. They didn't actually tell me 48 hours, they said I was being held incommunicado for as long as they wished. At a later stage I asked a police guy, 'How long can I be held incommunicado for?' He said, '48 hours'. Now I don't think he was supposed to say that, it sort of gave me support – at least I knew it was only for 48 hours whereas the other guys were trying to convince us they could hold us for as long as they wanted without telling anybody. (522F/88, 115 hours, released)

As we have seen, the cells in Paddington Green and some cells in other police stations in which PTA detainees are held contain toilets. Most police cells in Britain do not have this facility. These facilities are normally justified in terms of the longer period of detention which PTA detainees experience. They can also be seen as part of a deliberate strategy to increase the person's sense of isolation. The provision of an inside toilet means that they must remain inside their cell until summoned to come out. The one opportunity to control an aspect of their custody environment – asking to go to the toilet – has been taken away from them.

One detainee was under no illusions about the role of the inside toilet.

> They've got it all worked out, they've got a toilet built in – I understand that in jail they don't have toilets in cells. They can safely lock you away and forget about you. You're never going to

bother them. You see that's the whole idea, it's not in the interest of whether you might want to use the loo, that's not their concern. It's the mere fact that they can lock you away and forget about you. (311M/81, 7 days, released)

Inside toilets also serve to increase a person's sense of dependency. The flushing mechanism inside often doesn't work and the detainee has to get the police officer to flush it from outside the cell. Thus the most private tasks which everyone performs everyday are in the hands of the police. Detainees in these types of cells are therefore entirely dependent on their captors.

The Role of the Doctors

It appears to be common practice to have a doctor carry out a medical check or checks on all PTA detainees. The position of the doctor, however, is anomalous. In principle, their only concern as a medical practitioner ought to be the health of the detainee and they should do everything in their power to prevent the detainee suffering physically or mentally. But this would inevitably require them to challenge a number of aspects of the detention regime and in many cases demand the release of the person. In practice, they have three very different functions. First, they are required to confirm that the detainee is still able – however that may be defined – to continue to be detained. Second, by carrying out inspections of the detainee on entry and, if necessary, on exit, they provide a safeguard for the police against any allegations of physical abuse. Third, in some cases they play an even greater policing role by carrying out intimate body checks. In such a context it is not surprising that many people's experiences of doctors were negative.

I was medically examined. All this happened before I was told why I had been arrested. I was stripped and the doctor who I understand lived locally and was quite old with spectacles and balding, briefly looked at me for marks and took my blood pressure. He asked me if I had any illnesses. The medical examination took a couple of minutes. (205M/83, 6 days, released)

I had to see the doctor every night before going to bed. It was a man, he wasn't really that bothered I don't think, and the thing was that he said that my blood pressure and temperature was normal but I don't see how it could have been, I mean I had basically come down with flu and being pregnant as well. He knew I was pregnant, I told them. I thought they may try and do an internal examination so I told them that straight away. The next night, that's when I saw the doctor, he was a different doctor from the previous day, and he told the person, the woman that was looking after me at that time, to give me some cream. By that time my lips had all dried up and I was dehydrated, I felt absolutely awful ... He said I wasn't to have greasy food or anything like that. I was to have a cup of water or better still, tea. The next morning they came round and tried to give me a greasy breakfast – everything he had said not to give me. (397F/85, 4 days, released)

In one case a women who still had on dressings from an operation received only perfunctory attention at Birmingham police station.

I was taken to another room to be examined by an elderly police surgeon who treated me with extreme hostility and contempt, he made a perfunctory examination of my chest and announced his intention of examining my varicose ulcer. He ordered me to drop my trousers although he could easily have seen my leg if he had asked me to roll up my trouser leg. I refused to allow him to remove the dressing from my ulcer as, when my vascular surgeon in London had put it on the previous day he had told me to keep it on for two weeks. He prescribed the tablets for which I already had a prescription given by the vascular surgeon, but I was given these tablets for only two days. (182F/85, 4 days, charged)

In another case the medical examination was conducted in the presence of two Special Branch officers.

After the first interview they sent for a doctor. I didn't ask to see the doctor. He examined me and said that he would come back the next morning and examine me again. When the doctor examined me there were two Special Branch present all the time so I couldn't have said anything to him even if I wanted to. (422M/87, 168 hours, excluded)

Another person, a hospital porter, described his experience in extremely negative terms.

I saw the police surgeon who gave me a medical examination, but quite frankly, to call it a medical examination is a farce. I could do better myself as a hospital porter. All they do is to look you up and down and look at your feet and see if there is any bruising.

Later he explained to the doctor that he had a problem getting to sleep and that he was unable to eat. On about day two or three, he cannot recall, he was prescribed valium.

This enabled me to sleep and I was grateful for that. It made me feel a bit drowsy during the day. It didn't affect me then because I wasn't answering questions. (900M/1988, 168 hours, charged and acquitted)

Role of Lawyers

Lawyers, too, are placed in an anomalous role. Their principal function is to look after the interests of their client and it is generally assumed that they will advise their client not to answer questions and will therefore inhibit the work of the police. Recent research into the ordinary criminal justice system has shown that this common sense view is wrong.[12] Provision of legal advice at police stations must be seen in the context of continuing long-term relations between legal advisers and the police. The joint interests of police and legal advisers produce mutually convenient arrangements which may not be in the best interests of the detainee, particularly when police officers perceive that there are considerable advantages to be had from a legal adviser's presence.

Although the research cited above concerned only those detained under the ordinary criminal law, the desirability of producing a mutually convenient set of arrangements will be similar. The main difference is that the climate of fear which surrounds PTA detentions may give the police even greater power in negotiating the arrangements. Unless the detainees obtain a solicitor who is committed to and has experience of representing those detained under the PTA, their interests may be even less likely to be represented adequately by the chosen solicitor.

The study provides some evidence to support this analysis. Except where the detainee used an expert in the field, the experience of solicitors was generally negative.

I saw a solicitor on what I think was the third day, for about 10 – 20 minutes. I was taken downstairs into the place where the sergeant's desk was. The solicitor told me that he was there to see my rights were upheld but there was nothing he could do for me. All he knew was that I was being held under the PTA and no charges were being preferred against me. (255M/83, 7 days, excluded)

In another case the detainee knew from previous experience that he could be held for up to 48 hours without access to a solicitor and he therefore did not ask for one immediately. The police eventually found him a solicitor on the second night of his detention and he saw him the following morning. His feelings were generally very negative.

I asked him what was going on and for him to sum up what had been happening. He said that I had been arrested under Section 12 and that I was going to be held for seven days. He asked me what the questions I had been asked were like and advised me that it would be in my interest to talk. This was my solicitor telling me to talk – his attitude was if you have nothing to hide then you might as well talk as you have nothing to lose. From my experience in Northern Ireland, your solicitor will always advise you to say nothing. So I felt really confused by this stage. He also explained to me that from now on he could sit in on each interview. The consultation took place in private in the interview room.

During one interrogation he asked to have a word with his solicitor.

I told him that I was not going to talk to them any more as I had answered all the questions which they had asked about being in England. He said, it's up to myself. I felt that he was not doing very much to help me. I came to think that this solicitor was working for the police as at stages he was asking me questions that the police were not even asking me. (419M/86, 168 hours, excluded)

In a similar case the police informed the detainee that he could see a solicitor now that 48 hours had elapsed. But he wanted to talk only to his own solicitor.

He asked whether I wanted to see a duty solicitor and I said that I had my own solicitor. However the inspector said that he wasn't on the duty list and I didn't have his home phone number. A duty solicitor arrived about 5.30 p.m. but I didn't even want to talk to him. I asked him to get in contact with my own solicitor and told him generally what had happened. (421M/87, 72 hours, excluded)

In another case, a woman whose husband had been arrested tried to seek help from a local solicitor before she was arrested.

Since I was virtually under house arrest, I didn't ring for a solicitor until after the WPC left. I rang from next door as I was afraid that they had tapped our phone. I went to Chorley to see a criminal solicitor. He rang Chorley police station but the desk sergeant had not heard of the officer in charge of the case and could not give the solicitor any information. At 5.00 p.m. the solicitor wanted to go home so I went to the police station myself. I was not allowed to see my husband. (415F/85, 10 hours, released)

Not all people's experiences of solicitors were negative. Some people clearly found a visit from a solicitor helpful.

I saw my solicitor in private for about ten minutes in the interview room. She explained my rights and told me not to answer any questions. I found her visit reassuring. (165F/83, 31 hours, excluded)

Conclusions

This chapter has described people's experiences of three aspects of police custody under the PTA: the initiation into detention, the detention conditions and the detention regime. We have documented some of the painful processes of entry into custody, the appalling conditions of detention (which appear to have altered little since the recommendations of the various official reviews) and the carefully constructed rules and procedures which make up the detention regime. We have also seen how individuals working in other professions such as doctors, lawyers and social workers, are forced into a policing role in relation to people detained under the PTA. The power of the police therefore combines with the power of professionals to act in the interests of the state and against the individual being detained.

We know from experimental and laboratory findings that many of the features of detention that have been described cause considerable stress and anxiety, whether the person is innocent or guilty.[13] The police are familiar with the psychological research and police interrogation manuals describe how the physical features of detention can be manipulated to maximise their impact on the suspect.[14]

All the processes add up to a highly oppressive system of detention. The police 'take control over the body of the citizen'[15] and manipulate the whole environment within the police station. It is an environment which is totally hostile to the suspect and favourable to the police. The person's command over their world in terms of their self-determination, autonomy and freedom of action is at best disrupted and at worse defiled. In such an oppressive institutional *structure*, leaving aside the oppressive techniques which the police use during interrogation (dealt with at length in the next chapter), people experience coercion.

What is very clear from the descriptions of people's experiences is that as long as the length of custody, the conditions and the carefully constructed detention regime remain unaltered, codes of practice designed to provide some safeguards to those in custody will have little or no effect. The focus of the debate about the reform of the criminal justice system therefore needs to shift away from the details of the codes of practice to the circumstances which permit the widespread use of arbitrary arrest of large numbers of people (who are subsequently released without any action being taken against them) and the oppressiveness of custody system itself.

8 Interrogation: Gathering Information

Introduction

The last chapter described the conditions of detention and the detention regime. It illustrated the considerable power of the police to take over the control of the 'body of the citizen' and the powerlessness of the person being held. It showed how a range of factors from confinement and isolation to manipulation of a person's self esteem may adversely affect detainees and cause considerable distress. In this chapter we examine the interrogation process and the enormous power which the police exercise in this area of police work. This power is further underpinned by the sanction under the PTA that if a person fails to provide answers to police questions, they may be charged with the offence of withholding information.

Interrogation is an activity which is shielded from public scrutiny. There have, however, been a number of studies of interrogation tactics and techniques used by police officers in England and Wales. Some of these have been observational studies.[1] One has involved analysing the tapes of recorded interviews.[2] There have, however, been no previous studies of people interrogated under the PTA.

The form which the interrogation takes varies according to the circumstances of the arrest. A large proportion of the people in this study appear to have been arrested as part of trawling operations. In a few cases people were arrested after a report from a member of the public about something suspicious. In other cases, the person was arrested because they knew others connected in some way, however tenuously, with someone suspected by the police.

In practice, irrespective of the Codes of Practice, there is a huge disparity of power between the detainee and the police. One is powerful and the other is powerless. The impact on the mental state of the detainee of the detention conditions, the detention regime and interrogation is likely to be considerable. A review of the psychological literature on interrogation techniques and theory for the Royal Commission on Criminal Procedure in 1980 concluded that the implicit threat of detention and interrogation, the unfamiliarity of the situation and the confinement effects, are likely to produce a state of anxiety sufficient to impair decision-making. It pointed out that at that time there were no studies of suspects undergoing custodial interrogation and its conclusion could not therefore be proved or disproved.[3]

The aim of this chapter is to examine people's experiences of their interrogations under the PTA and to draw out a number of aspects of the process, focusing in particular on the differential in power between the detainee and the interrogator. It must be emphasised that no attempt is being made to present a representative picture of the whole process; this would be difficult not only because of the extreme variation between the interrogations but also because of limited space. The approach is deliberately selective in order to highlight the way in which coercion can be and is exercised on many totally innocent people in the confinement of the police station. The physical and psychological impact of detention and interrogation on people is examined in Chapter 11.

The Context

It is possible to build up a reasonably clear picture of the general interrogation routine under the PTA. Detainees are taken from their cells to a room which is specifically reserved for the task. Normally, it is a very bare room with just a desk and the exact number of chairs required for the detainee and the people conducting the interviews. In Paddington Green it has been observed that there is provision for an electric clock in some of the interview rooms, but the clock has been taken out. If the person has been granted access to a solicitor, then the solicitor will be present during the interview.

All the evidence illustrates the inherently coercive nature of interrogations. If a person refuses to go into the interrogation room, the police can attempt to interview the person in their cell. There is no right to decline an interview so an interrogation is not voluntary but coercive. Moreover, once a person is under interrogation, they are in a double bind. On the one hand, they have the right to remain silent in the face of police questioning. On the other, if they remain silent they may be charged with withholding information.

A number of people drew attention to this double-bind situation. They expressed it in a number of different ways. In one case the detainee (whose solicitor was present throughout the interrogations) exercised his right to silence after he was asked the same questions over and over again. This is what happened next.

> Having done that they began threatening me with withholding information and that sort of thing. They kept interrogating me and my response was that I wasn't making any more comment. I had properly answered all the questions; I wanted to be released. (900M/89, 168 hours, charged, acquitted)

Ironically, even where a person decides to talk to the police because they feel that they have nothing to hide, this can subtly be turned against them and used to coerce them into supplying even more information. This is illustrated in one case in which a man was arrested in London and taken to Paddington Green where he was interviewed. He was asked if he wanted to make a statement.

> 'I do, of course I do.' And this was the big mistake I made. I would advise anybody never to open their mouth when they go to a police station, any police station. Ask for a solicitor and reserve the right to remain silent. That is what I would do if I was ever arrested again. ... I would stand over that. But because I said, 'Of course I want to give a statement', I started on the Friday night that I got on the boat and I must have been talking for two hours – I don't know how long I was talking for – every single thing I done in England. And then I said, 'And then I was arrested. And that's my statement.' The man at this stage jumped up, he banged his two hands and said, 'You haven't even started.' He said, 'Go back down to your cell and when we come back to you we want answers.'
>
> I couldn't keep my mouth shut, I was yapping away to them and talking and they just kept writing. I was sure this was to get me out as quick as I can. And at this stage we could still make the boat, the boat wasn't till 11, so it was then really when I realised, I think I was two hours down in the cell, 'Well that's it, you're here for the night.' So they brought me back up, I haven't a clue, I couldn't tell you what time it was. I just don't know. He said, 'Right Paddy – right Patrick' – he kept calling me Patrick, he says, 'Now this is your statement.'
>
> I hadn't told them anything of value, anything they asked me I just said, 'That's right'. So then he started saying, 'What are you doing in London?' and I said I was over for my sister. He said, 'What was your other reason for being in London?' so I just said, 'I'm not answering any more questions.' So he said to me, 'Your wife's

Maureen and you've two young lasses', and I said, 'That's right', and, 'You have your own business' and I said, 'That's right'. 'What are you doing in London?' 'I'm not answering any more questions.' 'You're as guilty as hell.' I said, 'What do you mean?' He said, 'You'll answer questions about your family but you won't answer questions about London.' I said, 'My statement is finished', he said, 'You were making a statement when you were talking about your family.' I said I wasn't. I said I wasn't making a statement when I was talking about the family. He said, 'Well how come when we asked you about London?' I said, 'That's to do with me statement. I've finished my statement.' He said, 'Look sunshine, you've actually been talking about your family for the last ten minutes and he's been writing it down so that's your statement', and he said, 'Now when that goes to court it's yours to see. You're prepared to talk about your family but you won't talk about London.' And that's really when I got frightened, I got frightened as hell and then ... at this stage I said, 'Don't say any more'. I found it very hard not to say anything. I said, 'I can't remember'. I told myself to look on the floor. So I did that and I couldn't see them. I started twitching my fingers and he smoked a cigarette ... and I'll always remember this, he lit the other cigarette then and when he lit the other cigarette he said, 'No reply, twiddling his thumbs' and your man wrote 'No reply, twiddling his thumbs'. So he asked me another question and still the same ... and then he said, 'No reply, looking at the ceiling'. Then they let me down for I don't know how long and I was going mad to talk to somebody. I wished they would come and talk to me. After he smacked his hands on the table, after that interview, when I come back the next time I thought they were going to give me a hiding because I kept saying, 'I'm here for seven days, all the marks will be gone.' But they didn't, they just sent me back. (521M/88, 96 hours, released)

Another person articulated the dilemma which faces a detainee in a different way.

You get this fellow – a mouthpiece for the police – coming on telly and saying, 'Oh, well you know, you've got nothing to fear from us.' I mean that was an interesting thing because during part of the questioning this guy said to me, 'Well if you've done nothing you've got nothing to worry about.' Now he couldn't see the irony of the whole thing, the stupidity of his statement. Because there I was banged up in a jail and I hadn't done anything, and I was being taken away from my place of work, I'd been separated from my family, I'd been living under threat because two people had unfortunately died – I wasn't aware of the second death at the time. Here was a policeman telling me that I had nothing to fear from him and he couldn't see the stupidity of his statement. (311M/81, 72 hours released)

Within this generally coercive context the police have a variety of interrogation strategies to increase the pressure on the detainee. They may alter the number, length, form and content of the interviews at their discretion. They may alter the form and style of the questions and the same questions can be asked repeatedly over and over again. The mode of the interrogation can be friendly and supportive, outrightly aggressive or a mixture of the two. Threats can be used and the PTA provides plenty of ammunition. The reluctant talker can be threatened with an extended period of detention, a charge under the Act, or an exclusion order. If these are deemed to be insufficient, they can be threatened with a long prison sentence or threats can be made against their family. All these strategies were experienced by one or more people in the study.

Frequency and Length of Interrogations

There was wide variation in the length of time between when a person was initially put in a cell and their first interview, and the number and length of the interrogation sessions.

Sometimes I was interviewed every 24 hours for about two hours. At other times you might get dragged out about twice a day with a space of about six hours just to put more and more pressure on you; give you time to go back to your cell and get a bit worried. You'd think well I've got to think about this now for another 24 hours and they'd be back in a couple of hours later and start all over again – just trying to get a charge up. (373M/81, 168 hours, released)

I was questioned about three times a day for the first three days and then there were periods of 'chit-chat' twice a day for the next four days. The men interviewing me slowly changed over the seven days until there were people I had not seen originally. (255M/83, 168 hours, excluded)

Where a large number of people had been arrested at the same time, detainees were left in their cells for a considerable period of time before being interrogated.

I was seen first after – I would guess it was about midday of my first day there. So I had been there 14 or 15 hours I think before they saw me. The interrogations weren't regular. I think just the fact that there was so many of us in there all connected somewhat. There was a lot of officers involved and there was a shift system working and obviously back-checking what people were saying. Sometimes you might have two interrogation sessions a day and other times you might have one and another time you might have three. They tended to last two or three hours. I'm guessing but I think two or three hours. (401M/81, 168 hours, released)

But in another case, after having been checked in, fingerprinted and photographed, the person was interviewed almost immediately.

I was left in the cell for about half an hour before they took me out for questioning. Two officers questioned me at a time. One of them took notes and the other questioned me. It was mainly the same officers involved. There were four or five officers in all and the three arresting officers were among those interviewing me. I was only interviewed once the first night. The next day I was interviewed about four or five times for around one to two hours each time. (418M/86, 50 hours, excluded)

Typically, people would be interviewed by two police officers. Occasionally, the numbers would be increased without any explanation to the detainee.

I was usually interviewed by two police officers but on one occasion about six. They were always the same. (373M/81, 168 hours, released)

Interrogation Techniques

The most prevalent interrogation technique deployed in PTA cases appeared to be what is popularly known as the 'Mutt and Jeff' or the 'Starsky and Hutch' routine. This involves one police officer being friendly and supportive and the other being tough, nasty and aggressive. People described the technique in a variety of different ways.

> The same inspector was always present and after the first interview he was accompanied by the same sergeant – who got quite aggressive during his first interview. I felt they were trying the old ploy of the bad guy and the good guy: 'If you don't cooperate I'll turn him loose on you – he'll maybe rough you up.' I just laughed at it. They really only took this attitude at the start of the second interview. When they realised it was not having any affect on me they were just what I saw as their normal selves. (245M/79, 168 hours, excluded)

> One police officer acted 'heavy', the other 'nice'. They told me that they had telexed Northern Ireland and were aware that I had 'done time' – I was interned in 1971–2 for an 8–month period but I have not been either charged or convicted of any crimes and I pointed out that thousands had been lifted and interned in the early 1970s. (253M/83, 48 hours, released)

In some cases all the officers would be either soft or hard.

> The tempo of the interviews would change. First of all they would come in and say something quite friendly and then the next minute they would start shouting and roaring, 'You're a terrorist and you're involved in such and such'. They would get very aggressive and start banging and slamming tables until they realised it was hopeless and that I wasn't going to start talking to them so they would stop their banging and start talking amongst themselves, they were very intimidating. However I was never physically abused. (422M/87, 168 hours, released)

Another fairly common practice was to use a variety of threats. These took many different forms. In some cases it simply involved increasing the number of officers involved in the interrogation.

> Every occasion involved one or two officers and on one occasion they brought in two more, by way of a threat, although I answered all the questions and I argued with them and kept saying things like, 'You're crazy', and 'What am I doing here?' and, 'That's not true' or, 'That's true but'. (401M/81, 168 hours, excluded)

The most common threat was to tell the detainee that if they did not supply all the information which was required they would be detained for the full seven days.

> Most of the questions were personal. For example: what's your Grandmother's name, parents' names, brothers and sisters also as well as dates of birth and addresses. All information had to be supplied or I would be detained for a further seven days. He asked me to write on a blank piece of paper all the names of any friends I had. I refused to do this. The officer stated that he had to have some names and that I could write down at least five names of anybody I know. (253M/83, 48 hours, released)

People were also threatened with long periods of imprisonment.

> I was also threatened. 'At the bottom of this space, there's a gap here – you see that? There's a space there for your name. I hope you haven't bought any Christmas presents for your kids next year because you won't be seeing them. We don't have to hang you by your ankles out of the window to make you talk in here. We've got other ways and means of making you talk.' 'What do you mean by that?' 'You can find out.' (189M/84, 82 hours, released)

Some were threatened with being sent back to Belfast with the implication that someone would deal with them there.

> I was taken to a different interview room and introduced to two officers, supposedly from London. Their whole manner was completely different to the previous interviews. They asked such questions as: 'What are you going to do when we send you back to Belfast?' One officer sat behind a desk, the other walked around the room. This latter officer said that he wasn't happy with the answers he was being given. His manner was very threatening. He said that he had cruder ways of extracting the information he wanted. This was the worst part of the whole thing. (164M/83, 31 hours, released)

In a number of cases reference to the person's family was employed as a means of increasing pressure on the suspect. This strategy took a number of different forms. In some cases threats were made that members of the family might be arrested.

My mother was brought in and spoke to me on Christmas Eve for a couple of minutes. She looked very worried and the officer told me that my mother and father could be arrested and interviewed in those conditions. As far as I know nobody had tried to contact a lawyer or to ensure that a lawyer went to Paddington Green police station. (205M/83, 144 hours, released)

In another case, false information was given about the health of the detainee's father. The detainee reacted by cutting his wrists.

Before I went to sleep a plain clothes policeman came to see me and told me my father had taken a heart attack. I was sick with worry and frightened so I decided to slash my wrists and that way I would be taken from the police station and to a hospital. I asked to go to the toilet and when washing my hands I noticed directly behind the sink, small panes of glass in a window. I smashed my two fists into two of the panes and scraped my wrists back and forth against the broken glass. A policeman in uniform was in the room with me at the time. I was taken to a local hospital and had six stitches inserted in my right wrist. I was then returned to the police station and remained overnight there. (197M/85, 57 hours, released)

The case study in Chapter 5 describing the detention experiences of the mother of a seven year old, illustrated how the police withheld information about her daughter's whereabouts and on one occasion deliberately misled her. In other cases deliberate threats were made about what may have happened to detainees' children.

Many people were confused about the status of the statements taken by the police during the course of the interrogations. Typically, the detainee was asked to sign the statement at the end of the interrogation. Many were unhappy about doing so and if they refused, they were often threatened.

He tried to make me sign some type of statement but I wouldn't sign it. They tried to make me sign another form which I wouldn't sign either. That was for my possessions. (253M/83, 48 hours, released)

Anti-Irish Racism

There have now been a number of important studies into racism within the police in Britain.[4] These studies have concentrated on the racism towards black and Asian people. There have been no studies focusing specifically upon anti-Irish racism within the police, despite allegations of discrimination from the Irish community over many years.[5] In the previous chapter we showed how certain police practices in detention were anti-Irish. The interrogations provide further evidence of anti-Irish racism within the British police.

> They were very aggressive in the second interview, especially with the prejudice towards the Irish. One in particular, a Welsh fella, was more or less saying that we were all scum and that if he had his way this wouldn't be the only thing that he'd be happy with. It was just ear-bashing you know, nothing that I hadn't been through before. So they put me back in the cells, that had lasted an hour and a half. (264M/79, 168 hours, excluded)

> The next few interviews were spent insulting me about anything they thought of. I was called an Irish bastard, mad gunman, etc, etc. (196M/80, 168 hours, excluded)

In the case of an Englishwoman who was married to an Irish person, she reported that one police officer:

> ... was also very racist, making comments like, 'You're a bright girl to be hanging around with thick Paddies'. (165F/83, 51 hours, released)

Anti-Irish racism emerged in other ways. A person with an English first name was referred to throughout the interrogations as 'Paddy' (419M/86, 168 hours, excluded). In another case, it was assumed that the Irish had a particular propensity to commit rape.

> They also told me there were a lot of rapes in the area that were carried out by 'Paddies'. (243M/83, 168 hours, excluded)

In another, a police officer, who clearly wanted to be fair, implied that the Irish were likely to have a prison record.

> He seemed to be under the impression that because I was Irish I would have been in and out of many prison cells and he was trying to assure me that no matter what other prisons I have been in or what the conditions may have been, he ran a decent, proper police station –

he obviously took great pride in his work and I have no complaints in that regard. (247M/84, 12 hours, released)

Protestants from Belfast were no less likely than Catholics to experience anti-Irish racism.

They kept getting at me saying, 'If ever there is a united Ireland you'd be stuck there with them and you'd not be able to move because you'd not be allowed here, you'd be excluded from here, and if your family moves to the mainland, if there's a united Ireland, you'd be left because you'd not be welcome – you've an exclusion order and there's no way you'll get in, so you'd be as well telling us names', and this and that and the other. And I kept saying to them, 'Well, if you're that certain I'm not involved, why ask me these names?' And they kept coming back to the same thing; I lived in the district so I was bound to know what was going on. (269M/83, 168 hours, excluded)

Types of Questions

All the evidence suggests that most of these various interrogation tactics were directed at intelligence gathering. As with the examinations at ports, which were analysed in Chapter 3, the questions were mainly directed at obtaining background information on Irish people, their friends and relatives, and exploring people's involvement in politics.

The questioning about a person's family and background was often extensive.

The police asked me about everyone, my sister, my brother-in-law, other members of my family, my friends, where I drank, who I drank with (I'm not a drinker, I would go to a wedding but that's it). It was just the same routine, the same old questions over and over again – about your family, have you anybody living in England, where are they living? I have a sister living in England and others who have lived there on and off. (255M/83, 168 hours, released)

The questioning started off with details about my family in Ireland and myself here. I told them they had all that from a previous inter-rogation but they said they wanted it again. People as far away as second cousins, far distant relatives in Ireland and that took up most of the first one (interview). (401M/81, 168 hours, released)

They just went through everything – my mother's name, my father's name, my sister's name, did I have any brothers? Where my parents were born, where my sisters were born, where I was born? Cousins, uncles and aunts, people in Ireland, did I have any relations in America? Had I ever been to any Eastern bloc countries – people who I knew. I didn't know what they were talking about and still don't. That lasted about four hours, two hours – two separate interrogations of approximately two hours each. (373M/83, 168 hours, released)

The date of birth of every close relative was often sought by the interrogator. As has been pointed out, this is a crucial piece of information in any intelligence gathering exercise because it means that people of similar names can easily be distinguished – essential for any computerised database.

The type of questions they wanted to know – your name, your date of birth, your address, your wife's name, her date of birth, the kids' names and dates of birth, your mother and father's names, her mother and father's name; all your brothers and sisters, their kids' names if you knew them. (201M/85, 31 hours, released)

In a number of cases the questioning was focused on the political involvement of the detainee and it was clear that the aim was to build up intelligence on perfectly legitimate political organisations.

After that ... they got into the nitty-gritty about conspiracies and membership of proscribed organisations, supporting proscribed organisations and they asked me what kind of political affiliations I had. I told them that I was legitimately a member of the Irish Republican Socialist Party, had since resigned, and that I was contemplating taking up membership of the English Labour Party and that I'd never come into contact with anybody with a military nature. Then they insisted that the reason why I had resigned from the IRSP was because the military wing and the political wing are separate and you couldn't be in both. I just said that is not true, you've got it all wrong. They can't have it both ways, either they're separate or they're all the same, they just wouldn't have it. (373M/81, 168 hours, released)

We then talked about Marxism, Socialism, religion and what did I think of the IRA and the INLA. He informed me that I was being released. I was released four hours later. (253M/83, 48 hours, released)

I particularly remember being asked questions about an article on prisoners in the *Troops Out* magazine. 'What's POW then?' 'Prisoners of War'. 'Who fights wars?' 'Men.' 'You bastard, it's soldiers, and you're a member of the Irish Republican Socialist Party.' 'I'm not, I've never been a member of the Irish Republican Socialist Party and if you'd done your homework you'd know that the Irish Republican Socialist Party don't allow members in this country – associate members maybe, but they don't allow membership because of their voting rights in Ireland. You don't know much about the Irish Republican Socialist Party.' 'You're a member of the Irish National Liberation Army.' 'No I'm not.' I was asked about my involvement in political activities. 'What's your involvement in Irish politics?' 'I used to be in Clan na hEireann years ago although I'm not a member of any political party now since I left Clan na hEireann.' 'Why did you leave Clan na hEireann?' (189M/84, 82 hours, released)

A further factor which supports the view that the objective of the PTA is intelligence gathering is that in very few cases were people asked about specific incidents. A number of people commented on this feature.

I was asked my name and address, about my family – my wife's name, the names, addresses – jobs and places of work of my brothers and sisters, about their children, the names of my mother and father and where they lived. I was asked if I was a member of certain organisations and general questions about my friends and my social life – where I drank and who with, etc. I was not asked any questions about any specific incidents. (252M/83, 23 hours, released)

Recruiting Informers

Although the principal function of the interrogation process appears to be the gathering of intelligence, there is another function: the recruitment of informers. Informers have long been an essential source of information for the police in the investigation of ordinary crime and it would be surprising if they were not considered an equally valuable source in the police's fight against the political violence. Because of the clandestine nature of this aspect of police activity there is very little information about how informers are recruited, how many are used at any one time, what they are paid and what they are required to do in return. In Northern Ireland it is clear that informers have played a crucial role in policing both republican and loyalist violence. The recent prosecution of Brian Nelson provided a rare glimpse into the murky waters of undercover work.[6] Little information has, however, emerged in Britain concerning the role of informers in policing political violence. One exception concerned the case of Kenneth Lennon, who was found shot dead at Barnstead in England in 1974. Three days before his death he told Liberty that he had been blackmailed into becoming an informer for the Special Branch in England.[7] The evidence from this study suggests that the police are always on the look out to recruit informers.

In three cases in the sample the detainee claims that a direct approach was made to them during their interrogation.

> On the second day they were interested in me turning tout – in becoming an informer – they made certain advances. I have a brother living in Australia, I was asked if I wanted to go to Australia, that they would get me to Australia. I was told that if I wanted to go to Canada they would set me up in Canada if I gave them information about certain people they wanted to know about. 'We can get you set up anywhere in the world.' (255M/ 83, 168 hours, excluded)

Conclusions

This chapter has attempted to describe some key features of interrogations under the PTA. It has illustrated the inherently coercive context of the process and described the various strategies and techniques which are deployed. All the evidence suggests that the primary objective is to gather intelligence information and, to a lesser extent, recruit informers. The impact of the process on those detained can be considerable.

In Chapter 4 we referred to the current debate about the role of the Codes of Practices under PACE. Because most of the cases reported in this study occurred prior to the introduction of the Codes, it is not possible to produce evidence to assess how they would operate in a PTA detention. However, they will have done little to alter the overall coercive context of detention and interrogation and will have made no significant impact on the fundamental imbalance in power between the detainee and the police. In particular, the record–making requirements of the Codes, such as making a full account of the suspect's detention and a contemporaneous record of the interrogation, are unlikely to have altered the position of the detainee significantly. Indeed, this study adds support to McConville et al's view that they are inherently flawed. As they point out, 'No record can faithfully reproduce the environment which the suspect is required to confront; no system of contemporaneous notes can capture the suspect's predicament. But the police record is especially distorting, leaving out of account the critical social and environmental stimuli which influence the suspect's decision making.'[8] They go on to argue that in such a context any confession should not be seen as a joint product but a police product because of the dynamic imbalance in the power in favour of the police. 'Interrogations are best understood therefore as social encounters fashioned to confirm and legitimate a police narrative.'[9]

Although McConville et al's remarks were principally concerned with the production of confessions during interrogation, their insights would appear to be equally applicable to interrogations which are principally directed at gathering information.[10] As we have seen, most people are interrogated about their friends and relatives. They in turn then become suspects through association. Many of them will then be detained and examined at ports or arrested inland. The suspect community is therefore constructed in the interrogation rooms of the police stations.

There are numerous problems with attempting to deal with an approach to a political problem which relies on trawling a suspect population, making large scale arrests, subjecting people to coercive detention and interrogation practices and then releasing most of them without charge. It is likely, at best, to be totally ineffective and at worst, counter-productive. These arguments will be developed in the concluding chapter.

9   Exclusion: The Law

Introduction

The PTA contains powers for the Secretary of State to issue exclusion orders prohibiting people believed to be involved in violence connected with Northern Irish affairs from residing in or entering Great Britain. In 1976 the power was extended to provide exclusion from Northern Ireland to Britain. This was introduced to meet demands from Unionist MPs for reciprocity between Britain and Northern Ireland, notwithstanding ministerial debates which had identified this form of exclusion to be inappropriate and pointless.

Exclusion was not a new idea in 1974. The powers available to the Executive under the PTA are similar to those contained in the Prevention of Violence (Temporary Provisions) Act (1939), also passed by Parliament in response to an IRA campaign mounted in Britain. During the 15 years that this Act was in force, a total of 268 expulsion and prohibition orders were authorised by the then Home Secretaries. These provided for the removal of suspected terrorists from Britain (unless residency of more than 20 years could be proven) or prohibited their entry from either part of Ireland.[1]

This chapter examines the powers of exclusion in detail. In addition, it considers some of the more important offences which were introduced by the PTA in 1974 and subsequent renewals.

The Power to Exclude

Exclusion is legally permissible if a Secretary of State believes that a person is involved in political violence associated with Northern Ireland. It provides the only statutory restrictions on the right of entry, exit or place of residence of UK citizens and certain citizens of the Republic of Ireland.[2] Neither deportation nor exclusion measures can be used against British-born or naturalised citizens who are believed to be involved in terrorism associated with international situations. However, the majority of foreign nationals may be refused entry or deported under the Immigration Act 1971.

In practice, responsibility for exclusion orders rests with two ministers: the Home Secretary and the Secretary of State for Northern Ireland. Exclusion may, however, be legally exercised by *any* Secretary of State, irrespective of their responsibility for policing or security matters, or their direct ministerial experience of the issues involved. This inbuilt flexibility has, on occasion, been used to accommodate the pressures ministerial absences place on a provision operating within tight deadlines.[3]

A Secretary of State may exercise the exclusion powers conferred on him or her:

> in such a way as *appears* to him expedient to prevent acts of terrorism ... connected with the affairs of Northern Ireland [emphasis added].[4]

This is a very subjective judgement and the Secretary of State is legally obliged to be *satisfied* that the person:

> (a) is or has been concerned in the commission, preparation or instigation of acts of terrorism; or
> (b) is attempting or may attempt to enter Great Britain with a view to being concerned in the commission, preparation or instigation of such acts of terrorism.[5]

Parliament and the police are advised that involvement in the commission, preparation or instigation of acts of terrorism in the United Kingdom almost invariably constitutes a criminal offence and that the criminal law should therefore ordinarily be applied where someone may have committed such an act or conspired or attempted to do so.[6] This reflects the legislative intention that criminal charges should take precedence over exclusion wherever possible.

Nevertheless, relatively few criminal charges result from detentions under the Act. This is in turn acknowledged and defended as understandable on the grounds that the invocation of criminal proceedings may be restricted by certain considerations. Indeed it is for this reason that exclusion exists. As a pre-emptive power it is held to be appropriate where the successful prosecution of a known terrorist is felt to be precluded by the sensitivity of information or standard of available evidence.[7]

Like the powers of arrest and detention, however, exclusion does not require suspicion of a criminal offence. Indeed the Act allows for the

detention of travellers at certain ports simply because exclusion is con-
templated.[8] In all other cases, criminal prosecution or extra-judicial
exclusion are not mutually exclusive. People who have been tried and
acquitted, as well as those released from imprisonment following
conviction and sentence, have been excluded.[9]

Exclusion also revolves around terms and definitions that are less
technical and wider in application than those which generally apply in
criminal law. The use of such subjective terms as 'appears', 'expedient'
and 'satisfied', combined with the absence of any legal requirement that
the Secretary of State gives the reasons behind an exclusion order, makes
an exclusion order virtually unchallengeable.

The courts have compounded the situation by refusing to interfere.
In one appeal against an exclusion order the courts announced:

> ...we are simply not competent to set aside the Secretary of State's
> decision not to give reasons. To do so would be fraught with
> difficulty and danger.[10]

Before deciding to issue *any* type of exclusion order, the Secretary
of State must *consider* whether the person has appropriate connections
with that part of the United Kingdom to which they will be sent or,
in the case of non-UK citizens, with a country other than the United
Kingdom. This is intended to ensure that consideration is given as to
whether the person would be excluded as a complete stranger to
somewhere which is not their natural home.[11] It does not, however,
provide a legal exemption to exclusion. These are limited and apply only
to UK citizens.

The Act permits the exclusion of citizens of the UK from either Britain
or Northern Ireland but not from both parts of the United Kingdom
simultaneously. The Jellicoe Report considered that such a development
would be unacceptable. In any case it would probably contravene
international law.[12]

Certain categories of UK citizens have always been legally exempt
from exclusion by virtue of their place and period of residence. These
criteria are matters of fact rather than opinion or judgment and are
therefore more susceptible to judicial control and overview, although
the onus rests on the person affected to prove their exemption. Under
the PTA 89, only UK citizens who have been ordinarily resident in Great
Britain[13] or Northern Ireland throughout the previous three years are
exempt from exclusion. Previously, the residential period providing

exemption was 20 years.[14] Even before this change in the law, exclusion from Northern Ireland was not a realistic option since the vast majority of those believed to be involved in terrorism in Northern Ireland would have been, and are, legally exempt.

This substantial change in the legal definition of those exempt from exclusion followed a recommendation by the Jellicoe Report, which judged the 20 year period to be of decreasing value to the authorities in Britain.[15] Against this background, it recommended that the Act should only provide for the return to Northern Ireland of those who belonged there. Its intention was to end criticism that Northern Ireland was being used as a terrorist dustbin. It considered it wrong that Northern Ireland should bear the brunt of the further alienation of those uprooted and excluded from Britain. At the same time it suggested that the continued terrorist involvement of those excluded from Britain to Northern Ireland may well be reduced, given an increased awareness of police interest in their activities. These two points of view do not easily coexist. In any event, the implications of the Jellicoe Report's recommendation for security in Britain were clearly believed to be minimal: the Act continues to legislate for the return to liberty in Northern Ireland of people considered too dangerous to be at liberty in Britain.

Exclusion orders made against foreign nationals ban them from the United Kingdom as a whole[16] and may take effect without exemption, although the longer the residency the less appropriate is exclusion. Certain exemptions to exclusion may be secured should British citizenship be obtained, a relatively easy process for a citizen of the Irish Republic who has been living in the United Kingdom for a substantial number of years.[17]

Certain categories of citizens of the Republic of Ireland are otherwise exempt from statutory deportation. Exclusion therefore provides the only restriction on the travel and settlement of these groups within the United Kingdom, which is provided by right of the Common Travel Area that exists between the United Kingdom, the Republic of Ireland and the Channel Islands.[18]

The 1984 Act did not extend exclusion to cover international terrorism, since the vast majority of foreign nationals believed to be involved in such activity may be deported on grounds conducive to the public good. This permanent and almost unlimited power is available to the Home Secretary for reasons of national security or for other political reasons under the Immigration Act 1971.

Making the Decision

The decision-making procedure involved in exclusion is similar to that for granting extensions of detention, except that applications relating to exclusions in Scotland are referred to the Home Office.[19] Special Branch officers at the National Joint Unit at New Scotland Yard therefore consider all applications for exclusion from police forces throughout Britain and prepare the relevant papers for consideration by Home Office officials and ministers. There is very little publicly available information on the procedures followed or criteria employed within New Scotland Yard or the Home Office. In his 1987 review, Lord Colville considered that the system of police and Home Office submissions to the Secretary of State contributed to a consistency in decision-making and a common approach which would be harder to ensure through the courts.[20] These stages of preparation are seen to act as a *de facto* filter and are obviously significant. There has, however, been no serious exploration of the dangers imposed by pressures of time or the potential for the case-hardening of those involved.

Time constraints clearly do give rise to specific problems:

> Experience in operating the comparable problems in earlier legislation has shown the difficulties which tight time-limits can present. There have been cases in which applications for exclusion orders have come forward to the Joint Unit late in the detention period, when the reason for this, even allowing for the need to make the necessary enquiries, has not been readily apparent.[21]

It is also inexplicable why applications for the exclusion of those due to be released from imprisonment are only made within a fortnight of their release date. The risks of mistakes occurring under such circumstances are obvious. The Colville Report has since advised that particular scrutiny is required when assessing the expediency of exclusion following imprisonment.[22]

For applications arising from detentions under the Act, the police are advised to allow not less than 48 hours before the expiry of the seven day detention period for assessment and processing.[23] The probability that mistakes occur is certain to be enhanced the shorter the period available. The content of the original police application and the associated Home Office submission is therefore crucial.

The Submission to the Secretary of State

In 1978, the Shackleton Report provided an assessment of the information included in applications made to the Secretary of State.[24] This critical area of concern has not been reported on in any detail in subsequent reviews, even though it is fundamental to the existence of exclusion as a non-judicial power. There has been no exploration of the adequacy of Home Office guidelines to the police or the extent to which these are followed; little is known of the processes or criteria involved.

The Colville Report advised, however, that the decision to exclude is ultimately based on the existence of intelligence that the person is concerned in terrorism.[25] The four basic categories of information which are reportedly included in police applications are outlined below:

Intelligence Information

The police are advised to give emphasis to intelligence about the person's involvement in terrorism in any exclusion application and to include a brief account of their relevant background, covering any connections with terrorist organisations such as the IRA and related organisations, and relevant associations with individuals.[26]

Describing this information as 'sensitive and highly classified', the Shackleton Report recognised that the intelligence would be insufficient to bring a criminal charge against the person. Intelligence may, however, strengthen the police's view that the person concerned would present a danger in Britain. The Report warned, however, that any conclusion drawn from intelligence required careful judgement since its value was dependent on the way in which it was graded, assessed and used.[27] No review of the Act has, however, provided an assessment on whether existing police training or procedures are adequate, or the extent to which intelligence is supported by any other information, factual or otherwise.

Gathering intelligence, including hearsay and low grade information, has always been part of policing. In recent years, new methods of processing have further divorced its collection and collation from the way in which it is used and interpreted. Increasingly sophisticated computerisation adds to the inherent likelihood of inaccuracy and misinterpretation arising from an over-reliance on intelligence. Police intelligence on terrorist activity may be obtained from informers and other unnamed sources. Much of this intelligence could be provided

by an *agent provocateur* out of malice, for financial gain or some other
suspect motive. It could simply include information gleaned from the
interrogation of others held under the Act. By the very nature of its
source, content and processing, intelligence is intrinsically unreliable and
largely unverifiable.

Police Interrogation Reports

Police interrogation reports are likely to draw on the results of the questioning of detainees over a number of days in custody under the Act.
As was shown in previous chapters, detention and interrogation is a highly
coercive process. The interrogation reports are therefore likely to
contain subjective interpretations of statements and events, and unreliable
and even false information. The Shackleton Report again attached
importance to the need for police judgement during interrogation and
in forming a view of the person detained; the value of their judgement
being once again based on experience and training.

Factual Information

Recognising the limitations of an over-reliance on intelligence or interrogation reports, the Shackleton Report stressed that police applications
also contained a great deal of factual information, quoting, by way of
example, information detailing any past convictions of terrorist offences.[28]
   The police are advised to provide a range of other personal particulars covering, for example, the person's nationality, place and length of
residence in Britain, and the personal details of any dependants.[29]
These factual details are relevant to the task of establishing whether or
not the person is legally exempt from exclusion or whether certain
matters should be taken into consideration prior to a decision being made.
They are unlikely, however, to provide any indication of involvement
in terrorism.

Forensic Evidence

The results of forensic tests are included in applications for exclusion
only where they are insufficient to serve as the basis for a prosecution
since, where traces of explosive material have been revealed, it could

be expected that charges will be brought. According to the Shackleton Report, therefore, the results of forensic examination are largely subsidiary to the results of interrogation and intelligence reports. Any difficulties associated with the inclusion of such information in applications for exclusion would be brought to the attention of the Secretary of State. The nature of these difficulties, however, were not explored by the Shackleton Report.[30] It has become increasingly apparent that certain types of forensic tests conducted in 1970s are now considered to have been unreliable.[31]

Reviews have variously referred to the application of fairness and integrity in the decision-making process leading to an exclusion order and have concluded that any application studied was based on reliable intelligence which had been assessed for trustworthiness and recent involvement. Satisfaction has generally been expressed over the care with which applications are prepared and processed, with meticulous and strict regard paid to the interpretation of the grounds specified in the legislation.[32]

At the same time, no review has provided a critical assessment of the breadth of the terms and definitions employed in exclusion, or otherwise adequately responded to criticism that this power is over-inclusive and open to abuse. This is despite the fact that the expediency of certain exclusions has been questioned and many cases recognised to be finely poised, even within the broad terms allowed by the Act.[33] Instead, a general reference is made to the fact that the law merely requires the Secretary of State to be personally satisfied of the suspect's involvement in terrorism before making a decision to issue an exclusion order. The Colville Report has most recently stated that exclusion carries no room for a test of reasonable suspicion.[34] This is despite the fact that a proportion of all exclusion orders follow inland arrests which in themselves require reasonable suspicion of involvement under the terms of the Act.

Reviews have accepted and reiterated assertions that disclosure of the grounds for exclusion would involve unacceptable risks and that this must be accepted, despite the possibility of inaccuracies. The secrecy that surrounds the entire exclusion process is seen to rest on the use made of intelligence. It is argued that disclosing intelligence would endanger the life of the informant and the flow of information to the police, and information must therefore be withheld from the suspect. If revealed, the source of police intelligence could easily be traced, since the suspect's involvement in terrorism is likely to be known only to two or three people. The cost of denying access to such information is said to be the price of dealing with terrorism. Secrecy, however, covers not only intelligence information, it also includes the content of police inter-rogation reports. Should any factual information, in the form of forensic tests or weight given to any previous criminal record, family or employment connections elsewhere be considered, this is also kept secret.

The degree to which exclusion orders are influenced by political and security considerations is also generally not revealed. Yet these factors are fundamental to the operation of exclusion as a secret, non-judicial power. The Jellicoe Report, rejecting criticisms that the ultimate decision to exercise such a power should not rest with the Executive, outlined exclusion as:

> ... a matter of public policy. It is based not merely on the conduct of the excluded person, but also; once his terrorist involvement is estab-lished on matters such as the security situation at the time ... Neither the courts nor any form of tribunal could properly be expected to carry out an examination of all these issues and to reach a binding decision.[35]

Similarly, the Colville Report rejected the argument that the judiciary rather than the Executive should control such an infringement of civil liberties, believing that the process of exclusion was such that any such change would be cosmetic rather than substantial and would only involve the courts in a political process, bringing them into disrepute.[36]

Failure to Comply

It is an imprisonable offence not to comply with the exclusion order once it has been served and the opportunity to make representations has passed. It is also an offence to assist knowingly someone to enter or be in the territory from which they have been excluded. Both these offences carry the possibility of imprisonment or a fine.[37]

The Lifespan of an Exclusion Order

The PTA 84 provided a statutory life of three years for all exclusion orders, after which a new order is required if the exclusion is to continue. This fixed lifespan followed a recommendation by the Jellicoe Report that the Secretary of State should justify the continuation of an exclusion, at least on the basis of a review of intelligence.[38] Previously, exclusion orders were indefinite unless revoked by a Secretary of State. From 1984, therefore, instead of being continuous subject to revocation, exclusion may be continuous only subject to renewal.

The Use of Exclusion Orders in Britain

In the period from 29 November 1974 to 31 December 1991, 401 people have been excluded from Britain. Of these, 312 were removed to Northern Ireland, 64 to the Republic and another 13 were already outside Great Britain when served with an exclusion order. The statistics do not reveal the circumstances of the remaining 12. Over this period the Secretary of State has refused to support only 62 – or 13 per cent – of the 462 applications made to him by the police.

Figure 9.1 records the cumulative total in force, the number of new orders made and the number of exclusion orders made against both those detained at ports or airports and elsewhere. The number of people subject to exclusion orders reached a peak in 1982 and has since declined. The number of new exclusion orders shows wide variation over the period. In the early years of the PTA around 50 exclusion orders per year were issued. The number had declined by the mid-1980s, increased a little in 1987 and 1988 and then declined again. The number of exclusion orders which are issued after detentions at ports and airports exceeds those issued against people detained elsewhere by a ratio of 2 to 1.

Notification of Rights and Power of Removal

Once an exclusion order has been issued, the Act requires that the person must be served with a notice of the order which sets out their rights and how these may be exercised.[39] This notice must be served as soon as possible if the person is in the United Kingdom or enters at a later date. Table 9.1 shows the content of an exclusion order. As can be seen, the wording is extremely vague and legalistic. The person is not informed as to whether the Secretary of State believes that he or she is still involved or whether they are suspected of being involved in the past. The form which sets out their rights is reproduced in Appendix II. It too is highly legalistic and very complex.

208

Figure 9.1 Number of Exclusion Orders Following Detentions at (a) Ports and Airports (b) Elsewhere, and Number in Force, 1974-1991.

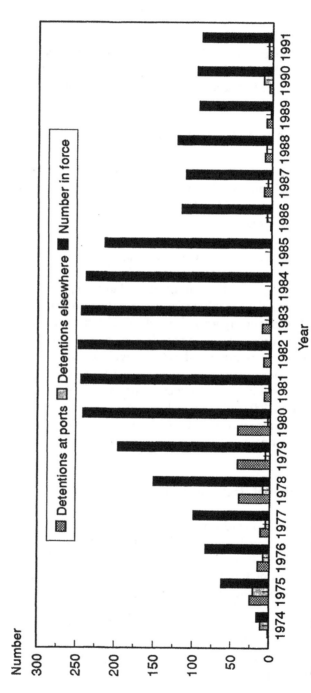

Source: Home Office Statistics

Table 9.1 An Exclusion Order

PREVENTION OF TERRORISM (TEMPORARY PROVISIONS)
ACT 1989 EXCLUSION ORDER

Whereas I am satisfied that .... is or has been concerned in the
commission, preparation or instigation of acts of terrorism connected with
the affairs of Northern Ireland:
And whereas it has not been shown that the said .... is entitled to
exemption under section 5(4) of the Prevention of Terrorism (Temporary
Provisions) Act 1989:
Now, therefore, in pursuance of section 5(1) and (2) of the said Act of
1989, I, by this order, prohibit the said .... from being in, or entering,
Great Britain:
And in pursuance of paragraph 7(1) of Schedule 2 to the said Act of 1989 I
hereby authorise .... to be detained pending the giving of directions for
his removal from Great Britain under paragraph 6 of Schedule 2 to the Act,
and pending his removal in pursuance of such directions

One of Her Majesty's Principal
Secretaries of State

Home Office
Queen Anne's Gate

The person is detained pending arrangements for their removal.[40]
Detention in certain designated places may, however, continue for 24
hours beyond the seven day period normally allowed by the Act if the
person is to be removed within that period. If, however, detention is
necessary for more than eight days following the initial arrest, the
person should be transferred to prison.[41]

If the person consents, they may be removed from the territory
immediately. In the absence of consent or written representations
against the exclusion order, removal may take place seven days after notification. Removal is also automatic following representations which have
been unsuccessful.[42] Normally the person does not have the right to
choose where they are sent, since their destination is defined by the Act.

Representation

The right for those excluded to make representations against their
exclusion order has always been subject to statutory time-limits. These
have been progressively extended since 1974.[43] The Act allows repre-

sentations to be made before removal if these are received within seven days of the exclusion order being served. The Act also allows representations made within 14 days of the date of removal.[44] The PTA 76 Act allowed only 96 hours either before or after removal for the receipt of representations, doubling the 48 hours provided by the 1974 Act. In practice, administrative flexibility has provided additional time beyond these statutory deadlines.

Advisers are appointed by the Secretary of State to consider any exclusion referred to them and to advise the Secretary of State on the exclusion. They are given access to the information on which the decision to exclude is based and the freedom to conduct interviews as they wish. No guidelines have been issued and the procedures advisers choose to adopt remain unspecified. This has been considered appropriate by the various reviewers of the Act, although certain anomalies have been recognised in the treatment of excludees. Basic matters, such as whether the case material should be considered before or after the interview, or whether or not the excludee may have a solicitor present, remain at the discretion of the individual adviser. The standard of advice received by the Secretary of State therefore rests solely with the adviser, who choses the procedures to be followed and the criteria considered relevant.[45]

The right of those making representations to have an interview with an adviser has also progressively been extended. Under the PTA 89, there is a legal right to such an interview either before or after removal (where the Secretary of State considers it is reasonably practicable within a reasonable period from the date on which representations were made). An interview must be requested in properly made representations[46] and may be held in Britain, Northern Ireland or the Republic of Ireland, depending on the nature of the exclusion order. Interviews may be refused for reasons of expense, inconvenience or other unspecified grounds. Under the PTA 76 an interview had only to be granted prior to removal. There was no explicit right to an interview with an adviser under the 1974 Act, although it was an administrative practice to grant any such request.[47]

The increased opportunity of obtaining a personal interview with an adviser under the PTA 84 marks an attempt to make representations more meaningful and increase the participation of those excluded. It follows from a recommendation from the Jellicoe Report which advised that those facing exclusion should not be constrained by having to remain in custody in order to activate a right, which was not only a safeguard to the individual, but also of crucial assistance to the Secretary of

State.[48] The Colville Report indicates that these interviews play a significant part in the recommendations made by advisers to the Secretary of State on whether or not the exclusion should be revoked.[49] Advisers and the interviews they conduct are therefore of critical importance. The overall role of the adviser system is, however, severely limited.

The Shackleton Report argued that it was erroneous to think of this system of representation as an appeal. The basic nature of the law has not altered since. The system of advisers is not intended to provide a reasoned assessment in the judicial sense. Advisers are not required to have any legal experience or indeed any knowledge of British-Irish history. They have no power to intervene and offer an interview and no power to interview anyone other than those excluded. At the same time, the value of these interviews has always been constrained by the requirement not to disclose the grounds for any exclusion. The system is understood, therefore, to provide:

> ... a means of taking account of any points the subject of the order might wish to make (at his own instigation) and of obtaining a second opinion on the case, based upon a personal interview ... the object of the system ... is to enable the adviser to form a first hand impression of the subject.[50]

The Colville Report, while agreeing with previous reviewers that the process is not, and cannot be, judicial, expressed the view that representations constitute a real method of appeal. It considered the process to be a method of reviewing executive decisions as the reports of advisers are conscientious and almost always accepted. The Secretary of State is not bound, however, to follow the recommendation of their advisers. In reality, advisers cannot be considered to be strictly independent, since they are appointed by the Secretary of State. Their role merely reinforces the secret and essentially subjective basis on which the power of exclusion operates.

The possibility that the exclusion is based on inaccurate information cannot, however, be ignored. By its very nature, the information considered relevant to an exclusion warrants close, independent scrutiny to ensure that clearly defined criteria are met. At present there is a danger that interviews are merely a mechanism for obtaining a general assessment of the character and credibility of those excluded. It is therefore understandable if existing procedures are perceived to be cosmetic and designed more to allay public and parliamentary concern than to provide justice to the individual.[51]

The question of whether the individual could have been brought to justice is one which rests with the police. The Crown Prosecution Service has no remit to intervene and advise on whether a prosecution could have been brought.

Reconsidering the Decision

Once representations have been received, the Secretary of State must reconsider the exclusion 'as soon as is reasonably practicable', taking into account the representations, the report and advice of an adviser and anything else which *appears* to be relevant.[52] The final decision on whether or not to revoke an order rests with the Secretary of State who is only obliged to notify the excludee of this decision 'if it is reasonably practicable to do so'. This caveat applies only to those excluded within the United Kingdom.

The Review Process

The exclusion must be reviewed prior to expiry of the three year exclusion order. If a new order is issued following a review, the right of representation is also renewed. Prior to 1984, reviews only took place at the discretion of the Home Office following a request by the individual concerned. There was no right to make representations against the continuation of an exclusion following a review.

Reviews have no statutory basis. They are administered by the Home Office and initially occurred only on an ad hoc basis when requested by the person concerned. It was not until March 1979 that the Home Office, in response to a recommendation by the Shackleton Report, began to operate a system intended to inform and encourage those excluded for more than three years to seek a reassessment of their case.[53]

The system introduced by the Home Office in 1979 had inherent problems. It depended largely on a response to a letter sent to the last known address of the person concerned, explaining the review system and inviting participation by way of a questionnaire enclosed for completion. Where the person agreed, it was also possible to obtain interviews with members of Special Branch if this was considered to be useful. These interviews were normally held at Castlereagh Holding Centre. The decision on whether or not to continue an exclusion was made on the basis of a report submitted by the Special Branch to the Home Office, and rested with the Secretary of State. In the absence of any approach to the Home Office, exclusions continued without any assessment of their merits.

Despite criticisms by the Jellicoe Report, Home Office review procedures did not change with the introduction of the PTA 84, beyond ensuring that a review became automatic before each exclusion order was due to lapse.[54] As before, where addresses were not available to the Home Office or were out of date, the onus rested with those excluded to know about the review procedure and the options open to them to participate in it.

Further, and more forceful, criticism by the Colville Report eventually prompted the Home Office to place advertisements about the review system in the Irish press.[55] More recently, certain minor changes in administrative procedures have been made. Those in receipt of their first exclusion order should now also be invited to keep the Home Office informed of any change of address so that they may be contacted when their review is due. The relevant form is provided shortly after their exclusion and again, if necessary, at the time of their review. The authorities in Northern Ireland are requested to trace the current address of those who have become lost to the system.[56]

These additional procedures have been welcomed by the Colville Report which considered that they ought to result in important information being made available for the review process and reduce the number of persons not informed about the result.[57] Improved opportunities to learn about the review system may reduce ignorance and confusion but they do not increase the value of these procedures to those wishing to challenge their exclusion. The number of orders revoked on the basis of the advice received by the Secretary of State is considered to provide sufficient evidence that the system provides a real safeguard for the individual.

The various modifications made in law and procedure have provided a veneer of due process. At best they have provided those who have been excluded with greater opportunities to register their objections in the knowledge that their view will receive some consideration. It is, however, an illusion to consider such changes as increasing the ability of those affected to contest the grounds on which the Secretary of State is 'satisfied' that their exclusion is 'expedient'. The system of representation and review continues simply to ensure that the Secretary of

State must consider any objections the individual raises to counter the suppositions behind their exclusion. Under the present system, therefore, the individual is clearly presented with the same difficulties as before.

Conclusions

The political nature of exclusion has not altered since 1974. It is one of the central provisions of the Act, operating under the sole control of the Executive to form part of government policy aimed at containing terrorism associated with Northern Ireland. In practice, exclusion has been overwhelmingly used to prevent the travel or resettlement of United Kingdom citizens within the United Kingdom. It has resulted in a one-way flow of people from Britain to Northern Ireland on the grounds of their suspected involvement in terrorism. It has been used extensively where criminal prosecutions have failed. Like internment in Northern Ireland, exclusion has provided an executive safety net for the assumed inadequacies of the criminal justice system. The re-arrest of acquitted people outside the courthouse and their subsequent exclusion does little to enhance public confidence in the courts when the police, supported by the Executive, make such a public statement of their own lack of confidence in the system.

Many believe that exclusion orders have been made for inadequate or inappropriate reasons, not only where evidence is insufficient or unreliable but also where people have been attempting to break terrorist links and start a new life, or for political or other reasons. This is not surprising. The terms and definitions used are in fact wide enough to allow exclusion to be used not only against those on the periphery of terrorist activity, but also anyone involved in subversion, general political activity or otherwise.

The grounds for any exclusion order remain secret. Those excluded have no right to know or contest the alleged justification for their exclusion. The system of representation and review is little more than cosmetic. There are no safeguards against incompetence or abuse. At the same time, exclusion is a parody of justice.

The right of representation and the review procedures administered by the Home Office merely provide an opportunity for the individual to register any objections to their exclusion and bring any matters they feel may be pertinent to the attention of the Secretary of State. Beyond matters of principle, this offers the possibility of either providing infor-mation which may be self-incriminating or asserting that supposition of involvement is misplaced (but with no guarantee that such an assertion will be believed). At the same time the use of the term 'rights' is at best misleading and at worst dishonest. The term has no substance in the context of a system in which an individual has no right to know either the evidence against them or to have a public trial.

Successive governments have argued that exclusion has rid Britain of dangerous terrorists and otherwise impeded terrorist operations. It is, however, extremely difficult either to prove or disprove such an assertion. The official statistics on the use of the exclusion orders over the years provides little support for this view. While there may have been some displacement of political violence from Britain to Northern Ireland, there is no concrete evidence to suggest that they have curtailed political violence.

In the debate to continue the PTA 89 in February 1992, the Secretary of State used the case of Kevin Barry O'Donnell to illustrate the importance of exclusion powers. O'Donnell had been stopped in north London with Kalashnikovs in the boot of the car he was driving. He was acquitted of possession of firearms with intent to endanger life. Immediately after the acquittal he was excluded. He was subsequently shot dead in an incident in Coalisland. The IRA then admitted that he had been a member since 1988. The Secretary of State argued that he was a very dangerous man from whom people needed to be protected and that his decision to exclude him was the right one.[58] But he seemed to be singularly unaware that people in Northern Ireland have an equal right to be protected. As long as Ireland is used as a dumping ground through the use of exclusion orders, the racist nature of the PTA will be further entrenched.

The real issue which this case raises and which the Secretary of State should have addressed was how a jury reached what appears to be a perverse verdict. This can only be guessed, but it would be surprising if their decision was not affected by the long string of miscarriages of justice suffered by Irish people.

The authorities have also acknowledged that exclusion holds possibly drastic implications for the individual and entails the most severe curtailment of civil liberties provided by the Act. It is accepted that the power runs counter to the internationally recognised right of people to reside and travel freely throughout the territory of which they are citizens. It is also acknowledged that exclusion entails the abrogation of the rule of law and suspends the tenets of natural justice. At the same time, it is said that this is justified on the grounds that an exclusion order is issued on the basis of information which is too sensitive, too secret, or too damaging to national security to be subjected to any cross-examination, trial or any public, formal hearing or appeal. The Government has no plans to remove the executive and secret nature of exclusion, which has remained unaltered since 1974.

Against this, the Colville Report recommended that exclusion should not be renewed in 1988 or, failing this, not replaced by any new legislation brought into force following the expiry of the 1984 Act in March 1989. It advised that this would be correct both in terms of civil rights within the United Kingdom and for our international reputation.[59] Previously, the Philips Annual Report for 1985 had recommended that no new exclusion orders should be made against United Kingdom citizens and that this power should eventually be allowed to lapse. Both proposals reflect the shifting debate on counter-terrorist strategies which holds its own implications for civil liberties.[60] Sir Cyril Philips' earlier proposal emerged from the perception that the transfer of suspects from one territory to another was of diminishing application and significance, given the increased emphasis on a general and coordinated strategy against terrorism affecting, and influenced by, international developments. The Colville Report's more recent recommendation for the repeal of this power in turn supports a view that an increase in police and security service intelligence in Britain would be more acceptable than a system of internal exile which is no longer sufficiently valuable to be defended against continuing criticism.

10   Internal Exile: People's Experiences

Introduction

This chapter focuses on the exclusion process. It is based on the experiences of 30 people who were detained or arrested and subsequently excluded in the period between 1977 and 1990. Twenty-three were initially detained at ports or airports and seven were arrested inland. Of the 30 excluded, two were women. The details concerning their initial detention or arrest and subsequent interrogation have been described in previous chapters.

To be served with an exclusion order can be a very traumatic event. One moment a person may be living happily in Britain but within a matter of days may find themselves in exile. In one case a man who had moved over from Northern Ireland with his wife to take up a job was driving along the Kilburn High Road one Wednesday evening when he was involved in a car crash. He was taken to the police station where he was then arrested under the PTA. He was interrogated for two days and then:

> After the interview on Friday night I kept being told that I was being sent back to Belfast. From Saturday to Monday I was just left in the cell ... By this stage I felt that because I was going back to Belfast, what did I need a solicitor for? I felt that they were going to do what they liked anyway. However I haven't had any say in the matter. I was just being put out of England without getting saying what I wanted to or given a chance to make any representations or have any say in the matter. I didn't know for certain whether the exclusion order had been granted. They were giving me the impression that it had been granted and it was only a question of somebody coming and taking me to the airport. (422M/87, 168 hours, excluded)

Notification of Exclusion

Those facing exclusion were formally notified of the order made against them by the police or, if they were detained in prison, by the prison governor. None of those who provided statements received any official explanation for their exclusion beyond what was written in their exclusion order:

> I was not told the reason why I was being excluded other than what was written on the exclusion paper. (245M/79, 168 hours, excluded)

This corresponds with government policy that the grounds for any exclusion should not be revealed. While no substantive reason was forthcoming from the police officers responsible for the application, some made passing comments. One person claimed:

> All [the police] said to me was that [my exclusion] was in respect of being a member of an illegal organisation ... (264M/79, 168 hours, excluded)

Another was given his earlier refusal to cooperate as the reason for his exclusion:

> The Special Branch came and told me I was being deported because I would not cooperate with them. (195M/80, 168 hours, excluded)

There is also the concern that the police will use the exclusion powers to get rid of anyone whom they do not particularly like for political or other reasons. These sentiments were articulated in a number of cases:

> The Special Branch said that they didn't want me or my type in London and that they didn't want me walking the streets of London. (422M/87, 168 hours, excluded)

Others were simply told that they were considered to be undesirable (246M/79, 168 hours, excluded) or informed that somebody just took a dislike to them (269M/83, 168 hours, excluded).

The atmosphere created by the police often left strong impressions of the process behind such decisions. The general theme was summed up by a man excluded in 1979:

> A local MP, who knew me personally, made representations to the Home Secretary. The police ... were adamant that it did not matter what was said on my behalf, that they had requested an exclusion order

and they were in no doubt that it would be granted – I was given the impression that the signing of the exclusion order was just a formality. (245M/79, 168 hours, excluded)

It is not surprising therefore that the level of decision making was not seen as an important safeguard by those facing exclusion:

I don't know why the Secretary of State's even interested in my exclusion or if he even knows about it or does he even get it or does one of his secretary's just say – Leon there's something that needs your signature on it. (255M/83, 168 hours, excluded)

Explanation and Knowledge of Rights

A number of people did not read or understand the notice of exclusion and rights before their removal; some attributed this to their general confused state, others to a feeling of pointlessness. Often an inability to reflect clearly on their situation was apparent.

Just before leaving Paddington Green I was handed some papers. I cannot remember if I was asked to sign these and I only read them when I was on the plane. I felt there was not much point in reading them at the time – I felt there was little I could do about it. (246M/79, 168 hours, excluded)

At about 8.30 that evening I was allowed to wash, given back my clothes and told I was being excluded from Britain. At this stage this was the only thing I could understand, although I wrote 'I accept' and signed the form. (243M/83, 168 hours, excluded)

In addition to receiving the formal notice of their rights to representation as required by the Act, a number of those interviewed said that the police also explained certain of the procedures involved.

They explained the exclusion order to me and what it meant so I understood it all. (343M/78, 168 hours, excluded)

For another, the whole process appears to have been perfunctory:

They gave me some papers and told me I was going to be excluded. (265F/77, 120 hours, excluded)

The police are now expected by the Home Office to provide verbal explanations of the representation procedure. This need not constitute an informative exercise, however, or mean that a positive impression of procedures is conveyed. One person recently obtained an objective, but hardly informative, explanation:

[The Detective Inspector] asked me, after he had read [the order] to me, what I wanted to do. He told me that I could either appeal it within seven days in England or within 14 days if I went back to Northern Ireland. (422M/87, 168 hours, excluded)

In another recent case, while the person was fortunate enough to be able to understand the formal notice of rights, his comments illustrate how explanations can be couched in negative terms.

A Detective Inspector came in with papers which he wanted me to sign. He told me if I didn't sign them I could be put in jail for seven days and be excluded anyway. He didn't actually explain the exclusion procedure to me, but it was all in the documents. (418M/86, 50 hours, excluded)

The presentation of the system of representation as a pointless delay to inevitable exclusion was an experience shared by many of those interviewed, irrespective of when and where they were detained.

Making Representations before Removal

The priority of those interviewed was to be released from custody and the conditions under which they were being detained as soon as possible. This was felt equally by those facing exclusion. Everyone was well aware that to make immediate representations against an exclusion order meant remaining in custody. This seems to have been a frequently stressed part of the process that was clearly understood.

All those excluded under the PTA 76 who did not ask for an interview before being deported, lost the right to an interview with an adviser. Their comments correspond with the view expressed by the Jellicoe Report that the major preoccupation of those facing exclusion is the desire to be released and to return home as soon as possible. They indicate how legal rights can in reality be meaningless as safeguards.

I didn't want to stay in the cell another 96 hours – I wanted out of it. They have you for seven days and then they state if you want to appeal you must remain in custody – who wants to do that after seven days in custody? This is the position they put people in; that if they want to fight it they must stay under arrest for another so many hours. (255M/83, 168 hours, excluded)

I was asked to sign [the papers] which I did because I wanted to be back to Ireland without any more waiting. (196M/80, 168 hours, excluded)

I just wanted to get out. So I didn't take [the representations] up. I didn't care. Just get me out of here. (261M/78, 72 hours, excluded)

We were told we could either sign the papers now, or choose not to sign them, and not be released but stay and appeal from Liverpool. We both chose to sign the papers and get out. (256M/81, 168 hours, excluded)

Legal rights administered in a vacuum of supporting procedures can clearly create discouraging uncertainty. The continuing absence of any obligation on the authorities to hear representations within a set period was manifest in the different information provided about the length of time the process would take.

I was told if I wanted to appeal I would have to stay in prison another two days. (243M/83, 168 hours, excluded)

I was told ... I would be sent to Brixton Prison for anything up to three months until the appeal was heard – I was not having any of that! (251M/80, 168 hours, excluded)

They did tell me that I could make representations within seven days against the exclusion order. But they said that if I did not agree to sign the exclusion order then I would be remanded in custody for four days. So basically what they were saying was sign and accept it or be remanded in custody. There was no way I was going to prison for four days. So I decided to sign the exclusion order when the time

came ... I was never told I could make representations within 14 days
of return to Northern Ireland. (419M/86, 168 hours, excluded)

The police often presented procedures as mere formalities rather than
legal safeguards, with understandable results.

I was not too happy about signing the papers when I read that the
Home Secretary was satisfied that I was involved in acts of terrorism
or was about to become involved ... When I said I wanted to appeal
I was told ... I would only succeed in being held in prison for a few
extra days. (245M/79, 168 hours, excluded)

He said ... I would be held for 28 days in the gaol and even if I did
appeal, it would be turned down, so I would do another 28 days for
nothing. (196M/80, 168 hours, excluded)

This atmosphere can actively encourage acquiescence to the police
objective of a quick and uncomplicated end to the proceedings that they
had initiated:

... If you want to mess us about now we'll lock you back up in the
cell and we'll go away and you can wait ... the same thing's going
to happen, you're still going to get sent home on the boat. It scared
me ... because I hadn't seen nobody, I didn't realise I had any rights,
they didn't tell me what they were holding me for. I was just that
sickened. I'd have signed anything to get out, to tell you the truth.
(269M/83, 168 hours, excluded)

Others were provided with a graphic prospect of prison custody:

They told me that if I made representations I'd be taken to Brixton
Prison and held there. They said that Irish people were given a hard
time in Brixton Prison and that you'd find yourself living in Brixton
Hospital, that if I didn't agree to being excluded I was going straight
to Brixton. In the end I didn't make any representations. (303M/79,
168 hours, excluded)

Such experiences were typical. The interests and outlook of those
providing information on rights is clearly critical in determining the
overall message conveyed.

While influenced by a different range of factors, advice from a solicitor (when it was available) did not, in the main, particularly differ in substance to that generally received from the police, as these cases illustrate:

> I said I would not sign anything until I had contacted a solicitor. They allowed me to make a phone call to my solicitor at home [Belfast]. This was the first contact which I had with the outside world. He advised me to sign the papers as the end result would be the same. The only difference would be that I would go to jail for seven days. I signed the papers on his advice. (418M/86, 50 hours, excluded)

In one case, however, a person received considered legal advice that reflected the fact that statistically representations have been more successful when they have been made before removal. In this instance the prospect of spending time in prison was not presented as daunting nor was it initially considered an obstacle:

> [The solicitor] advised me to appeal [the order] and she thought I might have a better chance of success if I stayed in London. I was told if I stayed I would have to go to Brixton Prison. I said that was fine. The next day I changed my mind as I thought it was hopeless trying to challenge it in England as I would have been thrown in Brixton for seven days and then thrown out anyway. (422M/87, 168 hours, excluded)

One person, who was removed from Britain without challenging his exclusion order in 1978, was later considered to have left voluntarily by the judge hearing the case for a judicial review of his continued exclusion in 1987 (185M/85, 168 hours, excluded). For all those interviewed, however, accepting their exclusion in the first instance and agreeing to be removed was a pragmatic decision. They felt they had little choice – not signing meant remaining in custody, with apparently little hope of successfully challenging the order; signing meant immediate release. As one person put it:

> You have to sign ... you must accept, you must sign ... (255M/85, 168 hours, excluded)

The Journey

Once an exclusion order was signed by the Secretary of State, most people were removed from the country fairly rapidly. In one case the police made a detour to his house for him to pick up his belongings.

> They brought me handcuffed to the house I had been living in. There was nobody in the house so one officer smashed the front window and got in that way. Of course some of the neighbours were out to see what all the commotion was. I was brought into the house and told to collect what was mine. I did this putting it all in bin liners. The landlord of the house came down to ask the police what was going on so they told him that I was being excluded. He wanted to know how much money I had on me as I owed him rent. (419M/86, 168 hours, excluded)

The use of handcuffs was widespread and in a number of cases people were taken in handcuffs onto the boat or aeroplane in full view of other passengers – one woman felt particularly outraged, 'like Ronald Biggs or something' (265F/77, 168 hours, excluded). Most people were escorted on their journey by a police officer.

> They took the cuffs off in the public lounge where I'd spend my time on the journey. It seemed like a public spectacle. I said to myself, I'm not embarrassed, which they were trying to do. (264M/79, 168 hours, excluded)

> It was obvious to people around the airport that I was under arrest. It is very humiliating to be led through the airport with so many people looking at you and think what's going on here? (418M/86, 50 hours, excluded)

> When I got to Heathrow I was taken through the terminal and put on a bus which takes you to the plane with the rest of the passengers. I was handcuffed to one officer and surrounded by all three. The handcuffs were taken off when I got to the steps of the plane. The detective inspector asked the pilot whether he wanted an escort or would he take me over on his own. The pilot said he wanted an escort. So the forensic guy got on the plane and came with me to Belfast. It was obvious to the other passengers that something was going on. (422M/87, 168 hours, excluded)

Seven days in police custody often without a wash or change of clothes added to feelings of embarrassment:

> I felt conspicuous because of the delay and because I was escorted on to the plane – plus the fact I had not been allowed to shave, shower or bath for seven days and I felt dirty. I did not feel my best. (255M/83, 168 hours, excluded)

Apart from feelings of acute embarrassment, some feared they were being left in a situation of personal danger. A Catholic Celtic football supporter, for example, was taken in handcuffs onto a boat, in full view of the Protestant Ranger football supporters travelling on the same crossing. Similarly, a Protestant stated:

> We were frog-marched onto the boat. Everyone noticed, that was the worst of it because we were going to Dublin and I could just imagine someone asking me my name and saying – that's not a Catholic name. (245M/79, 168 hours, excluded)

Such scenarios suggest the police responsible have little understanding or regard for the feelings or potential dangers facing those who live in Northern Ireland or who frequently travel there. One person commented:

> Needless to say that if a loyalist gang had been on the ship I would have been lucky to reach Ireland alive. (253M/83, 168 hours, excluded)

Being able to travel back on the boat without personally holding a ticket was of little assistance to those who found themselves departing late at night, without money and without anyone being informed and therefore able to meet them at their destination.

> We were put onto a boat without any tickets. I asked how we were supposed to get from Larne to Belfast as it would be after midnight when we arrived at Larne. The police just laughed and said that was our problem. As they went they gave us the fingers sign and called us Irish bastards. (196M/80, 168 hours, excluded)

In one case a person had come over to England to buy a black taxi and he was stopped and detained on arrival. He had £800 on him to buy the taxi. When he was about to be put back on the boat after an exclusion order had been served on him, he was told that he owed them a certain amount of money.

> When I asked, 'What for', he says, 'For your ticket'. I says, 'You're putting me out of the country and you want me to pay, that doesn't seem very fair to me', but he said, 'Well that's the fact, you have to pay for this ticket'. They were putting me out of the country and I had to pay for the ticket. It seemed ridiculous to me. Just because I had the money on me I had to pay. It was my father's taxi money and I had to explain to him what had happened to it. I asked what would've happened if I had not had the money. The policeman said, 'Now that's a point, I don't know' – he didn't know what would happen. He said, 'You may go to a solicitor and see if you can claim it back because I don't know anything about it – all I know is that you have to pay it'. (255M/83, 168 hours, excluded)

Since 1987 steps have been taken to ensure that no one now arrives in Northern Ireland too late or with insufficient money to get to home or family. Where necessary, a small amount of money can now be paid out by the police. The cost of exclusion however extends beyond the amount required for travel.

> To get my car back I had to send £100 to my brother-in-law in London and he had to travel up to Liverpool and put it on the boat. (422M/87, 168 hours, excluded)

People released from prison have particular problems. This is acknowledged in the 1985 Annual Report of Sir Cyril Philips. He discovered that arrangements for the exclusion of prisoners provided only for a deportee's allowance of £2.50, even in the absence of any assurance that relatives would fill the breach.[1] The difficulties generally experienced by people released from prison are well documented. These can only be exacerbated if plans and support networks are disrupted at short notice by exclusion:

> After my release [from prison] I intended to live in Liverpool where I had two jobs to go to and a home with the friends I had been living with before my arrest and conviction. However, at 6.15 p.m. on the evening before my release … I was informed that I was to be excluded from Britain. (249M/85, 168 hours, excluded)

On arrival in Northern Ireland, excludees were seldom stopped as they passed through security and appeared not to be treated as a threat.

> At Aldergrove I was free to walk out and carry on with my life except I could not go back to Britain. (245M/79, 168 hours, excluded)

> I was free to wander around the boat and walk off it in Belfast. (255M/83, 168 hours, excluded)

> Once on the plane, I had no problems from then on. My wife met me at the airport. The solicitor had contacted her and told her what flight I would be arriving on. (418M/86, 168 hours, excluded)

Representations after Removal

Despite receiving a written notice explaining that representations could be made after removal, a number of people were clearly unaware that this had been possible:

> At the time I did not realise I could write to the Secretary of State and object to my exclusion ... I thought there was nothing I could do about it because I had chosen to go home rather than appeal and be sent to Brixton Prison (251M/80, 168 hours, excluded)

> I was never told I could make representations within 14 days of returning to Northern Ireland ... When I did get home I didn't know what to do. I just wanted to forget all about it. They had told me that this exclusion order lasted for three years and it would expire automatically. (419M/86, 168 hours, excluded)

One person, excluded at a time when only written representations were possible following removal, decided not to take up this opportunity or seek legal advice:

> I felt there was not much point in seeing a solicitor when I got back. (246M/79, 168 hours, excluded)

Another person in the same situation had his order revoked after seeking legal advice:

I was excluded for about six months, they revoked the order ... I just went to see a solicitor. (358M/79, 168 hours, excluded)

Another, amongst the first to be given the opportunity to see an adviser after removal, chose not to bother to see a solicitor since he felt that as he was employed he was ineligible for legal aid. He did not make any representations. (256M/81, 168 hours, excluded)

Two people excluded after 1984, one of them straight from prison, contacted solicitors who arranged a meeting with an adviser. Another, excluded in 1979 (and therefore before interviews after removal became a possibility) found his solicitor advising against his desire to challenge his exclusion in court:

I was advised ... that I probably would not get any satisfaction and I should just forget about it. At the time I certainly felt I would not get a fair hearing so I did not bother. (245M/78, 168 hours, excluded)

Another, finding himself in the same situation in 1983, found a lawyer willing to take his case but decided, in the end, not to bother (269M/83, 168 hours, excluded). This reaction was shared by a number of those excluded before 1984 who were not really interested in making written representations or who were simply glad that their detention was over and wanted to forget about their experience:

At the time I did not write to the Secretary of State about the exclusion – I could not be bothered, I was just glad it was all over. (250M/79, 168 hours, excluded)

Only one made representations with the assistance of his MP, who attempted to call the Secretary of State to account for his decision:

[My MP] brought it up in the House of Commons – asking for what reason I had been excluded. The British Government wouldn't give him a reason at all, they refused to answer, he was just told it concerned the Special Branch; it was their territory and they didn't answer questions on it. (259M/85, 168 hours, excluded)

Interview with Adviser

An adviser may be seen either before removal, after removal or after a new order has been issued. The main feature of interviews with advisers was that at no time was the person ever informed about the case against them. Most of the questions focused upon the person's lifestyle and family circumstances.

> Myself and the solicitor went to Castlereagh and the adviser just listened to my side of the story, asked questions about my family background and took notes. He was fairly vague about when I might hear if my exclusion order would be revoked, emphasizing that the decision to revoke was not his, but Douglas Hurd's. In fact he was really only a messenger who wasn't there to judge or make decisions. (418M/86, 50 hours, excluded)

> My solicitor accompanied me to Ladas Drive police station where I had an interview with the government's adviser that lasted from 11.45 a.m. to 12.25 p.m. At the outset he made it plain that he was there to assess my case and report to the Home Secretary who would make the final decision. He asked me my date of birth and questions ranging from the time of my first prison sentence to the present day. I was asked why I had been charged and what I had been charged with on both occasions. He particularly wanted to know why I wanted to go back to Liverpool to live when my roots were in NI. He asked me if my parents were still alive and who would look after them if I went back to Liverpool. He seemed concerned to establish that I was not thinking of going back to Liverpool to finish the job off or that the man involved would not try to get me ... At the end of the interview he summed up what had been said and gave what I thought was a clear, acute picture of the situation. He told me that he would be going to Liverpool for some interviews and would be on holiday for several weeks before making his written report to the Home Secretary. I thought he gave me a fair hearing but I consider my exclusion to be a double punishment. (249M/85, 168 hours, excluded)

Review

About half of those interviewed who took part in a review of their order or who knew a review was taking place had been contacted by the Home Office. The remainder had made their own enquiries to the Home Office or had been informed by Liberty that a review of their case was due. The majority made written representations to the Home Office or completed the Home Office form used for this purpose. There was, however, little enthusiasm expressed for the process, or belief that they would be treated fairly:

> I got a review paper but I ignored it. (343M/78, 168 hours, excluded)

> Later I received papers from the government stating it was time for a review and to fill in the appropriate forms. I took the bother of filling in the forms, just more or less reiterating what I had already said to the police – I did not bother forwarding them; so I have not really been through a review procedure and I have had no further communication whatsoever. If the three year procedure is followed I would say I am due another review sometime this year. (245M/79, 168 hours, excluded)

> About three years later [in 1982] I received a letter from the Home Office which I filled in and sent off. I got no reply and was not told whether the exclusion order had been lifted or not ... I have not heard anything from the Home Office since. (246M/79, 168 hours, excluded)

> I got a letter from the NI office saying I could appeal my case which I did. They sent me another letter saying to meet a chief policeman from England at Castlereagh Police Centre. (195M/80, 168 hours, excluded)

Another person wasn't really interested until:

> I got a letter from the Home Office saying if you wish, your case will be brought up again, just fill in and send it back, yes or no. So I filled in the form and sent it back. They asked me to an interview and I went to Castlereagh. (261M/77, 72 hours, excluded)

> I appealed, we got all the paper work during 1983 and they asked me to go to Castlereagh to be interviewed by two Metropolitan Police officers. (303M/80, 168 hours, excluded)

> I received no communication from the Home Office. I was expecting to hear about a review. Following advice from the Committee on the Administration of Justice [I] went in December 1984 to see a solicitor with the intention of writing a letter as a form of appeal against

my exclusion. I do not know whether the solicitor sent this letter and the police said they did not receive it. After my MP had approached the Home Office on my behalf I received a form to fill in at the end of April 1985, which I completed and returned ... saying I would be willing to attend an interview with a member of the Metropolitan Police. (256M/81, 168 hours, excluded)

For the review I had a solicitor. I got him through the Workers Revolutionary Party so he got all the gen sorted out for me, what I done was I just wrote a letter to them myself asking for an interview and they said they'd get in touch with me and get me information. They set up an interview for me. (380M/79, 168 hours, excluded)

All those who participated were offered interviews with the Metropolitan Police. Most were asked to attend an interview at Castlereagh Police Station in Ladas Drive, Belfast, although one was interviewed in Castle Street and another offered a venue of their choice.

A number declined to attend because the venue offered was Castlereagh Holding Centre:

The Home Office wrote ... saying if I wanted a review I had to go to Castlereagh for an interview. It is not a place I ever want to go to so I did not reply and I have heard nothing since. (250M/79, 168 hours, excluded)

... I refused [to go to the interview]. Then I got a letter saying that the appeal had been turned down and that the exclusion order still stood. They said they had refused it because I didn't go for the interview. I don't know why they had to choose Castlereagh – nobody would go to Castlereagh unless they were forced. (303M/80, 168 hours, excluded)

[Castlereagh] is miles from my home. I did not go to him [the police] as I thought it was just a ploy to get me up there to hold me for a couple of days. Also the last time I was in Castlereagh I was beat about ... I got no reply after that so I took it that I would have to wait another four years as that is the how long you have to wait. (195M/80, 168 hours, excluded)

One was arrested on the day of his interview and was prevented from attending.

After I had filled in and returned the forms sent by the Home Office I got another letter saying I was to go to Castlereagh at 1.30 p.m. on a certain day to be interviewed by a member of the Metropolitan Police. I intended to go – but I went a little earlier than expected. At 5 o'clock in the morning the RUC came to my house, told me I was under arrest and I was being taken to Castlereagh. I said I was going in at 1.30 anyway but I was told I was going in now – I thought the police were bringing me in early. In fact I was held for five days and questioned about something that happened when I was a kid. I was told the (Metropolitan) police officer was coming to see me that night, then I was told he would be seeing me later on. I think if he had come over he would have spoken to me – but under those circumstances even if he had he would not have gone away with a very high opinion of me anyway. It seems very strange to me that the RUC should take that particular day to bring me in and start talking about something that happened 10 or 11 years beforehand. Later on I got a letter saying the Home Office had decided not to revoke the exclusion order; it never mentioned the fact that I had not had my interview. This happened about (1983) ... I did see a solicitor about it but I have heard nothing since and I do not know if you can get legal aid to fight an exclusion. I do not think the decision really rests with the Secretary of State anyway since he does not know you and is likely just to go by what the police tell him. (251M/80, 168 hours, excluded)

Security is the reason given for the choice of Castlereagh as a venue for interviews although its use has been recognized as a problem. Not only do many not wish to attend because of its reputation, but being seen to go to Castlereagh could also involve a risk to personal safety: it is an environment where informers are actively encouraged to come forward by the authorities and where paramilitary organisations on both sides execute anyone who is discovered to be an informer.

One person who refused to attend an interview at Castlereagh was offered an alternative with a Home Office adviser at the Department of Employment building in Belfast: their new exclusion was successfully challenged and the order revoked.

The greater flexibility announced over interview venues may therefore encourage more participation, although the usefulness of the process also remained an open question for many who did attend.

Use of Solicitors

Few had taken advice from a solicitor about their exclusion or its review and fewer were accompanied to their interview by a solicitor. Three reasons were given; not aware that a solicitor could be present, belief that a solicitor was too expensive, and did not wish one to be present.

> I asked if a solicitor could come with me. I asked a policeman at Castlereagh. I didn't ask officially to the Home Office. I took their [the police officer's] word for it. I asked him about the solicitor and he said, 'Well I'll enquire'. He did enquire because I think they said at the interview, 'I hear you want a solicitor', and I said, 'Yes' and he said, 'Why do you want a solicitor?' But they wouldn't allow me one. (380M/79, 168 hours, excluded)

Type of questions

Questions varied from interview to interview. The method appeared to be anything from asking the same pattern of questions as asked during the interrogation directly preceding the exclusion, to a general conversation. All, however, were asked about their employment, friends, family and associates, their political views and their family's political views.

> I don't remember what questions they asked me very well, near on the same things as when I was held. The interview must have been an hour at least. They asked me why I wanted it revoked. I said, 'Just in case I want to go over to England for a holiday'. (261M/77, 72 hours, excluded)

One claimed that certain general allegations were made about his political affiliations and reasons for travelling when arrested and excluded: it was believed he had travelled to Britain to buy arms. This at least provided an opportunity to make a response.

> ... They told me then (at the interview) that I wouldn't get back (to Britain). At the interview they asked me what they'd asked me in Stranraer – they must have had a sort of copy of what had happened there. I remembered what they'd said to me in Stranraer and he was

more or less repeating what was asked over there, and he was wanting to see the answers to see if they were the same, they were following the same pattern of answers and questions ... They started off the interview just by saying, 'Look, before we go any further there's no use in you wasting our time because you have to tell the truth'. So he started asking questions, asking, 'Was I in the IRA'. I say, 'No'. And they say, 'We've got a dossier'. And so I say, 'How is it I wasn't in jail for something if you've got all this information?' And he says, 'Well you were in jail for 14 months'. And I say, 'That's right, remanded I mean'. And he said, 'What happened?' 'The judge threw out the case'. I said, 'I shouldn't even have been remanded. I was one of the lucky ones – there were guys in for two or three years'. They asked me if my feelings had changed. I just told them what I'd said in Stranraer ... I've got a good memory like that. (380M/79, 168 hours, excluded)

In another case, a person who had been served with an exclusion order shortly after coming out of prison made great efforts a number of years later to get his exclusion order lifted because he had been offered a job in France. After two years he received a letter saying that his case was up for review and he was called to a pre-exclusion order review interview. The case illustrates the type of questions which are considered to be important and the extent of the information which the authorities collect, from informers and others, on individuals.

They seemed to be more interested in – the interview wasn't like the same interview you'd get if you were being held in England under the PTA. It was an entirely different interview altogether. I wasn't even prepared for it because I thought it was going to be the same intelligence gathering interview, where it would be menacing, they would be asking you specific questions, as they do when they hold you in England. But it was a more relaxed affair and it wasn't as menacing ... . But they did ask specific questions like did I know any paramilitary, did I drink in any clubs where any paramilitaries associate, and I just said, 'Look, I don't know any paramilitary and as regards drinking in any paramilitary clubs, I don't even know where there are any paramilitary clubs' and things like that, you know. They asked me specific was I a political. I said, 'No'. They asked me what I thought of Gerry Adams and various aspects of atrocities that have happened recently. They were asking me what my views were on such things and they said, 'Would you go to England if you got the order lifted?' and I said, 'Not necessarily. The reason I want the order lifted is not specifically just to go to England, it's the principle of the thing'. I told them I had an objection because it was an infringement of my liberties and things like that and it wasn't the fact that I just wanted to cart off to England. I might never go to England, and they asked me why – and I said, 'Because I would probably be frightened of going, because I could be fitted up over there quite easily'. And they said, 'Do you believe that that sort of thing happens?' I said, 'Yes, it does happen', and they just laughed and said, 'It doesn't'. They were young, both of them were young. One did most of the talking, the other guy was sitting just futering through files and he was just adding the odd question. He just said two trivial little things, which startled me, because he couldn't possibly have known that kind of information, it was trivial. One was – when I was in prison in 1978 I got into a fight in a cell with a guy, now nobody outside the cell really knew about that, it was just a skirmish, right, the authorities didn't know about it, if they had it would have ended up in my record. And the guy's from Armagh, the fellow I was fighting with, so it never went any further than the prisoners in the wing, yet he mentioned it. Now I found that really amazing and I said to him, 'How do you know that kind of information?' Had it been on my file in prison, if I'd been adjudicated in prison for it, then he would have known that because it would have been easier to get, because I'm sure they've looked at my prison files anyway, but it wasn't, and I knew it wasn't and I was amazed. I've no idea how he knew it. He mentioned another trivial item. I can't remember what it was, but it was so trivial you wouldn't remember what it was, and I says to him, how do you know these two snippets of information – the other thing was concerning prison as well – he just mentioned another prisoner's name to me – a person I'd been in the cell with, on the blanket, but who I had never had any association with afterwards or anything. It was just a guy I met in transit and that was it. As was the other fellow as well. One was from Armagh and the other was another Belfast fellow who I've never laid eyes on from that time, and that's going back to 1978/79. So he mentioned those two specific items, which really startled me you know, and he looked at me when he mentioned it, to see how startled I was and I think what he was trying to say to me was the amount of information we have on you is staggering, so don't be sitting here trying to bullshit us, because we know everything. So I just said to them well, if you know that kind of information you must also know then that I'm not a member of any organisation or whatever, because let's face it, to be able to pick up on snippets of information like that there, if I was going into republican clubs, if I was guilty by association in any way, you'd certainly know about it, and they never elaborated on it, they never accused me of anything, they never even suggested – well, they tried to suggest in a way, but they never point-blank turned round and said, 'Well, we know you are a sympathiser, or we have seen you with sympathisers', they never said anything specific like that, they just kept asking me if I knew sympathisers and suchlike. (421M/87, 72 hours, excluded)

What is clear from this evidence is that the interview system does not enable the excludee to cross-examine any evidence or directly respond to any specific allegations. On the contrary, the purpose is to conceal the source and content of any information. Whatever the actual decision following a review, the net effect of asking for a review is that the Special Branch gets to update its security file on the person involved.

Conclusions

From all accounts exclusion orders are 'inherently arbitrary and oppressive'.[2] We have seen from the 30 cases described in this chapter how it is possible for a person and their family to be uprooted from one part of the United Kingdom and exiled to another part, or to the Republic of Ireland. Exclusion orders provide the police with the enormous power to remove anyone they wish. However careful the Secretary of State may be in granting an order and however thorough any subsequent review of the operation of these powers, the fact remains that the initial case against the person is constructed by the police and is at no time subject to any independent examination.

In Chapter 8 we described the huge imbalance of power which exists between the detainee and the police during police custody and interrogation. Much of the information on which exclusion orders are based will have been obtained during the interrogations of a wide range of people. It will be a product of supposition, suggestion and prejudice.

The law suggests that the person who is being excluded has a number of important rights, such as the right of representation before or after removal and the right to an interview with an adviser. But as we have seen, these have little or no substance in practice. It is a mockery to suggest that a person has a right to appeal against an exclusion order when that entails a penalty of a further period of detention. Similarly, to suggest that a person has a right to an interview with an adviser when they are never told what the evidence is against them is to confuse and distort. In practice, exclusion orders, as we will show in more detail in the next chapter, involve a serious deprivation of civil liberties. They affect people's freedom of movement, the right to family life, the right to associate freely with others, the right to participate in public affairs and the right to seek work.

Exclusion orders not only affect the person on whom they are served. The partner and children of the subject of the exclusion order also suffer considerable disruption. If they accompany the excludee, they suffer all the loss of rights that he or she has suffered. If they do not, family life is broken up. Moreover, the poorer economic prospects in Northern Ireland and the Republic further compound the stresses and strains which stem from exclusion orders.

11 The Impact of the Acts

Introduction

This chapter analyses the overall impact of the operation of the PTA on people's lives. There are a number of different dimensions which need to be explored. To begin with, the experience of an arrest, detention and examination may have a profound physical and psychological affect on those detained. While some may recover from the experience fairly quickly, others may not forget it in their lifetime. An arrest and detention may also directly affect people's relationships with their family and friends, their employment prospects and their attitude towards the law. At the same time, the PTA has an influence which goes beyond the impact on those who are directly affected by the use of its powers. In particular, there is strong evidence that it may restrict perfectly legitimate political activity and debate around the Northern Ireland question through the creation of a climate of fear, the direct harassment of people and groups involved in Irish politics, and by censorship.

The study relied upon people making their own assessment of the impact of the Acts: it was impracticable to conduct any independent medical or psychological tests on people's physical and mental health. It was also impossible, because of the focus of the study on those directly affected, to examine the impact of the Acts on those who have never been arrested or detained but nevertheless have altered their behaviour, changed their attitudes or have been affected in some other way by the existence of the legislation. But some people did report on the broader impact of the Acts and this information is included. The objective then is to draw together all the various ways in which people have been adversely affected.

Physical and Mental Health

Adults

There were a number of cases in which people reported a significant impact on their physical health. One person described how she felt after a relatively short detention of 10 hours.

I suppose you know, it drains you, and I had to go into work that afternoon because the painters were coming and I had to give them a key, and I sat and worked for two hours and I was just wrecked. There was no way I could do any work at all. I was just there for that sole purpose and once the painters came and took the key off me I was going to be out of the door. For the rest of that day I never ate a bite. It just shatters you altogether. (398F/85, 10 hours, released)

In another case, a person who had experienced considerable fear during his detention was unable to eat and lost weight.

I was so frightened. I never ate one thing for four days. I drank many cups of tea, but I never touched anything. I was 11 pounds lighter when I got home than when I left. (521M/88, 96 hours, excluded)

In other cases the consequences were more severe. Two weeks after her detention a woman started to have problems with her pregnancy.

The pregnancy had been great and then it was about a week or two after I came back that I started having pains – it was agony. I went to the doctor's and he said a slow labour had started, and then it was a ruptured membrane ... everything just went wrong after that – she was six weeks premature. It just went on – and this was all just after that had happened. I don't know for sure if it was related to the stress of the detention. I never told the doctor about it and whenever I think about it, it was silly. The doctors asked me if there had been anything that had annoyed me and I just said no, which was stupid. It isn't an easy thing to discuss. (318F/79, 72 hours, released)

According to one lawyer who has had considerable experience of handling PTA cases, women often experience irregularities in their menstrual cycle after being arrested and detained under the PTA.[1]
A detention is often deleterious to the person's mental health.

While my breakdown was related to the death of my husband, I believed my detention the previous June contributed to my illness and my general feeling of being unstable, upset and paranoid. In hospital I had been put in a side-room on my own. I thought I was back at the Bridewell and at times became very deluded. I thought many of the medical staff were police spies and I had a feeling of being surveilled. (165F/83, 31 hours, released)

Other people described a range of different psychological symptoms.

> After the detention I was off work for six or seven weeks. I was like
> a wreck, going to the doctor and getting tablets and on top of that
> my brother and myself started arguing among ourselves. I came out
> all jumpy, nervous and found it very hard to listen to people. It made
> me very self-conscious – you always think they're watching.
> (399M/81, 4 days, released)

In another case a person who had been held for seven days and charged
with conspiracy to cause explosions had a frightening experience while
on remand.

> My beard stopped growing and my hair started to fall out. When I
> went to see the prison doctor he asked me if I had experienced a
> serious shock recently. (900M/88, 7 days, charged and acquitted)

Two people are known to have died shortly after being arrested and
detained under the PTA. It is obviously impossible to say categorically
that their deaths were caused by their experience, however all the
evidence points in that direction.

A man and his wife were arrested by armed police in their house in
1981. They were taken to Rochester Road police station and seven days
later released without charge. They had been kept in solitary confinement in windowless cells with 24-hour artificial light, minimal toilet
facilities, daily interrogations by the Anti-Terrorist Squad, and no
access to a solicitor.[2] In 1982 the husband, who had no previous history
of psychiatric problems, committed suicide.

In the second case, two Protestants from Northern Ireland who
came to live in Britain in 1947 were arrested by armed police and accused
of being involved with the IRA and connected with the Harrods
bombing.[3] The wife was released six hours later but the husband was
held for 39 hours and then released on police bail. No charges were ever
brought against them. They began proceedings against the police for
wrongful arrest but were advised by Queen's Counsel not to proceed.
He died a year and a half after the arrest. In the words of his wife:

> At the moment I am totally devastated and feel that the incident and
> its aftermath probably contributed to my husband's death. ... My
> dearest wish now is to clear our names. (140F/84, 6 hours, released)

Children

It was pointed out in Chapter 3 that there is no official information on the number of children who are affected by the operation of the PTA. In this study a number of children were directly or indirectly affected as a result of their parents being stopped and detained at ports or being arrested inland. In Chapter 5 we described the psychological impact on one child. But there are other examples. In one case a woman and her children had been stopped and detained at a port.

> It even had a bit of an effect on the children afterwards ... you're afraid of them having an accident – he was wetting the bed every night. My husband put it down to the detention. (318F/79, 96 hours, released)

In another case a man was travelling over from Belfast to Scotland with his son to see a football match when they were both stopped. His son, however, was allowed to go on to Glasgow with a friend. His mother takes up the story:

> Although my son was with someone he knew in Glasgow he had been very frightened and cried on the phone to me when I had been contacted on the evening of my husband's detention. I tried to reassure him that his dad would be released, although at this stage I only knew that he had been detained at Stranraer. At 3 a.m. the RUC came to the house to tell me that my husband was being held in Stranraer under the PTA. Fortunately, I knew already or it would have been a terrible shock as they surrounded the house and banged on the door as if they were going to raid it. Although I knew my son was with a friend in Glasgow I did ask them if they knew where he was and if he was all-right. They said, 'We've hardly arrested him' – that was the only information they gave me about my son. If I could have got to Glasgow that night I would have gone. Afterwards he talked a lot about it. (252M/83, 23 hours, released)

In a third case, a widow was prevented from returning to her two children who were being looked after by her parents. She had attended a women's conference in London and was detained at Heathrow on the way out. She was then taken to Rochester Road police station. She asked if they could get in contact with her family, but her request was refused until some four hours after her initial detention (272F/81, 24 hours, released).

Family and Social Life

As well as affecting the physical and mental health of other members
of the family, an arrest or detention can wreak havoc with a whole
network of family relationships. As one person put it:

> It's a hell of a disruption in your family ... because it doesn't only
> affect – it should be a lesson, for the State really – that it doesn't only
> affect your family, yourself and your wife and child, it ricochets
> right round your own family, your own brothers and sisters are
> affected by it. People who are very reasonable and very liberal-
> minded people prior to that sort of thing happening to a member of
> the family suddenly become a little bit agitated and then they think,
> hang on a minute. They become critical. (311M/81, 72 hours,
> released)

The police will sometimes visit a detainee's parents and ask them
questions. This, of course, can be extremely worrying and traumatic for
them and may have an everlasting impact, as it did in one case, on the
relationship between members of the family.

> They questioned my parents. I don't know how many times. But
> when they released me they even had my parents at the station
> asking them to make statements, and they took my car as well for
> forensic tests. My relationship with my parents is very bad now. My
> mother nearly had a nervous breakdown about it, she'd never known
> anything like it in her life. My stepfather hasn't spoken to me hardly
> at all since though. At first he was very nice when I came out, he was
> very upset.

A detention can also affect friendships. The subject of the case above
continues:

> I haven't really kept in contact with my friends over the last few weeks
> with the police following me; I was frightened to get in contact with
> any of them because they might have contacted them as well. The
> police checked up on me at hospital ... I presume that they wanted
> to look at my medical records too because they also wanted to know
> why I was going to natal classes ... So the people at the hospital know
> all about it as well but I haven't had any come-back from them.
> (397F/85, 72 hours, released)

The way in which a detention may influence one's friendships was graphically described in another case.

> To have been the victim of the PTA is like being a carrier of a plague germ. You can never tell who will have heard about it, or what attitude they will take to you. This produces in one a fear of mixing in social circles where there is no experience of the PTA: and thus one slowly becomes ghettoised. When one meets people who have had direct experience of the PTA it is possible, and only possible there, to talk frankly about the situation produced by its operation. One finds, for example, those who have had their houses searched in an overt fashion in order to frighten them off from political activity and also to notify their neighbours that they are plague-carriers. In my particular way of life the threat is more subtle and less crude: the effects of it are exactly the same. (223F/80, 12 hours, released)

Another lived in a housing co-op of about 12 houses.

> So we all knew each other, and there was about 12 houses and afterwards a lot of people avoided any sort of contact with us. People tended to avoid us. I'm sure due to possible repercussions if we'd be arrested again and they'd be arrested possibly along with us because at that time not only people involved in the Irish Republican Socialist Party were arrested – two, possibly three people who had no involvement with the Irish Republican Socialist Party (IRSP) or any politics at all had been arrested with us, one Indian and two English people. (401M/81, 196 hours, released)

The most drastic consequences for family life and friendships occur when one member of a family is issued with an exclusion order, typically the husband. The rest of the family are forced to uproot. The wife may have to give up her job, children are taken away from school and their friends, the house has to be sold or re-let and the whole family forced to live in either Northern Ireland or the Republic. Since there has been a considerable amount of intermarrying between Irish and English people over the years, the making of an exclusion order may force one of the partners and their children to leave their country of origin.[4]

Once a person has been excluded, access to the extended family is blocked and the person cannot attend any family occasions such as births, weddings or funerals. For example:

This exclusion order has made my life very difficult. Apart from having my character blackened in my home country, Scotland, it upsets my family life as I can't go north to visit my in-laws and relations. I couldn't even go to the birth of my son in October 1984 in Belfast and I never saw him or my wife for nearly four weeks because of this. (389M/84, 120 hours, excluded)

Even when an exclusion order has been lifted, there may still be a reluctance to travel.

I was invited to a wedding last month – the end of July – in Paisley in Glasgow. I wanted to go. I should've gone because there was no exclusion order on me then but I didn't. I intend to go at Christmas or November or whenever it is and I'll have a number of a solicitor over there. The friends that I go to – one of them is married to a solicitor so it would probably be only a matter of arranging the two telephone numbers. But I've got a funny feeling that I would probably get through this time but again you would never know. (201M/85, 31 hours, excluded)

An arrest and detention followed by an exclusion order played havoc with one couple's honeymoon.

The exclusion didn't have any effect on my life but it obviously disrupted our honeymoon. We had things planned and we couldn't do them. Places to go, etc. We didn't lose any money over it apart from ruining our honeymoon. (261M/78, 72 hours, excluded)

Exclusion orders also prevent contact with brothers, sisters and other members of the extended family.

I have relatives over there (England) who I like to go and see and now I can't go. When I was young I used to go to England all the time because I had relatives there; I always felt part of it. (264M/79, 168 hours, excluded)

I'd obviously like to go and see my family in England but I can't. (307M/82, 72 hours, excluded)

I would like to go to England on holiday or visit my sister. My wife and I would like to go to Blackpool but I can't go. (255M/83, 196 hours excluded)

Employment

When an employed person is detained or arrested under the PTA they have no opportunity to notify their employer that they will be missing from work for an indefinite period. If they are held incommunicado for the first 48 hours, it may be three days before they can get a message through. Whatever happens, they are going to look very irresponsible. At the same time they are faced with the dilemma of what to say. Few people would wish to admit that they are being held under the PTA, not only because of the opprobrium attached to it but also because it might affect their future employment prospects.

There were a number of different ways the PTA affected people's work. Some were unable to go back to work because of the trauma of their ordeal.

When I came back I didn't go to work for a full week because it had knocked me back, I don't think I slept much while I was there, while I was in the cell. I must have slept a couple of hours maybe but no more. So when I got back I was exhausted so I just had to take a week off work. And I didn't get paid. (253M/83, 48 hours, released)

Other people lost their wages.

When I went back to work they said that they didn't have to account for my wages. Then I wrote to the police and I didn't get a reply ... So I lost my wages. (311M/81, 48 hours, released)

Others felt that their future job prospects were damaged as a direct result of being detained.

As a theatre worker, my career has been strongly affected. When I was first stopped under the PTA, I was carrying a letter from [a theatre] inviting me to discuss with them a major production of one of my plays. Subsequently this project was never mentioned: and I have had no further communication with that director. I can only assume the police got in touch with him. In 1980 I was invited by a theatre group in New York to go over there, stay on the premises, and work on a production of my plays about Ireland. After some time the people who had invited me cancelled all their part in the work and ordered me off their premises without explanation. (223F/80, 12 hours, released)

Of all the powers under the PTA it is perhaps the exclusion power which has the most impact on employment. Anyone who was working in Britain prior to being served with an exclusion order immediately lost their job as a result.

A number were travelling over to take up a job when they were stopped and consequently found themselves back in Northern Ireland, unemployed:

As a result of my exclusion I could not take up my job in London, where I had intended to settle for a while. Instead I found myself back in Belfast, unemployed. (251M/80, 196 hours, excluded)

If my exclusion order was lifted I would be able to find work. Whenever I want to go there (England) there's a job there for me if I want it or for when I can get over to take it. (303M/80, 196 hours, excluded)

One person in the study was following an academic career and found himself unable to attend conferences or meet other academics in his field, as well as being unable to attend any interviews or take up any job in Britain (185M/79, 196 hours, excluded).

Another, who found employment following his exclusion to the Republic, experienced difficulties because of his inability to travel to Northern Ireland:

I am employed in the border town of Dundalk as a mechanic; a lot of our ordinary breakdown, recovery work is in the north and as I can't cross the border my job is in jeopardy. (389M/81, 120 hours, excluded)

More generally, the fact that a person has been excluded makes it more difficult to find work.

When you go looking for a job after being excluded and your name has been in the paper and people read it, they start thinking that you must be a terrorist. It's impossible to get a job. The sad reality of the situation is that nobody now wants to employ me. (419M/86, 196 hours, excluded)

Not everyone falls on hard times. One exclusion order had little impact on one man's employment prospects.

It hasn't made the slightest difference to my business, no way. I have to go via Dublin now when I go abroad but it's an easy job to drive up to Dublin airport. But it's not always so easy for other people. (343M/78, 196 hours, excluded)

This case appears to be exceptional, however. All the evidence suggests that the impact of the PTA on employment prospects has been considerable and in some cases fear has even forced people to give up their current jobs in Britain and move back to Northern Ireland.

In England there were lots of people from Cookstown. After I was arrested, most of them came back to Northern Ireland even though they were working and had good jobs, because they were afraid that the same thing would happen to them. A lot of them returned to Northern Ireland and those who didn't moved to other parts of London. (419M/86, 196 hours, excluded)

Freedom of Movement

The PTA has had a significant impact on people's freedom of movement. Exclusion orders stop people from travelling within the United Kingdom or between the United Kingdom and Ireland. The extensive examination powers at ports and airports have forced people to alter their behaviour. People no longer carry their cheque books or other personal documents such as diaries, for fear of being stopped and forced to produce them for investigation by an examining officer. It is also now a common practice for people to carry the name of a solicitor and to phone home before the plane or boat departs and make arrangements to phone on arrival so that if there is any undue delay in the return call investigations can be started to find out what has happened to them.

The PTA has also forced people to avoid certain routes between Britain and Ireland. A number of people now try and avoid travelling via Heathrow, for example. One person who was last detained at

Liverpool airport but who had previously been examined at Heathrow said:

> These experiences have affected my attitude to using Heathrow and I feel discriminated against in terms of gaining entry to Heathrow as an international airport. I would now choose to travel to Dublin for an international flight. (235M/81, 25 hours, released)

> I have had problems with Heathrow in the past and I remember saying I was not going to England again because I was being held up each time I went. (240F/81, 48 hours, released)

Another person from Northern Ireland now flies into Heathrow via Dublin rather than Belfast.

> When I had to travel abroad I chose to go from Dublin not Belfast. I travelled to Dublin to go to Heathrow ... I thought there just wasn't so much pressure on people when they arrived from Dublin. I thought I would definitely have been picked up if I had come into Heathrow from Belfast and was travelling to Beirut. (272F/81, 24 hours, released)

> If I had the choice I would travel some other route rather than go via London/Britain if I was going to the Continent. However, as often or not you more or less have to go through Britain either because you have to contact other people there or because it is much more expensive to go by another route. (247M/84, 12 hours, released)

> It put me off coming back to this country in case I have to go through it all again. I think that I will go through Dublin, ... because unless I get a new passport I will be hassled. (393F/85, 3 hours, released)

As well as making people feel reluctant to travel via London it has also made people frightened about travelling over to Ireland.

> I feel that I would probably be stopped and maybe held for a couple of hours or something ... That's one of the things it does, makes people much more nervous about travelling to Ireland. (392F/79, 30 hours, released).

Freedom of movement is curtailed most, of course, by the making of an exclusion order, but the use of exclusion orders is not without a number of contradictions to which various people drew attention.

My initial reaction was to feel poorly done by to say the least. That although a citizen of Britain I was being denied access to it for no reason that I could see. (245M/79, 196 hours, excluded)

It seems that I, a British citizen who was born in Scotland, can't travel freely over all of the UK (i.e. not in NI) – it is after all claimed to be all part of the one country, although I don't necessarily agree with this. When I travel home to Scotland, instead of going north through Larne to Stranraer and Glasgow at a cost of about £35 return, I have to travel Dublin–Glasgow for £150. (389M/81, 120 hours, excluded)

I couldn't understand me holding a British passport and not being able to walk over to Britain. To me it's stupidity. They would class me as a British citizen and I'm not allowed into Britain. I can't understand it at all. (269M/83, 196 hours, excluded)

Financial Consequences

The operation of the PTA has had severe financial consequences for some. We have already pointed out that wages may be lost when a person is being held or in some cases they may lose the job itself. There are other financial consequences. Examinations may force people to miss their connections and as a result have to make alternative travel or accommodation arrangements.

A number of people who were arrested complained about the damage caused by the police on gaining entry to make the arrest. Others drew attention to the damage done as a result of house searches. Some received compensation but it was insufficient to cover their losses. In one case, a couple attempted to make a statement of claim against the police totalling over £4,500 but were advised by Senior Counsel that they would have little hope of success (140M/84, 39 hours, released). Others made no claims. In one case, a person who was charged, held on remand in prison and then acquitted found that his house had been ransacked by squatters while he was inside.

During the time I was detained my house was burgled and squatted by homeless people. All my belongings were either sold or thrown away. I literally lost everything that I owned in my past life. My photographs and things like were all gone. You know clothes, furniture, everything. I just sort of salvaged what was left. A few pictures on the wall, and a few clothes, and I moved house immediately I was released. (900M/89, 168 hours, charged and acquitted)

Confidence in the Law

Public confidence in the law is essential in a democracy, otherwise people may resort to other methods of seeking redress. The riots in Los Angeles in April 1992 – following the jury verdict which acquitted four police officers charged with assault – illustrated this starkly. Lack of public confidence in the law played a significant part in the development of the current round of conflict in Northern Ireland.[5] When widespread political violence occurs, the authorities face a dilemma: how to achieve law and order when order can be achieved only at the expense of law. As one person expressed it:

You see, the big moral dilemma for the British is how far can you push repression, how far can you hold down a struggling people? With unjust laws on a people you are not advancing civilisation, you're taking it back a hundred years until you arrive at a very primitive stage where justice becomes an unknown concept – unknown. Just try to visualise what the world would be like if there was no such thing as a sense of justice, and a sense of justice depends on respect, of being respected and having the respect and confidence of people. When you lose that you're lost everything. (343M/78, 196 hours, excluded)

There is much evidence from this study to show the way in which the use of the PTA has led to a decline in people's confidence in all aspects of the law, from the police to the courts.

After what happened to me in Scotland I could never have any confidence in [the police] in my life again; after them telling that they knew I wasn't involved in anything and yet that they went and done that on me.

He also wrote to the Prime Minister asking why it had happened to him. The Prime Minister's office passed the letter to the office of the relevant chief constable.

> I got a letter from the chief constable saying that the complaint that I had made against the police was being looked into and that they would be in contact about it. But I wasn't complaining about the police, because at no time did they hit me or anything, but I was writing to her [i.e. Mrs Thatcher] for her to explain to me why this had all happened to me. (269M/83, 196 hours, excluded)

A number felt a profound sense of injustice.

> I was stripped of my rights as a citizen. They can do what they like, tell you what they like. I felt I had no rights whatsoever. I am sorry I didn't just give my name and address and date of birth, because I still got excluded anyway, even when I did cooperate. These people don't believe you are telling the truth, even if you are telling the truth; they just don't believe you. As far as they are concerned, you are a terrorist, you are a 100 per cent terrorist. That's it ... you are a terrorist. (422M/86, 120 hours, excluded)

> I don't have much faith in British justice now and I think most people here feel the same. They don't think they'll be treated fairly. (380M/79, 196 hours, excluded)

Another expressed frustration at the limitations placed on challenging an exclusion order:

> I did speak to a solicitor with a view to taking my case to court but I was advised against this, that I probably would not get any satisfaction and I should just forget about it. At the time I certainly felt I would not get a fair hearing so I did not bother taking my case to court although I would have done so if I had been given the choice – quite definitely. I am quite willing and would really love to go to court on it. (245M/79, 168 hours, excluded)

While people may be considered a danger in Britain and hence made subject to an exclusion order, the authorities in Northern Ireland may take a very different view of the extent of the threat. In one bizarre case a man was excluded and then called for jury service.

In about early 1984, I was called to do jury service in the High Court in Belfast ... The day before I was expected to attend I went down and said that I had been charged with terrorist offences, that I was excluded from Britain. I was told that internment did not count, that exclusion did not matter, that the charges had been dropped, I had no criminal record and that I was therefore eligible for jury service. I did jury service every Tuesday and Thursday for a month in trials that involved charges of rape and other serious offences. (246M/79, 196 hours, excluded)

Politics

Many people over the years have argued that one of the major impacts of the PTA has been to curtail political activities, debate and discussion around the Northern Ireland problem. Some would go as far as to argue that this was a deliberate policy. Whether or not this is correct, there is much evidence from the study to show that the PTA has had an insidious and profound affect on politics and political activities in a number of different ways. In Chapter 3 we showed how a person's politics played a role in the decision to stop and examine them at a port or airport.[6] Similarly, the sole purpose of a number of arrests appeared to be to gather information on political activity.

There has been widespread surveillance by the Special Branch of a wide range of perfectly legal political activity. Student politics has been heavily monitored over the years together with a number of political organisations including Troops Out, the Irish Republican Socialist Party, Clann na hEireann. A number of people were in no doubt about the extent of the surveillance and the use of the PTA for political purposes.

It's quite obvious that what the authorities are using the thing for is to simply keep an eye on political opponents and they keep an intelligence dossier on all sorts of people who are involved politically, even people who have impeccable records of opposition to violence, trade union leaders, student leaders – there's no way they are involved in anything like that and yet they're still detained under all these things. (271M/81, 22 hours, released)

The impact of the undercover activity, together with the examinations and arrests has forced people to give up political activity in these areas.

I would say, however, that people who've had similar experiences to
me who were politically active have now stopped their political
activity. Well I would certainly say it, I can understand that people
did lay low because of the fact that they've been arrested. (404M/78,
196 hours, excluded)

Another person expressed a similar view.

Afterwards I didn't go back to doing any more of the Irish work that
I'd been involved in – things like Troops Out movement. People are
suspicious of you after you've been detained. They always feel that
you must have talked about them. Nobody ever said to me anything
like that but I think that was the feeling. ... People are worried that
anybody who's been detained may however innocently have
mentioned somebody else's name. Once your name has been
mentioned, even in an innocent context, you're then on a list. I am
involved in Irish politics now but only through the Labour Party.
(392M/78, 24 hours, released)

In another case the person described their feelings.

After the detention I was very nervous for about a year. I was
frightened that whatever I did politically I would be suspected of all
kinds of Irish politics. (373M/81, 7 days, released)

The special offences provided for in the PTA such as soliciting or
inviting support for a proscribed organisation, or providing forms of
financial assistance for terrorism or withholding information, have also
played a significant part in curtailing political activity and controlling
the amount of information which is freely available to the public on
Ireland. While there has been a number of prosecutions, the provisions
have also been used to intimidate and threaten people with prosecution.

The various offences relating to supporting a proscribed organisation
have made people reluctant to hold meetings or to sell republican
literature or other material for fear of prosecution. The insidious and
far-reaching nature of these offences can be seen in the case of a
freelance journalist who was arrested.

My story described how I had watched in amazement as a section of
the large audience substituted 'Rock on Brighton' for the customary
refrain of 'Rock on Rockall' during a song about the disputed island

which both Ireland and Britain claim. I was hence astounded when my interrogator observed that my article 'could be construed as advocating support for a proscribed organization'. The essential themes of his subsequent remarks were to the effect that the events I had described had not occurred and moreover I had made them up; not in the course of the usual journalistic licence to heighten a story but that I had deliberately 'created' this story with the intention of promoting support for a proscribed organization. (147M/84, 13 hours, released)

More generally, the powers of banning and prohibition have

helped create a climate of unease amongst anyone concerned with the current problems of Ireland about where the boundaries of legality are drawn. It comes to introducing 'thought crime' into British law.[7]

The impact of the offence of withholding information has been even more pernicious. It runs counter to the journalistic principle of the need to protect confidential sources. There have now been numerous direct threats of prosecution made against journalists reporting events in Northern Ireland.[8] In 1991, however, the use of the PTA against journalists was taken one step further. In October Channel 4 showed Box Productions' 'The Committee' in its *Dispatches* series. The programme reiterated the widespread allegation of collusion in sectarian killings between loyalist paramilitaries and the security forces, but it went further and alleged the existence of a secret organisation made up of key people in the Northern Ireland business and professional community who were directing operations.

After the programme, Box Productions offered the RUC material on its allegations. The RUC subsequently obtained a court order under the PTA requiring Channel 4 and Box Productions to hand over more material. All the hearings were held *in camera* and the outcome was that more material was handed over. In January 1992 Channel 4 and Box Productions, however, informed the court that they were unable to hand over any more material because they could not reveal the identity of their principal informant. Channel 4 and Box Productions are now being sued for contempt of court. As Peter Goodwin has pointed out: 'For all its unique, and in many cases uniquely disturbing, features the C4 and Box case simply continues further along a path all too well-trodden in recent years.'[9] Increasingly, the PTA is being used to curtail the activities of investigative journalists.

Conclusions

This chapter has provided an overall assessment of the impact of the operation of the PTA on people's lives. Most of the evidence has been obtained from a small proportion of the 7,052 people who have been arrested and detained under the PTA and an even smaller group of those millions who have been examined. No information has been obtained from all those who have not been examined, arrested or detained under the PTA but who have nonetheless altered their behaviour and attitudes as a consequence of the legislation. Nevertheless, it has been possible to present a detailed picture of the impact of the legislation and to illustrate the widespread consequences of the legislation – ranging from shattered lives to small financial losses. In the majority of cases there has been no form of redress available whatsoever.

The chapter has also attempted to record some of the broader consequences of the PTA. All the evidence suggests that it has affected people's attitudes towards the law and the administration of justice, and has reduced their involvement in perfectly legitimate political activity. Democratic politics, particularly around the Irish question, have been severely curtailed. At the same time, the important role that journalists have in exposing wrongdoing and corruption is increasingly being challenged by the authorities under the PTA, either by the threat of prosecution for withholding information or, more insidiously, by using the courts to force journalists to disclose their sources.

12 An Assessment

Introduction

This book has focused upon the operation of successive Prevention of Terrorism Acts in Britain. It has attempted to describe how they have worked in practice, drawing on a unique study of over 115 people's experiences. The legislation has now been on the statute book for over 18 years. Yet the political violence in Britain stemming from the Northern Ireland conflict is still a threat.

On Friday 10 April 1992 the IRA planted two massive bombs in London. One exploded in the City of London and killed three people and injured another 91. It caused damage running into millions of pounds. The second destroyed the road junction where the M1 begins. An AA spokesperson said that 'It is likely to be utter chaos for several months at least'.[1] A few days later on 15 April a recruiting officer was shot in Derby at point-blank range with a hand-gun as he walked from an army careers office to his car. He later died and the Irish National Liberation Army claimed responsibility.

The police response – at least, from what can be gleaned from the media coverage – followed a familiar pattern. An unknown number of people were arrested for both incidents, most of whom were released without charge. The Government's response has been to expand the role of MI5. On 8 May 1992, Kenneth Clarke, the Home Secretary, announced that MI5 was to be given the lead responsibility in gathering intelligence on the IRA in Britain. The wider responsibilities, such as making arrests and preparing cases for prosecution, would rest with the police. It was a controversial decision.

MI5 – which was set up in 1909 but whose existence was not officially acknowledged until the introduction of the Security Services Act 1989 – has never been accountable to Parliament. Since 1989 a Security Service Commissioner has had responsibility for considering some aspects of MI5's activities. But the role of the Commissioner is very limited and serves only as a veneer of public accountability. Moreover, as a member of the judiciary has been appointed to the post, it calls into question the acclaimed constitutional separation of powers between the Executive and the judiciary.

In addition, a number of MI5's previous activities in relation to combating terrorism (particularly in Northern Ireland where it took over the key intelligence role from MI6 in 1973) have raised fundamental issues about the rule of law. There is, for example, still considerable doubt about whether or not MI5 was actively involved in the removal of Stalker from his inquiry into the alleged shoot to kill policy in Northern Ireland. All the circumstantial evidence seems to point to a conspiracy involving MI5.[2] There are also a number of unanswered questions about MI5's role in the shooting dead of three IRA members in Gibraltar.[3]

The principal finding of this study is that official responses so far to political violence have alienated the Irish community living in Britain or travelling between Britain and Northern Ireland. This alienation is likely to be further exacerbated by the involvement of a democratically unaccountable and secret organisation.

This community's sense of justice was further affected shortly after the announcement of MI5's extended role. On 11 May 1992 the Court of Appeal released Judith Ward from prison on the grounds that her conviction was unsafe and unsatisfactory. She had served 18 years in jail for crimes which she did not commit. She became the eighteenth person in Britain acknowledged to have been wrongly convicted in recent years in relation to political violence connected with Northern Ireland. She is another statistic in a long line of so-called 'miscarriages of justice' cases in the British criminal justice annals.

The issues of protecting the rule of law and responding effectively to political violence therefore remain as crucial today as at the start of this research project. This final chapter brings together some of the more important features which emerge from this study of the operation of the PTA in Britain. It also assesses some of the arguments which have been put forward in support of the draconian legislation.

The Construction of a Suspect Community

The most important feature of the operation of the PTA has been the way in which it has constructed a suspect community in Britain. The wide powers of examination, arrest and detention, the executive powers to proscribe selected organisations, the range of specific offences under the Acts, the power to issue exclusion orders and a whole new range of provisions covering seizure and investigation, have all played their part in making the Irish living in Britain, or Irish people travelling between Ireland and Britain, a suspect community. This community is treated in law and in police practices very differently from the rest of the population. To the extent that the legislation is principally directed at Irish people, it is an example of institutionalised racism.

More specifically, the wide powers of examination, arrest and detention have allowed the police to trawl the Irish community for information whether at ports or airports or inland. Who becomes a suspect within the community at any point in time appears to be a product of a number of interlocking and complex processes. To begin with, it appears to be commonplace for the police to try and pick up anyone who is related to, is friends with or has been connected with – however tenuously – someone who is suspected of a serious crime or has been charged with one. After this group has been arrested and interrogated, the police then focus on people related to, or connected with them, and so the process continues. This pyramid method of police investigation draws into the net a wide range of people and the main thread which links them all is the fact that most are Irish or are married to someone who is Irish.

Another investigative method involves carrying out selective interviews of members of the public. These do not involve arrest or detention but take the form of an interview at the person's home. This is a far less coercive method but people are still selected for interview simply because they are Irish. This point is well illustrated by a case in October 1990. Following the detonation of a bomb on the roof of the Army Careers Office in Derby, the police launched a large-scale inquiry. They requested and obtained the names and addresses of all Irish students studying at one particular college. The students concerned had no prior knowledge of the action of the college and did not give their consent. A number of students were subsequently interviewed by the police. One woman student was interviewed in her flat by a male officer and asked various questions, including her home address in Ireland and her date of birth. She was also asked to give an account of her movements in Ireland at the time of the Derby bomb incident. She was told that all Irish students were undergoing similar interviews. She felt that this was not meant to reassure her but to plant fear in her mind, and in the collective mind of England's Irish community, that they are under constant police surveillance. (595F/90, questioned)

The police, for their part, would argue that these methods are fully justified. The IRA has predominantly Irish membership and support. It is known that operatives are placed in the community and it is assumed that the IRA uses threats to enforce cooperation on law-abiding members of the community. It is therefore sound policing practice to interview people with Irish connections following any incident.

Apart from the widespread infringement of Irish peoples' civil liberties, the main problem with viewing a whole community as inherently suspect is that the policing techniques become more and more intrusive and intensified as political violence continues. In particular, the police have become much more proactive. For example, in October 1990 there was a report that the Bedfordshire police requested certain information from a mixed athletics team of Catholics and Protestants from Northern Ireland, which was due to take part in a championship in Britain. The police wanted the names and addresses of all participants, the registration numbers of the cars they would be using and the name and address of the hotel in which they were staying.[4]

A second problem associated with the police viewing the whole Irish community as suspect is that the public is also encouraged to do the same. In 1990 the *Mail on Sunday* carried a story in which a Deputy Assistant Commissioner is reported to have said :

We need the public to tell us about all Irish people who have arrived within the past year or so. They may be living with you or near you, or working with you. Just tell us and we'll check it out.[5]

The public has, of course, played an important role in the construction of suspicion for some time. Whether or not the Commissioner actually made the statement reproduced above, the fact that such a claim was reported will be sufficient to encourage some members of the public to report an Irish person's presence to the police. Often the trigger of suspicion is an Irish accent and an innocent conversation. In the case of three businessmen who were arrested in 1991, it appears that a barman had overheard them talking about bombs. But the conversation related to bombs in Colombia, which one of the party had visited 18 months previously (801M/91, 6 hours, released).

In the case of the five building workers arrested in Cheltenham, their Irish accents had created suspicion in the minds of the public. In another case, armed police burst into a woman's flat and began searching it. Her boyfriend, an ex-army medical orderly in Northern Ireland, had stayed the night. They had a horrendous row which she assumed had been overheard by the next door neighbour who then called the police.[6]

There have been a number of articles in newspapers promoting the view that all Irish people are suspect. In an article in the *Sunday*

Telegraph, for example, Peregrine Worsthorne argued that in the case
of terrorism the conviction of 10 innocent men was a lesser evil than
releasing a guilty one. He maintained that after any major IRA outrage
the police trawl for Irish suspects and many of those caught are
republican sympathisers rather than terrorists proper. He went on:

> Such people may not positively help the IRA. But nor are they
> properly speaking, innocent. Certainly they withhold information
> which would help catch the bombers, and serve the IRA in other
> ways. Many Irish priests do too, supplying safe houses. If they are not
> guilty themselves of acts of terrorism, all these hangers-on, as much
> on the mainland as in Ulster itself, are certainly accomplices either
> before or after the act.[7]

The argument then continued that a more ruthless state would
simply deport all republican sympathisers, pointing out that:

> As it is we make them welcome, allow them to vote and enjoy all
> the other privileges of citizenship.

These sorts of arguments are racist and inflammatory. They help
increase people's suspicion of the Irish living in Britain and lead to more
arrests and detentions of Irish people.

The PTA has gone further than constructing a suspect community:
it has also *criminalised* Irish people living in Britain.[8] The term 'criminalisation' has been used by criminologists to refer to the process by
which, through statute or case law, certain types of behaviour are
designated as prohibited acts and carry specified penalties. Anyone
engaging in any of these types of behaviour may be defined as criminal.
The process involves detecting and investigating alleged law breaking
and subsequently arresting, charging and prosecuting those under
suspicion. There have been a number of recent examples of this process,
including the criminalisation of miners during the coal dispute in
1984/85[9] and the New Age travellers in their annual attempts to reach
Stonehenge for the summer solstice.[10] The term can usefully be
extended to cover not only the processes by which certain *types of
behaviour* are designated prohibited acts by either statute or case law, but
also the way certain *categories of people* are drawn into the criminal
justice system simply because of their status and irrespective of their
behaviour. There is now much research showing how the black

community has been criminalised in this broader sense.[11] This study has illustrated the process in relation to the Irish community.

Dual System of Criminal Justice

The second feature to emphasise about the PTA is that it has created, as we have seen in Chapters 2 and 4, a dual system of criminal justice in Britain. PACE is now used to deal with ordinary crime, which includes a very large number of horrific offences including murder and rape. Yet PACE is considered inappropriate to deal with political violence arising from Northern Irish affairs or international political violence. In terms of actual harm, ordinary decent criminals in Britain have caused far greater damage to people and property than terrorists. During the period that the PTA has been in force there have been nearly 9,000 homicides, over 3,200 attempted murders, 15,000 threats or conspiracy to murder, 100,000 woundings or other acts endangering life, 1.5 million other woundings of one sort or another, 250,000 indecent assaults on females and 30,000 rapes notified to the police in England and Wales.[12] None of these offences have had anything to do with the conflict in Northern Ireland.

The justification for the different procedures, however, does not rest on the amount of harm done, but on the different nature of the activity. For example, reference is made to the way in which the law deals with other types of crime, such as drug offences and fraud. While there are important differences in the motivation and types of crimes committed by ordinary decent criminals and those involved in political violence, it is hard to understand why arrest and detention powers, and codes of practice, have to be so different for those suspected of political violence (and many of those drawn into the PTA are not suspected of very much) compared with those suspected of being serial killers.

The different procedures have helped create a very distinct culture and atmosphere around a PTA arrest compared to an arrest under PACE. PTA arrests, as we have seen, are invariably carried out by armed police. Security in the police stations is much more intense, there is heightened tension and the dissemination of information to the media is more carefully handled. The mere use of the PTA, therefore, helps to construct a particular view of and orientation towards the case. If a person is subsequently charged – which, as we have shown, is rare – there is intense security at the remand hearings and at the trial. Thus even before a shred of evidence has been heard by the jury, the behaviour of the authorities suggests that the person is an active terrorist. It is in this very different context, with an intense pressure on the police to produce results, that miscarriages of justice are more likely to occur.

The Terror of Prevention[13]

The third feature characterising the operation of the PTA has been its violence. Although, as its title suggests, it is designed to prevent terrorism, there is ample evidence from this study to show that it often creates terror. The armed arrests of people either in their homes or on the streets, as described in Chapter 6, was, for most, a terrifying ordeal. The prolonged detention and interrogation, as described in Chapters 7 and 8, carried its own terror. Even the examinations at ports and airports, as described in Chapter 3, were not without fear of what might happen: for example, the possibility of exclusion, a prosecution for non-disclosure or suffering sexual harassment. The impact of these experiences on people's lives, examined in the last chapter, can be devastating. Two people died not long after their arrest and it is possible that their deaths were related to their experiences. Others have suffered physically and mentally, and some have lost their jobs and their friends. It has affected men, women and children. And very few have received any compensation for their ordeals.

The terror is often compounded by the activities of various actors – the police, police doctors, social workers, solicitors, law officers, ministers and the media. Together they act against the interests of the detainee. It is a formidable array of force. It was, of course, a similar combination of actors – forensic scientists, police, prosecution lawyers and a prison doctor – that the Court of Appeal most recently identified as being responsible for the miscarriage of justice in the Judith Ward case.[14] Similar agents were typically responsible in other miscarriages of justice cases.

It is commonplace to counterpose the rule of law to the abuse of power or acts of violence. Law, from this perspective, is seen as the antithesis of violence. This study has set out to show this dichotomy to be false. The use of successive Prevention of Terrorism Acts has often constituted the terror of prevention. Law is thus an integral part of the repression and organisation of state violence, whether it takes place in a person's home or in police custody.

Recently an eminent Professor of Law called for a jurisprudence of violence.[15] By this he meant that it was time to shift the focus of legal thinking away from law's words – the nature of rules, principles and the interpretative activities of judges – to law's deeds; in particular, the awesome, physical force that the law deploys. He called for studies of the effects of legal force, not just on those who suffer it, but those who inflict it – namely, legal officials. Hopefully this study makes a contribution to the jurisprudence of violence.

Normalisation of Emergency Legislation

A fourth feature to emerge from the study is the way in which, after a period of time, the emergency or temporary legislation becomes normalised in a number of different ways. To begin with, it shifts from being a piece of temporary legislation to a permanent piece of law which is constantly re-enacted and extended. This has certainly been the statutory history of the PTA.

Secondly, a symbiotic relationship develops between the ordinary criminal law and the emergency legislation. On some occasions emergency powers become incorporated into the normal criminal law. On other occasions powers in the ordinary criminal law are incorporated into future enactments of the temporary legislation. As a result there is a general tightening up throughout the statutory law. There are numerous examples of both processes in relation to the PTA.

For example, the decision to permit a maximum period of detention under PACE of 96 hours was influenced by the existence of the seven day power under the PTA. If the seven day power had not existed it would have been more difficult to argue for such a lengthy period of detention under the ordinary criminal law. The reformed ordinary law then becomes the standard to which the emergency legislation should aspire. As Jim Marshall pointed out in one of the renewal debates to the PTA: 'This is an example of an insidious circular process in which draconian laws soften us up to similar laws which become the desired standard for further measures.'[16]

Another example concerns police powers, which have been used principally against journalists, to obtain certain types of material. The general power was initially enacted in the ordinary criminal law in PACE.[17] It was first used against journalists to obtain press photographs after the Bristol riots in 1986. When the PTA was further consolidated in 1989, a more extensive power to obtain materials was incorporated.[18]

It was this power which was used in 1991 against Channel 4 and Box Productions.[19]

Thirdly, once on the statute book emergency powers are often used to deal with ordinary crime. There are now a number of examples of this happening with the PTA. In the mid 1980s it was alleged that a number of hunt saboteurs were arrested under the PTA. The section on criminal charges in Chapter 4 also showed that a number of people arrested under the PTA were subsequently charged with a range of ordinary criminal offences such as motoring and theft offences, which appear to have nothing whatsoever to do with political violence.

Violation of Civil Liberties and Human Rights

The final feature of the operation of the PTA which must be emphasised is the extent to which it violates international standards on human rights and infringes civil liberties. The detention power was shown to be in violation of the European Convention on Human Rights in the case of *Brogan and Others v United Kingdom*. In addition, the Act has effectively destroyed *habeas corpus* as a safeguard against unlawful detention. The exclusion power violates at least six fundamental human rights: the right to freedom of movement, the right to a fair and public trial, the right to family life, the right to freely associate with others, the right to participate in public affairs and the right to seek work and improved economic prospects. Already, the United Kingdom has been found in violation of the European Convention more times than any other signatory state.[20]

The power of the Executive to ban organisations and the vague offence of supporting proscribed organisations have substantially eroded freedom of association and freedom of expression. At a broader level, free and open public debate on the Northern Irish problem has been restricted as a result. People have been forced to give up their political activity for fear of being arrested, detained and possibly excluded. It has, therefore, had an insidious and long-term impact on the democratic process itself. Indeed, some have argued that the primary function of the PTA was to silence and politically neutralise the Irish community in Britain.[21]

Since the present round of conflict began in Northern Ireland, the United Kingdom Government has been faced on a number of occasions with how to reconcile the coercive legislation, introduced to deal with political violence in Northern Ireland and Great Britain, with the

European Convention on Human Rights. Its standard tactic in relation to Northern Ireland has been to enter a derogation from the Convention which is permissible under Article 15 and requires that there is a 'public emergency threatening the life of the nation'. It first entered a notice of derogation in 1957 but withdrew all its derogations in 1984 when it reviewed the circumstances in Northern Ireland. Internment had ended and it was felt that none of the rest of emergency legislation violated the Convention.[22] Following the European Court of Human Rights ruling in the case of *Brogan and Others v United Kingdom*, however, a derogation was again entered. Although the case arose in Northern Ireland, the section applies to the whole of the United Kingdom: it is hard to conceive how the Government can justify the derogation on the grounds of 'public emergency threatening the life of the nation' in Northern Ireland let alone in Great Britain.

It can be seen from this broader analysis of the operation of the PTA that there are a number of very negative consequences. The Government, however, argues that the legislation is successful in preventing terrorism and that the curtailment of civil liberties, for example, is a small price to pay in the battle against terrorism. It is a view held by the official reviews, a large section of the popular press and a sizeable section of the population. Before considering the specific and the broader arguments which have been put forward to justify the introduction and use of the various PTA powers, it is important to examine the assertion that 'terrorism is a threat to democracy'.

Terrorism and Democracy

These concepts, as has been pointed out in an excellent analysis,[23] can mean several things. They can be reduced to an authoritative statement: terrorism destroys democracy, which is also a value judgement implying that terrorism is bad and democracy is good. Finally, it is asserted that 'the good' must be defended at all costs against 'the evil'. The problem, however, is that 'complicated questions are oversimplified by approximations or attaching undue importance to one particular question'.[24]

The meaning of both concepts is open to considerable debate. 'Terrorism' itself is defined in very broad terms under the PTA. Moreover, the term 'democracy' is no less problematic. Democracy is made up of a political as well as a legal system. At the heart of the legal system is the notion of the rule of law and 'the recognition of human rights in the form of fundamental rights attaching to individuals who

may rely on them against the state'.[25] The issue then is how far
'terrorism' challenges either the political system or the legal system. In
regard to terrorism emanating from Northern Ireland, which is based
on a national claim to the territory, it 'does not seek to undermine
democracy as such, but is directed against the state ... it is the British
presence and domination which is at issue, not democracy. There is no
gun-powder plot threatening Westminster.'[26]

When the impact of terrorism, then, is considered in a broader
context, the main casualty is not the political system or the state but the
law: fundamental changes, as we have seen, are introduced to deal with
the political violence. The state, however, does not have an unfettered
discretion to change the law. There are limits and this principle was
upheld by the European Court of Human Rights in 1978 in the Klass
case:

> The Court, being aware of the danger such a law poses of undermining
> or even destroying democracy on the ground of defending it, affirms
> that the Contracting States may not, in the name of the struggle against
> terrorism, adopt whatever measures they deem appropriate.[27]

This judgment is clearly asserting that the real threat to democracy
is not terrorism itself, but *the response to terrorism* by the state. From this
perspective, it is essential that there is an open, informed and independent debate about the nature and efficacy of the laws introduced to
combat terrorism.

It is, however, extremely difficult to have an open and intelligent
debate about such legislation in contemporary Britain. Anyone who
questions the legislation is seen (particularly by the popular press) as
assisting terrorism. Moreover, the issue of legislation to deal with
terrorism has become a political football between the two major political
parties since the Labour Party announced its opposition to the PTA in
the early 1980s. At the Conservative Party Conference in 1989 the then
Home Secretary, Douglas Hurd, attacked the Labour Party on their
opposition to it. He said: 'They feel that they have to humour the friends
of Sinn Fein in their ranks. That will not do.' The implication of his
remarks, as Melanie Phillips has pointed out, is that if you do not
support the PTA you must support terrorism. During the renewal
debate on the PTA in February 1992 the Home Secretary, Kenneth
Baker, attacked Roy Hattersley for being responsible for the Labour Party
breaking from the bipartisan policy in 1983 and quoted the former Home

Secretary, Roy Jenkins, who had argued that if Mr Hattersley ever became Home Secretary 'he would be racked by a conflict between his genuine concern for public safety and the foolish commitments ... into which he has entered in opposition'.[28] During the recent election campaign, a number of Conservative candidates used the Labour Party's opposition to the legislation to suggest that if Labour gained power, terrorists would have a free rein in Britain.

A comprehensive and informed public debate over the operation of the legislation is further hampered by the lack of information. This study has revealed the limited value of official statistics and the fact that answers to parliamentary questions often tell only half the story. A major source of information for politicians and the public has been the reports of the official reviews of the legislation. Although these reviews are described as independent, however, they have been carried out by people closely associated with government and have relied almost exclusively on collecting information from those involved in implementing and enforcing the legislation. None of the reviews conducted any systematic research into the experiences of those people affected by the legislation.

In any event, all the reviews were given restricted terms of reference which precluded any discussion of whether special legislation is in fact necessary to deal with political violence. The danger identified by the European Court of Human Rights in the Klass case, namely that legislation designed to defeat terrorism may in fact destroy democracy, could not even be considered by the official reviews because the terms of reference began with the assertion that special legislation *was* necessary.

Over the years a number of specific arguments has been put forward to justify the introduction and continuance of each of the major provisions introduced under the PTA: controls at ports, proscription of selected organisations, extended powers of arrest and detention, exclusion and new investigative powers.

Controls at Ports

The extensive port powers, which were described in detail in Chapter 2 and their use in Chapter 3, were justified officially on the grounds of deterrence and protection.[29] As both grounds are used to support the PTA in general, they are examined in detail below. A more specific argument is that the port powers are required to determine whether or not a person is involved in terrorism.[30] On the surface this appears to be a reasonable objective. But the question is how this is to be achieved in practice. Those genuinely involved in terrorism are hardly likely to inform the authorities and no offence of withholding information is likely to make them change their minds. Moreover, an extended examination is most unlikely to make it any easier to separate the terrorists from the rest of the travelling public. The only way in which the authorities are going to determine whether or not someone is involved in terrorism is by having some prior information on them. But if this information gives rise to reasonable suspicion that the person has committed offences, then sufficient powers exist under the ordinary criminal law to make an arrest. In other words, is it really necessary to subject the *whole* of the travelling public to examinations, with all the consequent infringement of civil liberties, in order to find out if a person is involved in terrorism? .

In any event, the argument that the port powers are required to determine whether or not a person is involved in terrorism, is a red herring. This study has shown that the principal function of the port powers is to gather intelligence and a comprehensive system of surveillance has been developed to this end. Those involved in Irish politics, as well as those with a past record, are the subject of particular attention. Under the umbrella of executive powers and the operational imperatives of the police, a secret state has been developed which collects and stores information and which is subject to no independent scrutiny. At the same time, those subject to the surveillance are often totally unaware that their personal details are stored on a computer and even if they are, they have no right to check the accuracy of the information which is stored on them.

The amount of information which has been collected and stored from those examined at ports and airports over the years must be considerable. When all the information collected from those arrested inland is added to the database, it must be very large indeed and contain all sorts of different information. Much of the information collected is probably of no value whatsoever either because, as we have shown in this small study, many of those examined, detained or arrested are not connected in any way with political violence in Northern Ireland, or because some of it is inaccurate. Thus in practice the police must be overwhelmed with information and it must be an impossible task to sort out the wood from the trees. The usefulness of such vast databases must itself be open to question.

An internal police memorandum adds support to this view. It was leaked during the policy debate on whether or not MI5 should take over the principal role in the collection of intelligence in relation to IRA activity in Britain. It pointed out that there was very little intelligence 'at this stage'.[31] This is an extraordinary statement. At what stage is there likely to be intelligence? It is now some 18 years since intelligence gathering, employing a variety of draconian powers, was started. It can only be assumed that much of the information which has been collected on the Irish community is worthless.

Apart from the issue of the value of the information, the whole operation of the port powers, as we have demonstrated, alienates the very people from whom one seeks cooperation because of the infringement of their civil liberties and their differential treatment at the hands of the law.

Arrest and Detention Powers

Chapters 4 to 6 considered the extraordinary powers of arrest, detention and search under the PTA and examined in detail people's experiences. This exercise has shown all too clearly how coercive and repressive these powers are in practice. The principal argument in support of these powers is that terrorism poses such a threat to society that special powers are needed.[32] In particular, it is more difficult to obtain evidence on which to convict; hence a longer detention period and less stringent codes of practice are required in order to obtain the necessary evidence. Underlying the argument is the belief that terrorists are trained in anti-interrogation methods.

But these arguments justifying the special powers of arrest, detention and search all rest on the assumption that the main purpose of the extraordinary powers is to secure a conviction after an arrest. In reality, as we have shown, the principal purpose of an arrest and detention is to gather information and the detention regimes are specifically devised for this end. The argument that special powers are needed to gather evidence to put before a court apply in fewer than five per cent of all arrests.

Much of the evidence presented in the study is drawn from people's experiences going back over a number of years. No doubt it will be argued that many aspects of operational policing, the criminal law and criminal procedure have changed in the period and therefore it would be wrong to draw conclusions about what is currently happening. It will be pointed out that the number of people now being arrested and detained is substantially fewer that in the period of the late 1970s and hence the operation of the powers is nowadays much more targeted.

While the numbers arrested and detained have indeed declined, there is no evidence that the operation of the PTA is more targeted. The proportion of those detained and charged or excluded is still as low as ever, with nine out of every ten being released without charge.

It will also be argued that PACE has radically transformed the rights of suspects and imposed important supervisory controls over the whole detention process. According to this view, abuses are now a thing of the past and the whole of the administration of justice has been improved. Chapter 8, however, argued that PACE and the codes of practice have done little to alter the imbalance of power between the police and the detainee in police custody. The codes can all be accommodated without radically compromising the power of the police. Indeed, the central argument of that chapter was that they have actually facilitated the construction of the suspect population. In any event, they have done little to alter the terror of detention and interrogation. They have, on the other hand, given legitimacy to these often brutalising physical and psychological processes.

Exclusion Powers

Exclusion has been justified on a number of grounds. The Jellicoe Report suggested that it prevents terrorism by getting rid of the person and preventing those excluded from travelling legally across the border.[33] More recently, exclusion has been justified on the grounds that it both limits the area where terrorists can carry out their activities and helps offset the fact that it is often impossible to charge people when the information comes from sources which cannot be disclosed without risking people's lives.[34]

These arguments can easily be challenged. The suggestion that exclusion prevents terrorism by getting rid of the person is highly dubious. It may stop some incidents in Britain, but the person excluded – assuming that the intelligence is accurate and they are involved in political violence – is still free to pursue their activities in Ireland. Ireland thus becomes the dumping ground for discarded terrorists. In addition, no exclusion law is likely to deter the highly-motivated terrorist from crossing borders. Finally, to support exclusion in order to protect sources of information is highly questionable. It privileges the rights of an informer over the rights of others to have a public hearing of the alleged charges against them.

Proscription

The executive power under the PTA to proscribe certain organisations
has been used to ban both the IRA and INLA. As we have seen, there
are various offences under the PTA connected with proscribed organisations, such as being a member or collecting money on behalf of the
organisation. In addition, proscription has been supplemented by other
legislation which bans direct broadcasts of representatives of proscribed
organisations or those speaking in support of such organisations.

The grounds for proscription are most succinctly presented in the
Jellicoe Report.[35] First, the legislation enshrines 'public aversion to organisations which use, or espouse, violence as a means to political ends'.
This is a statement of fact and its practical impact is impossible to
assess. Those who believe that violence is a legitimate means to political
ends are unlikely to be influenced by a statement of opposition enshrined
in the law, and those who are already opposed merely have their
position re-enforced.

The second argument in support of proscription and the broadcasting ban is that the ban prohibits public displays by, or in support of, such
organisations and thereby prevents the expression of public outrage which
may itself lead to disorder. The Home Secretary justified the broadcasting
ban on similar grounds and argued that broadcasts can be deeply
offensive to viewers and listeners.[36] While proscription certainly prohibits
public support, it does not automatically follow that it prevents the
expression of public outrage which may lead to disorder. In any event,
the major impact of the ban is to push support for proscribed organisations underground and hence make them less visible.

The third argument is that proscription stems the flow of funds to the
organisations concerned. This can not be proven one way or the other.
It may certainly stem the flow of funds from public collections, but other
sources of funding are likely to be secured. The effect, then, is to
displace the collection activity from one form to another.

While the Jellicoe Report accepted that the practical impact of the
ban is probably limited, it considered that the presentational objective
has been beneficial. The Report also considered that the ban might be
wrong in principle and is an unacceptable infringement of the freedom
of speech. In particular it took note of the argument that proscription
had inhibited free discussion about the future of Northern Ireland
because of the fear of police action. In fact it argued that if this were
'the necessary and inevitable result of proscription', the power should
lapse forthwith. But without producing any evidence, it simply asserted

that it did not 'believe' this to be the case.[37] Freedom of speech is eroded simply on the basis of belief.

General Prevention

All the arguments in support of the specific powers under the PTA can therefore be challenged on one or more grounds. The final argument that needs to be considered is whether the PTA as a whole has been effective in preventing terrorism principally through deterrence. As we have seen, this is the position taken by the Jellicoe Report in regard to the main function of the port powers.[38] The Home Secretary in the debate on the renewal of the PTA in February 1992 also appealed to the deterrent argument to justify the port powers, as well as the wide powers of arrest and detention.

> What these powers do among other things, is to provide a sizeable deterrent to the movement of terrorists and of their materials. I am entirely satisfied from what I know that these powers do deter. They make life more difficult for terrorists. I am not prepared to remove deterrents from these people and I do not think that Opposition Members should do so either.[39]

The problem with the deterrent argument is that the people involved in political violence, as was pointed out by the Home Secretary, 'have a ruthless commitment to their cause'.[40] With such motivation even the most draconian of measures are unlikely to be an effective deterrent. The measures may certainly 'make life more difficult' and impede their activities, but are unlikely to deter those involved; they are likely to find ways of circumventing the powers.

The deterrent argument therefore has little substance. But this does not destroy the prevention argument altogether. The powers may prevent political violence in other ways. For example, people involved may have been arrested or detained or the special powers provided the police with information which would have been impossible to obtain under the ordinary criminal law; and this information may prevent a number of incidents. In other words, the level of terrorism would have been higher had it not been for the legislation.

The difficulty with this argument is that it is impossible to prove. As Walker has pointed out, prevention is especially difficult to assess since it involves the proof of an omission. But one crude indicator of success is the overall level of terrorist activity, which he analysed in some detail. He concluded that the enactment had no immediately discernible effect and that while political violence was now less frequent but more carefully targeted, factors other than the PTA were important.[41] He suggested that most of the successes in terms of prosecutions were attributable to chance, routine police work and terrorist incompetence.[42]

Conclusion

All the available evidence, together with a broader understanding of the dynamics of why people become involved in political violence, indicates that the Government's current strategy of dealing with political violence is not working. The dominant feature of this strategy lies in its coerciveness and repressiveness. It relies on arresting large numbers of mainly Irish people, holding them in police custody, interrogating them and then releasing them without charge. At ports and airports the position is little different. Examining officers have enormous powers to stop, question and take away information which they consider relevant. The approach is a far cry from policing by consent.

A suspect community has been constructed against a backdrop of anti-Irish racism. This community has suffered widespread violation of their human rights and civil liberties. As a consequence, the United Kingdom's reputation throughout the world in upholding human rights and civil liberties has been constantly compromised. At the same time, the PTA has had an insidious impact on the ordinary criminal law. Moreover, it has criminalised and silenced political opposition to Britain's role in Ireland.

Other less coercive strategies may be introduced with less negative consequences, but their effectiveness may be equally problematic. The lessons of history are that political violence can never be dealt with through the law. Ultimately a political solution has to be found to the Northern Ireland problem.

Appendix I Research Methodology Used in this Study

It was not possible, for obvious reasons, to select a random sample of the 7,052 people who have been arrested or detained under the PTA between 29 November 1974 and December 1991. It was therefore necessary to adopt a different approach. To begin with, efforts were made to contact people who had experience of the PTA by placing advertisements in newspapers read by the Irish community. The official reviews had used a similar technique to encourage people to come forward to give evidence on the operation of the Acts.

The response to our advertisements was poor and we assumed that this was because people were unwilling to come to an organisation of which they had probably never heard and make a statement about what was, for most, a traumatic ordeal.

While waiting for a response from the advertisements, time was spent preparing information sheets on the PTA and providing advice to individuals and organisations. As a result of this work, various contacts were made with people who had been examined, arrested or detained under the PTA. A number of them were prepared to provide information on their experiences. At the same time, the newspapers were searched regularly for any reports of arrests under the PTA. When a report was found, efforts were made to contact the people concerned. In addition, a number of solicitors were approached and this source produced a number of new contacts. As the project became better known, more and more people came forward who had either been arrested or detained themselves or knew of someone who had been.

This networking approach to the construction of a sample is unusual but it slowly produced results. Its major limitation is that it is impossible to tell whether or not it is representative of all those arrested or detained and, as a result, it is impossible to generalise from the experiences. It may be the case – but there is no way of knowing – that all those detained or arrested have had similar ordeals. The key issue for the study, is whether or not it is acceptable in a democratic society for anyone to be subject to such experiences. The issue therefore shifted from being about representativeness to broader moral and political issues.

Once people had been contacted, the next research question was: 'What type of method should be adopted to record their experiences?' Initially it was decided to adopt a quantitative approach and use a structured questionnaire asking a series of questions about people's experiences at different points in the legal process. In particular, it attempted to ascertain whether people knew about their rights and whether or not their rights were upheld. After a number of the questionnaires had been completed, it was apparent that this legalistic approach to people's experiences was inappropriate. Most people did not know their rights and, more importantly, they did not know what was happening to them or what their official status was at any particular point in time. The different legal statuses such as an examination, detention or arrest, had no meaning for them. All they knew was that they were kept in custody by someone in authority.

Another limitation of the structured questionnaire quickly emerged. When talking to people about their experiences, the detail was so rich that it became apparent that a questionnaire simply could not capture the depth and intensity of the experience. It was therefore decided to switch to a qualitative approach and let people tell their experiences in their own words and only ask questions about key areas at the end if they had not been covered. Most interviews were taped and then transcribed.

The transcribed interviews came to many hundreds of pages and the next research problem was how to analyse and present the data. There are now a number of computer programmes which have been developed to systematically analyse qualitative data. Limited time and resources, however, prevented the use of these programmes and most of the analysis was carried out using the search facility in conjunction with a split window on Microsoft Word. This approach had a number of advantages. First, no time was required to prepare and structure the data for a special programme. Second, it was a very rapid method of searching a large body of text for key points. Third, once a section describing a particular experience was identified it could be added to a file covering the topic.

It was decided to present most of the data under key headings to illustrate people's experience of a particular aspect of the process. This approach, however, has had the disadvantage of losing the sense of a person's overall experience. To overcome this problem, three case studies are presented in full, one examination at an airport, a three-day detention at Paddington Green and a one-day detention at a provincial police station.

Appendix II Exclusion Order Notice under the Prevention of Terrorism (Temporary Provisions) Act 1989

Notice under paragraph 2(1) of Schedule 2 of the making of an exclusion order prohibiting a person from being in, or entering, Great Britain

The Secretary of State is satisfied that you, ... are or have been concerned in the commission, preparation or instigation of acts of terrorism connected with the affairs of Northern Ireland. In pursuance of section 5(1) and (2) of the Prevention of Terrorism (Temporary Provisions) Act 1989, the Secretary of State has made an exclusion order prohibiting you, ... from being in, or entering, Great Britain.

It has not been shown that you are entitled to exemption under section 5(4) of the said Act. This provision exempts a British citizen from an exclusion order being made against him if he is ordinarily resident in Great Britain and has been so ordinarily resident throughout the last three years. There is an additional exemption if the person concerned is a British citizen who is subject to an order under section 6 of the 1989 Act excluding him from Northern Ireland. (By virtue of paragraph 9(1) of Schedule 2 to the said Act it lies on the person concerned to prove that he is exempt under these provisions.)

In pursuance of paragraph 7(1) of Schedule 2 to the said Act the Secretary of State has authorised your detention pending the giving of directions for your removal from Great Britain under paragraph 6 of the said Schedule and pending your removal in pursuance of such directions.

If you object to the exclusion order you may make representations to the Secretary of State in writing setting out the grounds of your objections. You may include in your representations a request for a personal interview with the person who will be nominated by the Secretary of State to consider your case. The interview will be granted in Great Britain if you have not consented in writing to be removed. If you have so consented it will, if it appears reasonably practicable to the Secretary of State to do so within a reasonable period from the date of your representations, be granted in Northern Ireland or in the Republic of Ireland.

You have seven days from the time when this notice is served on you during which you may exercise your right to make representations. Unless you consent in writing you will not be removed from Great Britain until that period has expired or, if you make representations within that period, until the Secretary of State has notified you of a decision not to revoke the order. If you consent in writing to be removed from Great Britain you have 14 days from the time when you are removed to make representations.

Once you have been removed, or become liable to be removed, under the order you will commit a criminal offence, punishable by up to five years' imprisonment or a fine, or both, if you fail to comply with the order.

If you wish to make representations objecting to the making of the order, you should address them to F4 Division, Room 647, Home Office, Queen Anne's Gate, London SW1. You may either post them or, if you are still in custody, hand them (in a sealed envelope if you wish) to the officer in whose custody you are detained.

The exclusion order will expire three years from the date on which it was signed.

Notes and References

Notes to Chapter 1

1. *Review of the Operation of the Prevention of Terrorism (Temporary Provisions) Acts 1974 and 1976*, Cmnd. 7324, 1978 (cited as 'Shackleton Report'); *Review of the Operation of the Prevention of Terrorism (Temporary Provisions) Acts 1976*, Cmnd. 8803, 1983 (cited as 'Jellicoe Report'); *Review of the Operation of the Prevention of Terrorism (Temporary Provisions) Acts 1984*, Cm. 264, 1987 (cited as 'Colville Report').
2. In a Written Answer in July 1991 it was reported that the Home Office Research and Planning Unit had conducted research into the PTA, but this research has not been published. See *Hansard*, Written Answers, Col. 250, 8 July 1991.
3. See: Farrell, M. (1986) *The Apparatus of Repression*, Field Day Theatre Company, Pamphlet No. 10, Derry: Field Day, p. 5.
4. See: Farrell, M. (1983) *Arming the Protestants: The Formation of the Ulster Special Constabulary and the Royal Ulster Constabulary*, London: Pluto Press and Boyle, K., Hadden, T. and Hillyard, P. (1975) *Law and State: The Case of Northern Ireland*, London: Martin Robertson.
5. See: Bunyan, T. (1977) *The Political Police in Britain*, London: Quartet Books.
6. Palmer, S. H. (1988) *Police and Protest in England and Ireland 1780–1850*, Cambridge: Cambridge University Press, p. 528.
7. See: Miles, R. (1982) *Racism and Migrant Labour*, London: Routledge & Kegan Paul, pp. 135–50.
8. Jackson, J. A. (1963) *The Irish in Britain*, London: Routledge, p. 6.
9. Quoted in Curtis, L. (1984) *Nothing But the Same Old Story: The Roots of Anti-Irish Racism*, London: Information on Ireland, p. 51. For further reading on the roots of anti-Irish racism see: Lewis, P. and Curtis Jr. (1971) *Apes and Angels: The Irishman in Victorian Caricature*, Newton Abbot: David and Charles, and Darby, J. (1983) *Dressed to Kill: Cartoonists and the Northern Ireland Conflict*, Belfast: Appletree Press.
10. Sim, J. (1991) Review of *Proved Innocent* by Gerry Conlon and *Stolen Years* by Paul Hill in *International Journal of the Sociology of Law*, Vol. 19, No. 2, p. 238.
11. One early exception was Lambert, J. R. (1970). *Crime, Police and Race Relations: A Study in Birmingham*, London: Oxford University Press. In 1992 the first known study which attempted to explore the relationship between

the Irish, crime and policing was published. See: Woodhouse, T., O'Meachair, G., Clark, N. and Jones, M. (1992) *Policing the Irish*, London: Islington Council. It was partly based on a secondary analysis of the second Islington Crime Survey.

12. *Hansard*, Vol. 882, No. 24, Col. 35, 28 November 1975.

13. *Criminal Statistics for 1980*, Table 2.4, London: HMSO, 1981, p. 40.

14. This term was first used to distinguish between those charged in Northern Ireland with ordinary offences and those charged with schedule offences under the Northern Ireland (Emergency Provisions) Acts. Scheduled offences are those which principally arise in the course of some form of political violence. The authorities, however, have never admitted the distinction between ordinary crime and political crime. The phrase 'Ordinary Decent Criminal', which clearly assumes some other, unspecified, type of crime, is now gaining wider usage and was recently used by Lord Colville in his last review of the operation of the PTA. (See *Report on the Operation in 1990 of the Prevention of Terrorism (Temporary Provisions) Act 1989*, p. 11.)

15. See: Home Office Statistical Bulletins 1974–91. The figures refer to the period from 29 November 1974 to 31 December 1991.

16. See: Mullin, C. (1987) *Error of Judgement: The Truth About the Birmingham Bombings*, Dublin: Poolberg Press. See also Gilligan, O. (ed) (1990) *The Birmingham Six: An Appalling Vista*, Dublin: Literéire Publishers. This is a powerful and moving anthology of support by 55 writers and artists.

17. See: Conlon, G. (1990) *Proved Innocent: The Story of Gerry Conlon of the Guildford Four*, London: Hamish Hamilton, and Hill, P. (1990) *Stolen Years*, London: Doubleday.

18. See: Woffinden, B. (1987) *Miscarriages of Justice*, London: Hodder & Stoughton.

19. *Jellicoe Report*, paragraph 1.

20. *Colville Report*, paragraph 1.1.2.

21. *Jellicoe Report*, paragraph 8.

22. *Colville Report*, paragraph 1.2.6.

23. See: Sim, J. and Thomas, P. A. (1983) 'The Prevention of Terrorism Act', *Journal of Law and Society*, Vol. 10, No. 1, p. 77.

24. I will use the word Liberty to refer to NCCL except in the case of publications published before 1989.

25. See in particular: Scorer, C. (1976) *The Prevention of Terrorism Acts 1974 and 1976: A Report on the Operation of the Law*, London: NCCL; Scorer, C. and Hewitt, P. (1981) *The Prevention of Terrorism Act: The Case for Repeal*, London: NCCL; and Scorer, C., Spencer, S. and Hewitt P. (1984) *The New Prevention of Terrorism Act*, London: NCCL.

26. *Daily Telegraph*, 5 December 1983.

Notes to Chapter 2

1. Spencer, M. (1990) *1992 and All That: Civil Liberties in the Balance*, London: The Civil Liberties Trust, p. 30.
2. *Ibid.*, Chapter 2.
3. *Report of Her Majesty's Chief Inspector of Constabulary Annual Report (1983)*, *1983/84*, HC 528, London: HMSO, p. 31.
4. PTA 89, Schedule 5 Section 8.
5. *Reports of Her Majesty's Chief Inspector of Constabulary for the Years 1974 to 1989*, London HMSO.
6. *Report of Her Majesty's Chief Inspector of Constabulary, 1974*, HC 406, 1975, London HMSO, p. 37.
7. *Report of Her Majesty's Chief Inspector of Constabulary, 1989*, HC 524, 1990, London HMSO, p. 68.
8. *Ibid.*, p. 68.
9. *Report of Her Majesty's Chief Inspector of Constabulary, Annual Report 1984/85*, HC 469, London HMSO, p. 32.
10. *Report of Her Majesty's Chief Inspector of Constabulary, 1989*, HC 524, 1990, p. 68.
11. *Hansard*, Written Answers, Col. 357, 24 June 1991.
12. *Hansard*, Written Answers, Col. 355, 24 June 1991.
13. PTA 89, Schedule 5, Section 10(4).
14. PTA 89, Schedule 5, Section 10(1).
15. PTA 89, Schedule 5, Section 5(1).
16. In Northern Ireland members of the armed services are included in the definition of 'examining officers'.
17. PTA 89, Schedule 5, Section 2.
18. PTA 89, Section 14.
19. *Re Boyle, O'Hare and McAllister*, Divisional Court, 30 October 1980 (unreported).
20. Divisional Court, 30 October 1980 (unreported).
21. See: Walker, C. (1986) *The Prevention of Terrorism in British Law*, Manchester: Manchester University Press, p. 156. A second, and greatly expanded, edition of the book was published in 1992. Because this book was almost complete when the second edition was published, it has not been possible to incorporate references to it except in the concluding chapter.
22. Divisional Court, 30 October 1980 (unreported).
23. See Walker, C. (1986) *Op. cit.*, p. 157.
24. *Colville Report*, paragraph 8.6.3.
25. PTA 89, Schedule 5, Section 2(4).
26. Home Office Circular 27/1989, paragraph 5.6.
27. PTA 89, Schedule 5, Section 2(4).
28. *Colville Report*, paragraph 8.4.1.
29. *Ibid.*, paragraph 8.4.2.

30. PTA 89, Schedule 5, Section 3(2)(a).
31. *Ibid.*, Section 3(2)(b).
32. *Ibid.*, Section 3(3).
33. *Shackleton Report*, paragraph 97.
34. *Jellicoe Report*, paragraph 150.
35. *Colville Report*, paragraphs 8.5, 2-8, 5.3.
36. PTA 89, Schedule 5, Section 4(2).
37. PTA 89, Schedule 5, Section 4(5).
38. Home Office Circular 27/1989, paragraph 5.12.
39. PTA 89, Schedule 5, Section 4(1).
40. PTA 89, Schedule 5, Section 4(4).
41. PTA 89, Schedule 5, Section 11.
42. *Hansard*, Standing Committee B, Cols. 429-431, 12 January 1989.
43. PTA 89, Schedule 5, Section 6(1).
44. PTA 89, Schedule 5, Section 6(2).
45. PTA 89, Schedule 5, Section 6(3).
46. Home Office circular 27/89, paragraph 5.24.
47. See for example: Hugo Young, '59481 Reasons to Challenge this Act', The *Guardian*, 24 September 1987.
48. *Colville Report*, paragraph 16.1.2.
49. *Colville Report*, paragraph 16.1.4.
50. *Colville Report*, paragraph 16.1.5.
51. *Hansard*, Written Answer, Col. 356, 24 June 1991.

Notes to Chapter 3

1. Throughout the book all references to individual cases have been presented in a common format. The first three numbers refer to the case number followed by an 'M' or an 'F' to indicate the gender of the respondent. The next two figures refer to the year of the examination, detention or arrest. The next section refers to the length of the detention and the final section records the outcome.
2. See Chapter 2, p. 27–30.
3. The *Guardian*, 22 April, 1985.
4. *Jellicoe Report*, paragraph 131 and 152.
5. *Colville Report*, paragraph 10.1.8.
6. *Colville Report*, paragraph 8.4.1.
7. *Jellicoe Report*, paragraph 134.
8. *Colville Report*, paragraph 8.2.3.
9. *Jellicoe Report*, paragraph 140.
10. Walker, C. (1986) *The Prevention of Terrorism in British Law,* Manchester: Manchester University Press, p. 166.
11. *Shackleton Report*, paragraph 155; *Jellicoe Report*, paragraphs 140, 152.

12. Bierne, P. and Messerschmidt, J. (1991) *Criminology*, San Diego: Harcourt Brace Jovanovich, p. 315.

Notes to Chapter 4

1. PTA 89, Section 14.
2. PTA 89, Schedule 5, Section 6(1)(4).
3. Hall, P. (1989) 'The Prevention of Terrorism Acts' in Jennings, A. (ed) *Justice Under Fire: The Abuse of Civil Liberties in Northern Ireland*, pp. 171–2.
4. *Ibid.*, p.172, quote from per Hailsham *Re. W* (1971) 2 All ER 56.
5. *Shackleton Report*, paragraphs 84 and 135.
6. *Jellicoe Report*, paragraphs 67 and 232.
7. Home Office Circular 27/1989, paragraph 4.5.
8. *Ibid.*, paragraph 4.5.
9. *This Week*, June 1985.
10. Home Office Circular 27/1989, paragraph 4.12.
11. Home Office Circular 26/1984, paragraph 94.
12. Criminal Law Act 1967, Section 3(1).
13. Walker, C. (1986) *The Prevention of Terrorism in British Law*, Manchester: Manchester University Press, p. 124.
14. *Jellicoe Report*, paragraph 68.
15. PTA 89, Section 15(1).
16. PTA 89, Section 15(3).
17. PTA 89, Section 15(5).
18. PTA 89, Schedule 7, Section 2(1).
19. PTA 89, Schedule 7, Section 2(2).
20. PTA 89, Schedule 7, Section 2(3).
21. PTA 89, Section 17(1)
22. PACE 84, Sections 10 and 14.
23. These details were taken from correspondence between Liberty and the detainee's solicitors.
24. PACE 84, Section 24.
25. An amendment to Section 118(2) of PACE 84, is enacted in Schedule 8, paragraph 6(7) of the PTA 89.
26. Home Office Circular 27/1989, paragraph 23.
27. Magistrates' Court Act 1980, Section 43(1).
28. PACE 84, Sections 42 to 44.
29. *Colville Report*, paragraphs 5.3.2–5.3.5.
30. PTA 89, Schedule 3, Section 3(2).
31. PTA 89, Schedule 3, Section 5.
32. PTA 89, Schedule 3, Section 3.
33. *Jellicoe Report*, paragraphs 69–70.
34. PACE 84, Section 56.

35. PACE 84, Section 58.
36. PTA 89, Schedule 3, Section 7.
37. PACE 84, Codes of Practice, C Annex B, Section 8.
38. PACE 84, Sections 56 and 58.
39. PACE 84, Codes of Practice, C Annex B, Section 9.
40. *Hansard*, Written Answer, Col. 355, 24 June 1991.
41. *Hansard*, Written Answer, Col. 250, 8 July 1991.
42. *Shackleton Report*, paragraph 144.
43. *Jellicoe Report*, paragraph 106.
44. PACE 84, Codes of Practice, Code C, paragraph 8.1.
45. *Ibid.*, paragraph 8.2.
46. *Ibid.*, paragraph 8.3.
47. *Ibid.*, paragraph 8.4.
48. *Ibid.*, paragraph 8.5.
49. *Ibid.*, paragraph 8.6.
50. *Ibid.*, paragraph 8.7.
51. *Ibid.*, paragraph 8b.
52. *Ibid.*
53. *Ibid,* paragraph 11.5
54. *Ibid,* paragraph 11.3.
55. *Ibid,* paragraph 12.1.
56. *Ibid,* paragraph 12.2.
57. *Ibid,* paragraph 12.7.
58. *Ibid,* paragraphs 12.2 and 12.7.
59. Kaye, T. (1991) *'Unsafe and Unsatisfactory?'*, London: Civil Liberties Trust, p. 35.
60. PACE 84, Section 62.
61. PACE 84, Section 62(9) and Codes of Practice C, Annex A, paragraph 2.
62. PACE 84, Codes of Practice C, paragraph 4.1 and Annex A.
63. PTA 89, Section 14(4).
64. PTA 89, Section 14(5).
65. *Shackleton Report*, paragraph 78, and *Jellicoe Report*, paragraphs 40–44.
66. Home Office Circular 27/1989, paragraph 4.11.
67. Ewing, K. D. and Gearty, C. A. (1990) *Freedom Under Thatcher: Civil Liberties in Modern Britain*, Oxford: Clarendon Press, pp. 223–4.
68. *Brogan v UK*, (1989) 11 EHRR 117.
69. *Hansard*, Written Answer, Col 210, 14 November 1989.
70. *Ex parte* Lynch [1980] NI 126.
71. Stang Dahl, T. (1987), 'Women's Law: Method, Problems, Values', *Contemporary Crises*, Vol. 10, No. 41, pp. 361–71.
72. See in particular: Greater London Council (1986) Consultative Conference on the Effects of the Workings of the Prevention of Terrorism Act upon London's Irish Community, London: GLC, pp. 9–11.
73. *Hansard*, Written Answer, Cols 357–8, 24 June 1991.

74. *Ibid.*
75. Children and Young Persons Act, 1969, Section 28.
76. Child Care Act, 1980, Section 73(1).
77. Hill, P. (1990) *Stolen Years*, London: Doubleday, p. 56.
78. Walker, Op. cit., p. 138.
79. The contrast between the aims of the two systems can be seen in the outcome statistics. Under the ordinary criminal law, approximately 70 per cent of all arrests lead to some action, from a police caution to a charge. Under the PTA, fewer than 14 per cent of all arrests end in any formal action being taken against the person.
80. Hadden, T. and Hillyard, P. (1980) *Ten Years On in Northern Ireland: The Legal Control of Political Violence*, London: Cobden Trust, pp. 25–7.

Notes to Chapter 5

1. Bauman, Z . (1989) *Modernity and the Holocaust,* Oxford: Polity Press, p. 103.
2. *Ibid.*, p. 98.

Notes to Chapter 6

1. Many people in Ireland still refer to police stations as barracks and police officers as guards – a historical legacy of many years of military rule in Ireland. See: Palmer, S. (1988) *Police and Protest in England and Ireland 1780–1850*, Cambridge: Cambridge University Press.
2. Personal communication with the person's solicitor.
3. In *Re v Fisher* (1811) 2 Camp 563 at 570.
4. For a detailed analysis of the broader functions of the PTA see: Green, P. (1988) 'The Prevention of Terrorism and its Legislative Process', Occasional Paper, No. 3, Institute of Criminal Justice, University of Southampton.
5. Diplock Commission (1972) *Report of the Commission to Consider Legal Procedures to deal with Terrorist Activities in Northern Ireland*, 1972 Cmnd. 5185, London: HMSO, paragraph 84.

Notes to Chapter 7

1. There are other aspects of sexuality and custody which require further examination. In Northern Ireland women police officers take part in the physical maltreatment of both female and male detainees. Also, there are strong homosexual overtones in some of the ill-treatment of male detainees – especially young boys – by male police officers. There have been

reports of police officers sitting on their laps while hitting them, kissing them, humiliating them sexually and making them strip without any justification. See: Evidence submitted by Madden & Finucane to the Northern Ireland Human Rights Assembly, London, 7 April 1992 (copy held by Civil Liberties Trust Library, 21 Tabard Street, London SE1 4LA).

2. See: Goffman, I. (1961) *Asylums: Essays on the Social Situations of Mental Patients and Other Inmates*, Harmondsworth: Penguin, pp. 24–40.

3. See: NCCL (1986) *Strip Searching: An Inquiry into the Strip Searching of Remand Prisoners at Armagh Prison between 1982 and 1985*, London: NCCL; LSPU (1988) *Working Together to End Strip Searching: Report of a Conference, 5 December 1987*, London: GLC; UCASS (n.d.) *Strip Searching: Personal Testimonies, Report of an Inquiry into the Psychological Effects of Strip Searching*, London: United Campaign Against Strip Searching; Howard League (1989) *Strip Searching in HM Prisons*, London: Howard League.

4. *Jellicoe Report*, paragraph 96.

5. *Jellicoe Report*, paragraph 97.

6. Diplock Commission (1972) *Report of the Commission to Consider Legal Procedures to deal with Terrorist Activities in Northern Ireland*, Cmnd. 5185, London: HMSO, paragraph 84.

7. Compton Report (1971) *Report of the Inquiry into Allegations against the Security Forces of Physical Brutality in Northern Ireland Arising out of Events on 9th August 1971*, Cmnd. 4823, London: HMSO.

8. See: *Ireland v United Kingdom of Great Britain and Ireland* (Application No. 5310/71), Report of the European Commission on Human Rights (adopted 25 January 1976) and Judgment of the European Court of Human Rights (delivered 18 January 1978).

9. Bennett Report (1979) *Report of the Committee of Inquiry into Police Interrogation Procedures in Northern Ireland*, Cmnd. 7497, London: HMSO, paragraph 46. See also Taylor, P. (1980) *Beating the Terrorists: Interrogation at Omagh, Gough and Castlereagh*, Penguin Books.

10. Committee on Administration of Justice and Amnesty International (1991) *Ill-treatment of Persons Detained under Emergency Legislation in Northern Ireland*, Evidence presented to the United Nations Committee Against Torture, Belfast: CAJ.

11. Poulantzas, M. C. (1980) *State Power and Socialism*, London: Verso Press, pp. 76–7.

12. Dixon, D. (1991) 'Common Sense, Legal Advice and the Right to Silence', *Public Law*, Vol. xx, pp. 233–54.

13. See: Irving, B. and Hilgendorf, L. (1980) *Police Interrogation: The Psychological Approach*, Royal Commission on Criminal Procedure, Research Studies No. 1, London: HMSO.

14. See, for example: Inbau, F. E., Reid, J. E. and Buckley, J. P. (1986) *Criminal Interrogation and Confessions* (3rd ed), Baltimore: Williams and Wilkins.

15. McConville, M., Sanders, A. and Leng, R. (1991) *The Case for the Prosecution*, London: Routledge, p. 38.

Notes to Chapter 8

1. See for example: Softley, P. (1980) *Police Interrogation, An Observational Study in Four Police Stations*, Home Office Research Study, No. 61, London: HMSO; Irving, B. (1980) *Police Interrogation. A Case Study of Current Practice*, Research Studies No. 2, London: HMSO; and Irving, B. and McKenzie, I. R. (1989) *Police Interrogation: The Effects of the Police and Criminal Evidence Act*, London: Police Foundation.
2. Morton, S. (1990) *The Ever-So-Gentle-Art of Police Interrogation*, Paper presented at the British Psychological Society Annual Conference, Swansea University, 5 April.
3. Irving, B. and Hilgendorf, L. (1980) *Police Interrogation: The Psychological Approach*, Research Study No. 1 and No. 2, Royal Commission of Criminal Procedure, London: HMSO, p. 42.
4. See for example: NACRO (1986) *Black People and the Criminal Justice System*, Report of the NACRO Race Advisory Committee, London: NACRO; Shallice, A. and Gordon P. (1990) *Black People, White Justice: Race and the Criminal Justice System*, London: Runnymeade Trust; Smith, D. and Gray J. (1983) *The Police and People in London*, Vol. 4, London: Policy Studies Institute.
5. See: Scraton, P. (1991) 'Recent Developments in Criminology: A Critical Overview', in M. Haralambos (ed) *Developments in Sociology: An Annual Review*, Vol. 7, London: Causeway Press.
6. See: *Statewatch*, Vol. 2, No. 2, p. 4–5.
7. See: Kelley, K. (1982) *The Longest War: Northern Ireland and the IRA*, Dingle: Brandon, p. 190.
8. McConville, M., Sanders, A. and Leng, R. (1991) *The Case for the Prosecution*, London: Routledge, p. 78.
9. *Ibid.*, p. 79.
10. *Ibid.*, Chapter 2: Constructing the Suspect Population, pp. 14–35.

Notes to Chapter 9

1. House of Commons debates. Vol. 493, Col. 1209, 15 November 1951.
2. Walker, C. (1986) *The Prevention of Terrorism in British Law*, Manchester: Manchester University Press, p. 67.
3. *Jellicoe Report*, paragraph 162.
4. PTA 89, Sections 4(1) & 4(2).
5. PTA 89, Section 5.

6. Home Office Circular, 27/1989, paragraph 2.8.
7. *Ibid.*
8. PTA 1989, Schedule 5, Section 6(1)b.
9. See: Bonner, D. (1985) *Emergency Powers in Peacetime Britain*, London: Sweet and Maxwell, p. 169; Scorer, C., Spencer, S. and Hewitt, P. (1985) *The New Prevention of Terrorism Act: the Case for Repeal*, London: NCCL, p. 28.
10. *R. v. Secretary of State for the Home Department ex parte Stitt*, DC 28 January 1987.
11. *Hansard*, Standing Committee D, Col. 164, 16 November 1983.
12. Walker (1986), *Op. cit.*, p. 59.
13. PTA 1989, Section 5(4).
14. Twenty-three Orders were made against those resident between 3 and 20 years in the decade prior to 1984, see *Hansard*, Standing Committee D. Col. 115, 15 November 1983
15. *Jellicoe Report*, paragraphs 178 & 181.
16. PTA 89, Section 7.
17. British Nationality Act 1981, see Walker (1986), *Op. cit.*, p. 59.
18. Immigration Act 1971.
19. *Jellicoe Report*, paragraph 162; Home Office Circular, 27/1989, paragraph 2.10.
20. *Colville Report*, paragraph 12.1.5.
21. Home Office Circular, 27/1989, paragraph 2.11.
22. *Colville Report*, paragraph 11.8.2.
23. Home Office Circular, 27/1989, paragraph 2.10.
24. *Shackleton Report*, paragraph 39.
25. *Colville Report*, paragraph 12.1.3.
26. Home Office Circular, 27/1989, paragraph 2.9.
27. *Shackleton Report*, paragraph 41.
28. *Shackleton Report*, paragraph 39.
29. Home Office Circular, 27/1989, paragraph 2.9.
30. *Shackleton Report*, paragraph 39.
31. Mullin, C. (1986) *Error of Judgement: The Birmingham Bombings*, Dublin: Poolberg, pp. 165–71, 239.
32. *Jellicoe Report*, paragraph 187–9; *Philips Report* (1985), *Op. cit.*, paragraph 40; *Colville Report*, paragraph 11.5.2.
33. *Shackleton Report*, paragraph 38–9.
34. *Colville Report*, paragraph 11.8.1.
35. *Jellicoe Report*, paragraph 191.
36. *Colville Report*, paragraphs 12.1.3–12.1.6.
37. On summary conviction to imprisonment for a term not exceeding 6 months or to a fine not exceeding the statutory maximum, or both; or on conviction on indictment to imprisonment for a term not exceeding 5 years, or to a fine, or both. PTA 89, Section 8(4).
38. *Jellicoe Report*, paragraph 198.

39. PTA 89, Schedule 2, Section 2.
40. PTA 89, Schedule 2, Section 7.
41. Home Office Circular 27/1989, paragraph 2.16.
42. PTA 89, Schedule 2, Section 5.
43. Full objections need not be supplied within these time limits but a request to do so must be made.
44. PTA 89, Schedule 2, Section 3.
45. Scorer, C., Spencer, S. and Hewitt, P. (1985) *The New Prevention of Terrorism Act: The Case for Repeal*, London: NCCL, pp. 24–5.
46. PTA 89, Schedule 2, Section 3.
47. Scorer, C. and Hewitt, P. (1981) *The 1976 Prevention of Terrorism Act: The Case for Repeal*, London: Liberty, pp. 30–31.
48. *Jellicoe Report*, paragraph 195.
49. *Colville Report*, paragraph 11.3.1.
50. *Shackleton Report*, paragraph 47–8.
51. Bonner (1985) *Op. cit.*, p. 198.
52. PTA 84, Section 7(ii).
53. *Shackleton Report*, paragraph 127.
54. *Jellicoe Report*, paragraph 198.
55. *Colville Report*, paragraph 11.10.2.
56. *Hansard*, Col. 761–2, 29 July 1988; Home Office Circular, 26/84, paragraph 79.
57. *Colville* (1989), paragraph 4.4.
58. *Hansard*, Col. 689, 24 February 1992.
59. *Colville Report*, paragraph 11.6.1.
60. *Philips Report* (1986) *Report on the Operation during the Year 1985 of the Prevention of Terrorism (Temporary Provisions) Act 1984*, House of Commons Library.

Notes to Chapter 10

1. *Philips Report* (1985) *Report on the Operation during the Year 1984 of the Prevention of Terrorism (Temporary Provisions) Act 1984*, House of Commons Library.
2. *Shackleton Report*, paragraph 50.

Notes to Chapter 11

1. Evidence given by Gareth Peirce to the Northern Ireland Human Rights Assembly, London, 7 April 1992 (copy held in Civil Liberties Trust Library, 21 Tabard Street, London SE1).
2. See: The *Guardian*, 12 November 1981.

3. For more details see *The Times,* 14 December 1983.
4. See: the case of John McKenna reported in Scorer, C., Spencer, S. and Hewitt, P. (1985) *The New Prevention of Terrorism Act: The Case for Repeal,* London: NCCL, p. 26.
5. See: Boyle, K., Hadden, T. and Hillyard, P. (1975) *Law and State: The Case of Northern Ireland,* London: Martin Roberston, Chapter 2.
6. See: pp. 60–2.
7. Foley, C. (n.d.) *Temporary Provisions: The Case Against the Prevention of Terrorism Act,* London: Labour Committee on Ireland, p. 11.
8. See Curtis, L. (1984) *Ireland: The Propaganda War,* London: Pluto Press, pp.171–2 and Article 19 (1989) *No Comment: Censorship, Secrecy and the Irish Troubles,* London: Article 19.
9. Goodwin, P. (1992) 'Protect and Survive', *Broadcast,* May 1992.

Notes to Chapter 12

1. The *Guardian,* 13 April 1992, p. 7.
2. Although a highly respected investigative journalist on Northern Ireland argues that the evidence does not suggest a conspiracy (See Taylor, P. (1987) *Stalker: The Search for Truth,* London: Faber and Faber), the government should set up a tribunal of inquiry to establish the facts.
3. See in particular: Kitchen, H. (1989) *The Gibraltar Report,* London: Liberty.
4. The *Irish News,* 19 October 1990.
5. The *Mail on Sunday,* 23 September 1990.
6. *Today,* 5 April 1989.
7. The *Sunday Telegraph,* 29 October 1989.
8. See: Foley, C. and Moriarty M. (1989) *Justice Denied: Irish People and the English Law,* London: Connolly Association.
9. See: Green, P. (1990) *Policing the Miners,* London: Sage.
10. Thornton, P. (1989) *Decade of Decline: Civil Liberties in the Thatcher Years,* London: Liberty, pp. 86–8.
11. See in particular: Hall, S., Critcher, C., Clarke, J., Jefferson, T. and Roberts, B. (1987) *Policing the Crisis,* London: Macmillan; Institute of Race Relations (1987)*Policing Against Black People,* London: Institute of Race Relations; Cashmore, E. and McLaughlin E. (1991), *Out of Order? Policing Black People,* London: Routledge.
12. Criminal Statistics for England and Wales for 1981 and 1991, London: HMSO.
13. My thanks to Dee Coombes for this observation.
14. The *Guardian,* 12 May 1992.
15. Sharat, A. and Kearns, T. R. (1991) 'A Journey Through Forgetting: Toward a Jurisprudence of Violence' in *The Fate of Law,* edited by Sharat A. and Kearns, T. R., Michigan: University of Michigan Press.

16. Quoted in Sim, J. and Thomas, P. A. (1983), 'The Prevention of Terrorism Act', *Journal of Law and Society*, Vol. 10, No. 1, p. 75.
17. PACE, Section 9 and Schedule 1.
18. PTA 89, Section 17 and Schedule 7.
19. See: Chapter 11.
20. See Standing Advisory Commission on Human Rights: SACHR (1986) Twelfth Report of the Standing Advisory Committee on Human Rights, *Annual Report for 1985–6*, HC 151, London: HMSO, pp. 8–10 and *Independent*, 30 November 1988.
21. See: Reynolds, P. (1987) 'No Time for Love in the Morning', *An Pobal Eirithe*, No. 3, p. 5.
22. See the criticism of this position by the Standing Advisory Commission on Human Rights: SACHR (1986) Eleventh Report of the Standing Advisory Committee on Human Rights, *Annual Report for 1984–1985*, HC 394, London: HMSO, paragraphs 53–5.
23. Delmas-Marty, M. (1992) The *European Convention for the Protection of Human Rights*, Dordrecht: Kluwer Academic Publishers, p. 15.
24. *Ibid.*, p. 15.
25. *Ibid.*, p. 15.
26. *Ibid.*, p. 16.
27. ECHR case of *Klass and Others*, 6 September 1978.
28. *Hansard*, 7 March 1983, Vol. 38, Col. 576.
29. Jellicoe Report, paragraph 116.
30. Colville Report, paragraph, 3.1.4.
31. The *Guardian*, 23 April 1992.
32. Colville Report, paragraph 3.1.3.
33. Jellicoe Report, paragraph 176.
34. *Hansard*, 24 February 1992, Vol 204, Col. 693.
35. Jellicoe Report, paragraph 207.
36. *Hansard*, 24 February 1992, Vol. 204, Col. 691.
37. Jellicoe Report, paragraph 212.
38. Jellicoe Report, paragraph 116.
39. *Hansard*, 24 February 1992, Vol. 204, Col. 694.
40. *Ibid*, Col. 694.
41. Walker, C. (1992) *The Prevention of Terrorism in British law*, (2nd edn), Manchester: Manchester University Press, p. 244.
42. Nevertheless, Walker concluded, without presenting any evidence to support this view, that the Acts had achieved some preventive influence over terrorism in Britain, *Ibid.* p. 250.

Bibliography

Article 19 (1989) *No Comment: Censorship, Secrecy and the Irish Troubles*, London: Article 19.

Bennett Report (1979) *Report of the Committee of Inquiry into Police Interrogation Procedures in Northern Ireland*, Cmnd. 7497, London: HMSO.

Bierne, P. and Messerschmidt, J. (1991) *Criminology*, San Diego: Harcourt Brace Jovanovich.

Bonner, D. (1982) 'Combating Terrorism in Great Britain: The Role of Exclusion Orders', *Public Law*, pp. 262–81.

Bonner, D. (1983) 'Combating Terrorism: The Jellicoe Approach', *Public Law*, pp. 224–34.

Bonner, D. (1989) 'Combating Terrorism in the 1990s', *Public Law*, pp. 440–76.

Boyle, K., Hadden, T. and Hillyard, P. (1975) *Law and State: The Case of Northern Ireland*, London: Martin Robertson.

Boyle, K., Hadden, T. and Hillyard, P. (1980) *Ten Years on in Northern Ireland*, London: Cobden Trust.

Bunyan, T. (1977) *The Political Police in Britain*, London: Quartet Books.

Cashmore, E. and McLaughlin E. (1991) *Out of Order? Policing Black People*, London: Routledge.

Colville (1989) *Report on the Operation in 1988 of the Prevention of Terrorism (Temporary Provisions) Act 1984*, House of Commons Library.

Colville (1991) *Report on the Operation in 1990 of the Prevention of Terrorism (Temporary Provisions) Act 1989*, House of Commons Library.

Colville Report (1987) *Review of the Operation of the Prevention of Terrorism (Temporary Provisions) Act 1984*, Cm. 264, London: HMSO.

Compton Report (1971) *Report of the Enquiry into Allegations against the Security Forces of Physical Brutality in Northern Ireland Arising out of Events on 9th August 1971*, Cmnd. 4823, London: HMSO.

Conlon, G. (1990) *Proved Innocent: The Story of Gerry Conlon of the Guildford Four*, London: Hamish Hamilton.

Connolly Association (nd) *The Prevention of Terrorism Act*, London: Connolly Association.

Curtis, L. (1984) *Nothing But the Same Old Story: The Roots of Anti-Irish Racism*, London: Information on Ireland.

Curtis, L. (1984) *Ireland: The Propaganda War*, London: Pluto Press.

Darby, J. (1983) *Dressed to Kill: Cartoonists and the Northern Ireland Conflict*, Belfast: Appletree Press.

Diplock Commission (1972) *Report of the Commission to Consider Legal Procedures to Deal with Terrorist Activities in Northern Ireland*, Cmnd. 5185, London: HMSO.

Dixon, D. (1991) 'Common Sense, Legal Advice and the Right to Silence', *Public Law*, pp. 233–54.

Ewing, K.D. and Gearty, C.A. (1990) *Freedom Under Thatcher: Civil Liberties in Modern Britain*, Oxford: Clarendon Press.

Farrell, M. (1983) *Arming the Protestants: The Formation of the Ulster Special Constabulary and the Royal Ulster Constabulary*, London: Pluto Press.

Farrell, M. (1986) *The Apparatus of Repression*, Field Day Theatre Company, Pamphlet No. 10, Derry: Field Day.

Foley, C. (nd) *Temporary Provisions? The Case Against the Prevention of Terrorism Act*, London: Labour Committee on Ireland.

Foley, C. and Moriarty, M. (1989) *Justice Denied: Irish People and the English Law*, London: Connolly Association.

Gilligan, O. (ed) (1990) *The Birmingham Six: An Appalling Vista*, Dublin: Literéire Publishers.

Goffman, I. (1961) *Asylums: Essays on the Social Situations of Mental Patients and Other Inmates*, Harmondsworth: Penguin.

Goodwin P. (1992) 'Protect and Survive', *Broadcast*, May 1992.

Greater London Council (1986) Consultative Conference on the Effects of the Workings of the Prevention of Terrorism Act upon London's Irish Community, London: GLC.

Green, P. (1988) 'The Prevention of Terrorism and its Legislative Process', Occasional Paper, No. 3, Institute of Criminal Justice, University of Southampton.

Green, P. (1990) *Policing the Miners*, London: Sage.

Hadden, T. and Hillyard, P. (1980) *Ten Years On in Northern Ireland: The Legal Control of Political Violence*, London: Cobden Trust.

Hall, P. (1989) 'The Prevention of Terrorism Acts' in Jennings, A. (ed) *Justice Under Fire: The Abuse of Civil Liberties in Northern Ireland*, London: Pluto Press.

Hall, S., Critcher, C., Clarke, J., Jefferson, T. and Roberts, B. (1987) *Policing the Crisis*, London: Macmillan.

Hill, P. (1990) *Stolen Years*, London: Doubleday.

Hillyard, P. (1987) 'The Normalisation of Special Powers' in Scraton, P. (ed) *Law, Order and the Authoritarian State*, Milton Keynes: Open University Press.

Hogan, G. and Walker, C. (1989) *Political Violence and the Law in Ireland*, Manchester: Manchester University Press.

Howard League (1989) *Strip Searching in HM Prisons*, London: Howard League.

Hugo Young, '59481 Reasons to Challenge this Act', The *Guardian*, 24 September 1987.

Inbau, F. E., Reid, J. E. and Buckley, J. P. (1986) *Criminal Interrogation and Confessions* (3rd edn), Baltimore: Williams and Wilkins.

Institute of Race Relations (1987) *Policing Against Black People*, London: Institute of Race Relations.

Irving, B. (1980) *Police Interrogation: A Case Study of Current Practice*, Research Studies No. 2, London: HMSO.

Irving, B. and Hilgendorf, L. (1980) *Police Interrogation: The Psychological Approach*, Royal Commission on Criminal Procedure, Research Studies No. 1, London: HMSO.

Irving, B. and McKenzie, I. R. (1989) *Police Interrogation: The Effects of the Police and Criminal Evidence Act*, London: Police Foundation.

Jackson, J. A. (1963) *The Irish in Britain*, London: Routledge.

Jellicoe Report (1983) *Review of the Operation of the Prevention of Terrorism (Temporary Provisions) Acts 1976*, Cmnd. 8803, London: HMSO.

Jennings, A. (ed) (1990) *Justice under Fire* (2nd edn), London: Pluto Press.

Kaye, Tim (1991) *'Unsafe and Unsatisfactory'?* Report of the Independent Inquiry into the Working Practices of the West Midlands Police Serious Crime Squad, London: Civil Liberties Trust.

Kelley, K. (1982) *The Longest War: Northern Ireland and the IRA*, Dingle: Brandon.

Lambert, J. R. (1970) *Crime, Police and Race Relations: A Study in Birmingham*, London: Oxford University Press.

Lewis, P. and Curtis Jr. (1971) *Apes and Angels: The Irishman in Victorian Caricature*, Newton Abbot: David Charles.

London Strategic Policy Unit (1988) *Working Together to End Strip Searching*, Report of a Conference, 5 December 1987, London: GLC.

London Strategic Policy Unit (1988) *Policing the Irish Community*, Police Monitoring and Research Group, Briefing Paper No. 5, London: LSPU.

McConville, M., Sanders, A. and Leng, R. (1991) *The Case for the Prosecution*, London: Routledge.

Miles, R. (1982) *Racism and Migrant Labour*, London: Routledge & Kegan Paul.

Mullin, C. (1987) *Error of Judgement: The Truth about the Birmingham Bombings*, Dublin: Poolberg Press.

NACRO (1986) *Black People and the Criminal Justice System*, Report of the NACRO Race Advisory Committee, London: NACRO.

NCCL (1986) *Strip Searching: An Inquiry into the Strip Searching of Remand Prisoners at Armagh Prison between 1982 and 1985*, London: NCCL.

Palmer, Stanley H. (1988) *Police and Protest in England and Ireland 1780–1850*, Cambridge: Cambridge University Press.

Philips (1985) *Report on the Operation during the Year 1984 of the Prevention of Terrorism (Temporary Provisions) Act 1984*, House of Commons Library.

Philips (1986) *Report on the Operation during the Year 1985 of the Prevention of Terrorism (Temporary Provisions) Act 1984*, House of Commons Library.

Poulantzas, M. C. (1980) *State Power and Socialism*, London: Verso Press.

PTA Research and Welfare Association (1987) *The Prevention of Terrorism Act: A Massive and Ongoing Breach of Civil Liberties*, Submission to Viscount Colville in conjunction with the Irish Chaplaincy Scheme in Britain and the Irish Commission for Prisoners Overseas, Birmingham: PTA RWA.

Suspect Community

Reynolds, P. (1987) 'No Time for Love in the Morning', *An Pobal Eirithe*, No. 3, p. 5.

Rose-Smith, B. (1979) 'Police Powers and the Terrorism Legislation' in Hain, P. (ed), *Policing the Police*, Vol. 1, London: John Calder.

Scorer, C. (1976) *The Prevention of Terrorism Acts 1974–1976: A Report on the Operation of the Law*, London: Cobden Trust.

Scorer, C. and Hewitt, P. (1981) *The Prevention of Terrorism Act: The Case for Repeal*, London: Cobden Trust.

Scorer, C., Spencer, S. and Hewitt, P. (1985) *The New Prevention of Terrorism Act: The Case for Repeal*, London: NCCL.

Scraton, P. (1991) 'Recent Developments in Criminology: A Critical Overview, in Haralambos, M. (ed) *Developments in Sociology: An Annual Review*, Vol. 7, London: Causeway Press.

Shackleton Report (1978) *Review of the Operation of the Prevention of Terrorism (Temporary Provisions) Acts 1974 and 1976*, Cmnd. 7324, London: HMSO.

Shallice, A. and Gordon, P. (1990) *Black People, White Justice: Race and the Criminal Justice System*, London: Runnymede Trust.

Sim, J. (1991) Review of *Proved Innocent* by Gerry Conlon and *Stolen Years* by Paul Hill in *International Journal of the Sociology of Law*, Vol. 19, No. 2, p. 238.

Sim, J. and Thomas, P. A. (1983) 'The Prevention of Terrorism Act: Normalising the Politics of Repression' in *Journal of Law and Society*, Vol. 10, No. 1, pp. 71–84.

Smith, D. and Gray J. (1983) *The Police and People in London*, Vol. 4, London: Policy Studies Institute.

Softley, P. (1980) *Police Interrogation, An Observational Study in Four Police Stations*, Home Office Research Study, No. 61, London: HMSO.

Spencer, M. (1990) *1992 and All That: Civil Liberties in the Balance*, London: The Civil Liberties Trust.

Stang Dahl, T. (1987) 'Women's Law: Method, Problems, Values', *Contemporary Crises*, Vol. 10, No. 41, pp. 361–71.

Street, H. (1975) 'The Prevention of Terrorism (Temporary Provisions) Act' in *Criminal Law Review*, Vol. 192.

Taylor, P. (1980) *Beating the Terrorists: Interrogation at Omagh, Gough and Castlereagh*, Harmondsworth: Penguin.

Thornton, P. (1989) *Decade of Decline: Civil Liberties in the Thatcher Years*, London: Liberty.

United Campaign Against Strip Searching (n.d.) *Strip Searching: Personal Testimonies, Report of an Inquiry into the Psychological Effects of Strip Searching*, London: UCASS.

Walker, C. P. (1984) 'Prevention of Terrorism (Temporary Provisions) Act 1984', *Modern Law Review*, Vol. 47, pp. 704–13.

Walker, C. P. (1983) 'The Jellicoe Report on the Prevention of Terrorism (Temporary Provisions) Act 1976', *Modern Law Review*, Vol. 46, pp. 484–92.

Woffinden, B. (1987) *Miscarriages of Justice*, London: Hodder & Stoughton.

Woodhouse, T., O'Meachair, G., Clark, N. and Jones, M. (1992) *Policing the Irish*, London: Islington Council.

Index

Adams, Gerry, 234
Amnesty International, 170
Ancient Order of Hibernians, 48
Anti-Apartheid Meeting, 47, 58, 61
Archer, Peter, 26
Armstrong, Patrick, 7, 88
arrests: at home, 1, 123–7
    at work, 132
    force used, 71–2
    mass arrests, 86–8, 128, 183
    media coverage of, 140–7
    on the streets, 127–31
    powers of, 68–72, 269–70
    released, 1, 5, 86, 147, 199
    statistics on, 86–8
Astra, 57
Attorney General, 27

Baker, Kenneth, 266
banning orders, 91, 94, 254, 271
Barry, Tom, 118
Bauman, Zygmunt, 96
BBC, 142–4
Benn, Tony, 101
Bentham, Jeremy, 67
Birmingham pub bombings, 1,
Birmingham Six, 7, 10, 111, 149,
    155, 170
Box Productions, 254–5, 264
Brittan, Leon, 70
broadcasting ban, 271–2
Campbell, Glen, 118
carding, 17, 38, 43, 44, 45, 52
Castlereagh Holding Centre, 49,
    213, 229–30, 231, 232
cells, condition of, 113, 115, 160–8
censorship, 238

Channel Four, 142, 264
children: and exclusions orders, 237
    and house searches, 136
    at ports and airports, 49–51
    impact of PTA on, 109–10, 241–2
    on arrest of parents, 85, 133–5
    placed in care, 49, 50, 95, 103
    threats about, 190
civil liberties: arrest, 90, 259
    censorship, 238
    exclusion, 42, 206, 215–16, 235,
        237
    freedom of movement, 30–1,
        39–43, 43–9, 63, 65, 235 247–9
    privacy, 24, 66, 39–43, 54–8, 155,
        175
    proscription, 91, 254–71
Clann na h'Eireann, 195, 252
Clarke, Kenneth, 256
Collins, Gerry, 116
Collins, Michael, 40
Colombia, 131, 259
Colville Report: flaws in, 8–9
    on accommodation at ports, 51
    on examination rights, 19
    on examination statistics, 28, 29–30
    on exclusion, 202, 203, 205, 206,
        211, 213, 216
    on extensions to detentions, 81–2
    on power to see documents, 24
    on questions at ports and airports,
        23
    on random searches, 58
    on review procedures, 75
    on suspicion, 60, 205
Committee for the Administration
    of Justice, 170, 214, 230

confessions, false, 7
Conlon, Gerry, 7
conspiracy charges:
  to cause explosions, 129, 240
  to murder, 145
Court of Appeal, 7, 19, 88, 200, 262
crime: political, 77
  ordinary, 4, 68, 77, 261, 264
criminal justice system:
  dual system of, 4, 68, 93
  racist bias in, 159–60, 191–3,
    260–1
  research on, 4
custody:
  abuse of power in, 5
  death in, 7
  initiation rituals, 151
Criminal Law Act, (1977), 71
criminalisation, 151, 154, 260–1
Crown Prosecution Service, 212

Data Protection Act, (1984), 17
date of birth,
  for intelligence gathering, 42, 53,
    98, 194, 251
Denning, Lord, 10
Department of Employment, 232
Department of Social Security, 131
detention:
  concessions in, 77–8
  conditions of, 78–9, 98–9, 113,
    160–9
  extensions to, 88–90
  length of, 81–3
  outcome of, 1, 5, 17, 59, 73–9,
    90–2,
  regimes in, 169–77, 269
  review procedures, 74–7
  rules, 73–7
Devlin, Bernadette, 118
Diplock, Lord, 148, 170
Director of Public Prosecutions, 27,
  75
Disraeli, 3

doctors, 96, 100, 101, 113, 116, 155,
  174, 177–9, 262
Donaldson, Lord, 18

Easter Rising, 48
Ellenborough, Lord, 142
employment, impact of PTA on,
  117, 245–7
European Convention on Human
  Rights, 82, 264
European Court of Human Rights,
  82, 108, 170, 265, 266–7
Ewing, Keith, 82
examinations at ports and airports:
  basis of suspicion, 59–64
  conditions, 40, 44, 51–2
  duty to comply, 25–6
  efficacy of, 43
  impact of, 64–5
  length of, 19, 21
  notice of rights, 19–21, 34
  people's experiences, 27–32,
    37–65
  power to detain, 21–3, 26, 69
  power to question, 23, 52–4
  power to see all relevant
    documents, 24, 54–8
  power to retain documents, 25
  random investigations, 19, 46
  statistics on, 27–32
  unfettered discretion to examine,
    18–19
exclusion:
  arbitrariness of, 236
  cost to excludee, 226–7
  courts' approach, 200
  criticisms of, 214–6
  impact of 243–4, 249
  intelligence information, 203–4
  interview with adviser, 228–9
  journey into exile, 224–7
  lack of reasons, 218–19
  lack of suspicion, 199
  making decisions, 202–3

notification of, 217–19
orders of, 69, 75, 146, 217
powers of, 13, 198–201
representation, 49, 129, 209–12,
220–3, 227–36
review process, 212–14
statistics on, 207–8
equal before, 85
exercise, 104, 175

family:
threats to, 187, 190
impact of PTA on, 43, 85, 242–5
Fenians, in C19th, 2
financial consequences of PTA,
249–50
fingerprinting, 80, 98, 108, 113,
150, 152–7, 188
food:
poor quality in custody, 168–9
deprivation of, 173
forensic tests, 7, 98, 152, 204–5
Fortress Europe, 14, 33

Gearty, Conor, 82
George, Lloyd, 40
Gibraltar shootings, 257
Goodwin, Peter, 254
Greater London Council, 9
Guildford Four, 7, 10, 88, 149, 155,
170

H-Block, 54, 139
Hall, Peter, 69
Hamilton, Bill, 143,
handcuffs, 105, 130, 175, 224
harassment:
of Irish, 66, 148, 238
sexual, 56, 66
Hattersley, Roy, 266
health, physical,
impact of PTA on, 238–41
health, mental,
impact of PTA on, 238–41

Her Majesty's Inspector of Constabulary, 16, 27, 51
Hill, Paul, 7, 88
house:
searches of, 98
damage to, 1, 108, 134, 138, 249
Hume, John, 43, 54
Hurd, Douglas, 229, 266

identity:
proof of, 14, 38, 41, 47, 48, 53,
58, 128
cards, 33, 45
use of passports, 39
immigrant workers, 14
Immigration Act, (1971), 13, 201
incommunicado, 77, 78, 94, 140,
176, 245
informers, recruiting of, 195–6
intelligence gathering, 30, 32, 66,
69–71, 77, 85, 93, 138, 148,
195, 203–4, 268
internal exile,
see exclusion
International Convent on Civil and
Political Rights, 82
international terrorism, 5, 13, 71, 73,
201
internment, 54, 63, 189, 214, 274,
252–65
interrogation:
after arrest, 79–80, 101
at ports and airports, 62
bigotry of, 114
length of, 187–8
methods of, 102
psychological research on, 182
rooms used for, 166, 184
techniques,188–9
threats, 189–91
types of questions, 193–5
Irish Embassy, 140
Ireland, Acts of Coercion in C19th,
2

Irish National Liberation Army, 194,
     195, 256
Irish people:
   as depicted in racist stereotypes, 3
   as a suspect community, 5, 13, 33,
     93, 146, 197, 257–61
   as suspects in criminal justice
     system, 7, 159–60
   attacks on, 1, 2
   born in Britain, 3
   invisible as an ethnic minority, 4
Irish Republican Army (IRA), 53,
     61, 118, 131, 146, 194, 258,
     260, 268
Irish Republican Socialist Party, 194,
     195, 243, 252
isolation,
   in custody, 151, 176

Jellicoe Report
   deterrence and PTA, 67
   flaws in, 8–9
   on accommodation at ports and
     airports, 51
   on exclusion, 200, 201, 202, 205,
     206, 210, 213, 220, 270
   on detention, 76, 78, 165
   on grounds for arrest, 72
   on port controls, 66, 67
   on power to see documents, 24
   on proscription, 271
   on suspicion, 65
   terms of reference, 8
Jenkins, Roy, 4, 267
journalists, curtailment of, 255
Judges' Rules, 74, 79

King, Tom, 143–6

law: abrogation of rule of, 71, 194,
     215
   as racist, 33, 258
   equal before, 85
   lack of confidence in, 250–2

normalisation of emergency law,
     263–4

Lawley, Sue, 143
legal advice, 77, 78, 179–81, 223
Lennon, Kenneth, 196
Liberty, 9, 229
London Boroughs Grants
     Committee, 9
Long Kesh, 41

MacBride, Sean, 42
Magee, Patrick, 90
Maguire Seven, 7, 10, 88, 106, 149
McConville, Mike, 196
media:
   bias reporting, 35, 140–8
   dissemination of information to, 5
   disclosure of sources, 254–5
MI5, 257, 268
migration, 3
miscarriages of justice, 26, 94, 150,
     215, 257, 262,
   see also Birmingham 6, Guildford
     4, Maguire 7 and Judith Ward
mortification processes, 151
Murphy, Dervla, 55, 60–1
Murphy riots, 2

National Council for Civil Liberties,
     9,
   see also Liberty
National Identification Bureau, 157
National Joint Unit, 16–18, 27–8,
     32, 33, 38, 48, 60, 66, 81, 202
National Ports Scheme, 13, 14–16
National Security Commission, 9
National Union of Students, 44, 62,
     63
Nelson, Brian, 196
Nuremberg, 120

O'Donnell, Kevin Barry, 196, 206
   of suspects at ports, 46, 59

Offences under the PTA,
  and exclusions orders, 199
  and proscribed organisations,
    90–1, 194, 254, 264
  charges brought, 91
  withholding information, 183, 184
Ordinary Decent Criminals (ODCs),
  4, 68, 73, 77, 261, 264
Paddington Green Police Station, 1,
  50, 95, 96, 104, 110, 132, 140,
  168, 171, 185, 191, 219
Parliament:
  European, 33, 45
  Westminster, 44, 76, 228, 256
personal belongings,
  taking away, 151
  return of, 107
Philips, Sir Cyril, 216, 226
Phillips, Melanie, 266
photocopying,
  of materials retained, 55, 58, 62
photographs:
  after arrest, 98, 113, 150, 152–7
  family, 42, 139
  of Bristol riots, 263–4
  of houses of detainees, 126
  on ID cards, 47
Place of Safety Order, 85
plastic bullets, 46, 54, 57, 61
police:
  abuse of powers, 71
  and media, 147–8
  armed, 1, 71, 112, 113, 124, 126,
    132, 137, 143, 147, 261, 262
  beatings, 7
  coerciveness of, 96, 184, 187, 196,
    273
  custody, 149–182
  discretion, 59
  National Police Computer, 17,
    27, 95
  with dogs, 133, 135–6, 138
Police and Criminal Evidence Act:
  and PTA, 83–4, 149

Codes of Practice, 24, 68, 73–4,
  77, 79, 183, 196
concessions for detainees, 270
fingerprints, destruction of, 156
Police Complaints Authority, 58, 59
potato famine, 3
power:
  focus of research, 11
  lack of for detainees, 11, 184, 270
  in interrogation, 184
premenstrual tension, 56, 239
Prevention of Violence (Temporary)
  Provisions Act, (1939), 2, 198
privacy, deprivation of, 175
PTA
  and creation of terror, 95–120,
    123, 124
  and policing politics, 57, 60, 63,
    65, 194, 233, 252–5
  as counter-productive, 67
  history, 2–4
  normalisation of emergency law,
    263–4
  research on, 1–2, 78
  symbolic functions of, 94, 147–8
  violation of civil liberties, 264–5

public outrage, 1, 271–2
racism: anti-Irish, 159–60, 191–3
  in media, 260
  in processing suspects, 159–60
  institutional, 33, 258
rape: cases, 155
  feeling like, 56
  intimate body search, 158–9
reviews of PTA, 8–9,
Richardson, Carole, 7
Royal Ulster Constabulary, 17, 153,
  232

samples: body, 150, 155
  hair, 155
Schengen: Agreement, 14,
  Information System, 4, 33

searches: of babies, 134
    of body, 62, 143
    of children's property, 136–7
    powers at ports, 24, 62
    powers inland, 72–3
    of anal passage, 80, 158–9
secret state, 28
security: in police stations, 5
    on court appearances, 145
    on journey to police stations,
    139–40
Security Service Commissioner, 256
Shackleton Report
    flaws in, 8–9
    on deterrence and PTA, 67
    detention conditions, 78, 165
    on exclusion, 203, 204, 211, 212
    on power to see documents, 24
    on suspicion, 69
    on port controls, 67
    terms of reference, 8
silence: abolition of, 25–6, 33, 146
    right to remain, 23, 94
Sinn Fein, 54, 61
sleep, deprivation of, 99, 172, 173
Social Democratic and Labour Party,
    43, 54, 57
Social Security Office, arrests at, 132
Social Services departments,
    and policing, 103
Social workers, 96, 103, 262
solicitors, 73, 77, 96, 103, 106, 113,
    138, 145, 179–81, 184, 217,
    223, 227, 228, 232, 233, 240,
    247–8, 251, 262
Special Branch, formation of Irish
    Special Branch, 2
Spencer, Michael, 14
Stalker, John, 257
statements, signed, 107, 185, 186
stormtrooper, 119

strip searches, 24, 72, 150, 157–9
students, examined at ports, 62, 258
suspect community, 5, 13, 33, 93,
    146, 197, 257–61
suspicion, reasonable:
    on arrest, 69, 205
    on examination, 59

television, controls on, 254–5
threats, during interrogation, 189–91
time, deprivation of, 161, 171–2
torture, 170
Troops Out Movement, 9, 195,
    252, 253

UN Committee Against Torture,
    170

Violence:
    concentration under state control,
    96, 262–3
    during interrogation, 170
    response to political violence,
    265–6

Walker, Clive, 19, 67, 72, 88, 272
Ward, Judith, 7, 149, 262
Winchester Three, 142–7
women:
    and pregnancy, 155, 178, 239
    and washing facilities, 173–174
    before the law, 85
    in custody, 115, 150
    number arrested inland, 85–6
    number detained at ports and
    airports, 30–1
    strip searched, 157–8
    with periods, 158, 174
    see also, children
Workers Revolutionary Party, 231
Worsthorne, Peregrine, 260

Printed and bound by CPI Group (UK) Ltd, Croydon, CR0 4YY

09/06/2025

14685867-0003